THE HISTORIC CHURCH

Phot. *Moscioni*

The Epitaph of Avircius

THE HISTORIC CHURCH

An Essay on the Conception of the Christian
Church and its Ministry in the Sub-Apostolic
Age

by

J. C. V. DURELL, B.D.

Rector of Patrington,
Late Fellow of Clare College, Cambridge

πιστεύω εἰς ἁγίαν ἐκκλησίαν
Old Roman Creed

CAMBRIDGE :
at the University Press
1906

CAMBRIDGE UNIVERSITY PRESS
Cambridge, New York, Melbourne, Madrid, Cape Town,
Singapore, São Paulo, Delhi, Mexico City

Cambridge University Press
The Edinburgh Building, Cambridge CB2 8RU, UK

Published in the United States of America by Cambridge University Press, New York

www.cambridge.org
Information on this title: www.cambridge.org/9781107615687

First published 1906
First paperback edition 2013

A catalogue record for this publication is available from the British Library

ISBN 978-1-107-61568-7 Paperback

TO MY WIFE

PREFACE.

IN 1888 and 1889 Dr Hort delivered a course of lectures on "The Early History and the Early Conceptions of the Christian Ecclesia." These lectures were published in 1897 under the title of "The Christian Ecclesia." Their purpose was to examine the evidence afforded by the writings of the New Testament as to the ideas underlying the Ecclesia of the Apostles. But the ground covered by the Lectures was only a preliminary to a much larger problem, the conceptions of the Christian Ecclesia as revealed in Christian history as a whole. It is with the second stage in this problem that the present investigation is concerned. The period we propose to examine, extending to the close of the second century, may be roughly called the sub-apostolic age. We shall give a careful consideration to all Christian writings that have come down to us from this period; and we shall set out in full the evidence, which they afford, as to the conception which their writers had of the Christian church.

This period, which covers upwards of a hundred years, necessarily exhibits growth and development. Circumstances change; and the church, being a living organism, adapts itself to new conditions. Our aim will be to pierce beneath the changing conditions and to seek for the permanent principles, which underlie the varied forms of outward expression. If we are to derive any help from the study of the early ages of the church in our attempt to solve the problems of our own day, it is essential that we should distinguish between the necessary conditions of the life of the church and the accidental forms in which at any time that life may be clothed. For these may be contingent upon changing circumstances, or may belong only to a stage in the growth of the body, whose fundamental possession is life.

In making this survey of the available evidence, I have been greatly indebted to Harmer's edition of Lightfoot's "Apostolic Fathers," in which so many of the texts with which we are here concerned are collected in an easily accessible form.

For the text of the Canons of Hippolytus I have used the edition of Dr Hans Achelis, published in the "Texte und Untersuchungen" (Gebhardt und Harnack), Band vi. 1891.

I wish to acknowledge very gratefully the generous help that I have received from Dr Swete, the Regius Professor, and Dr Stanton, the Ely Professor of Divinity in the University of Cambridge, in the revision of this volume for the press. To both I owe many valuable suggestions, which have enabled me to make the present Essay less faulty and incomplete than it must otherwise have been.

J. C. V. DURELL.

September, 1906.

TABLE OF CONTENTS.

CHAPTER I.

THE EARLIEST WITNESS: CLEMENT—IGNATIUS—POLYCARP.

D.   b

Section 3. Ignatius.

SECTION 4. IGNATIUS (*continued*).

SECTION 5. POLYCARP.

CHAPTER II.

FURTHER WITNESS: THE DIDACHÉ—BARNABAS—HERMAS.

SECTION 1. THE DIDACHÉ.

SECTION 2. THE DIDACHÉ (*continued*).

SECTION 5. THE SHEPHERD OF HERMAS (*continued*).

CHAPTER III.

FROM THE AGE OF THE APOLOGISTS TO IRENÆUS.

SECTION 5. THE MARTYRDOM OF POLYCARP.

SECTION 6. THE ANTI-MONTANISTS.

SERAPION—APOLLONIUS—AN ANONYMOUS WRITER—THE EPITAPH OF AVIRCIUS.

SECTION 7. DIONYSIUS OF CORINTH.

CHAPTER IV.

IRENÆUS.

SECTION 1. IRENÆUS.

SECTION 2. IRENÆUS (*continued*).

CHAPTER V.

THE CLOSE OF THE CENTURY.

SECTION 1. THE EPISTLE TO DIOGNETUS.

SECTION 2. APPENDIX TO THE EPISTLE TO DIOGNETUS.

SECTION 3. THE MURATORIAN FRAGMENT.

SECTION 4. THE CANONS OF HIPPOLYTUS.

SECTION 5. THE CANONS OF HIPPOLYTUS (*continued*).

SECTION 6. THE EARLY MINISTRY AT ALEXANDRIA.

CHAPTER VI.

CONCLUSION: THE LESSONS OF THE SUB-APOSTOLIC AGE.

SECTION 1. THE CONCEPTION OF THE CHURCH.

SECTION 2. THE MINISTRY OF THE CHURCH.

SECTION 3. THE DEVELOPMENT OF CHRISTIAN THOUGHT.

CHAPTER I.

THE EARLIEST WITNESS:
CLEMENT—IGNATIUS—POLYCARP.

SECTION I.

CLEMENT OF ROME.

Characteristics of the church: (1) Its holiness; (2) Its corporate life; (3) Its continuity; (4) Its unity; (5) Its brotherhood.—The doctrine of election in relation to the church.—The idea of sacrifice.

The Epistle to the Corinthians by Clement of Rome is probably the earliest Christian document that has come down to us, outside the Canon of the New Testament. It is written in the name of the church in Rome to the church in Corinth, and may be dated in the closing years of the first century.

We find in Clement's letter the foundation truth, which underlies the article of the old Roman Creed, " I believe in a holy church." This foundation truth rests upon the relation of the church to God. The members of the church are " an elect portion " unto God (Clem. 29). They are " the portion of the Holy One " (Clem. 30). The church therefore is God's possession. It belongs to One who is holy, and it must therefore

itself be marked by holiness. "Seeing then that we are
the portion of the Holy One, let us do all things that
pertain unto holiness" (Clem. 30). The church is holy as
belonging to God, and requires therefore from its members
a growth in holiness.

And this holiness, which should mark the lives of
members of the church, is not merely an individual
matter. It is to be realised through due recognition of
the duties of a corporate life. For life in the church is as
life in a kingdom, carrying with it duties of citizenship.

There is indeed an ambiguity in the use of the phrase
"the kingdom of God." Sometimes it means that realm
of heavenly sovereignty and overpowering majesty which
shall be revealed at the Last Day, when those, who have
been perfected, "shall be made manifest in the visitation
of the kingdom of God" (Clem. 50). This eschatological
sense, which has its basis in the eschatological parables of
our Lord, is very common, but does not concern our present enquiry. The phrase however is also used of present
conditions. Members of the church are reminded that
they belong to a spiritual polity, a "kingdom of God,"
a realm, within which obedience is due to God, as from
citizens to their king. So those who are true to their
obligations are spoken of as men, who "live as citizens of
that kingdom of God, which bringeth no regrets" (τὴν
ἀμεταμέλητον πολιτείαν τοῦ Θεοῦ, Clem. 54). So, then,
the church is presented as an organised society, a
spiritual polity, in which the members must recognise
a duty to the community, and must be ready to subordinate their own private interests to the welfare of all.

This principle underlies Clement's appeal to the
church in Corinth. He appeals to those whose self-
assertion, whether as leaders of the schism or as intruding

ministers, has caused the trouble. Let them remember this duty, and by a self-denying ordinance do what in them lies to restore harmony. "They also, who set themselves up as leaders of faction and division, ought to look to the common ground of hope" (Clem. 51). They ought to subordinate their private interest to the welfare of the community, the organised society to which they belong. So the appeal takes a specific form. "Who therefore is noble among you? Who is compassionate? Who is fulfilled with love? Let him say, If by reason of me there be faction and strife and divisions, I retire, I depart, whither ye will, and I do that which is ordered by the people: only let the flock of Christ be at peace with its duly appointed presbyters" (Clem. 54).

This character of the church is further emphasised by the analogy of a secular state, in which the individual citizen is often called to exercise self-denial in the interests of the state at large. "Many kings and rulers...have delivered themselves over to death, that they might rescue their fellow-citizens through their own blood. Many have retired from their cities, that they might have no more seditions" (Clem. 55).

So then the Christian life is the exercise of a citizenship (see also Clem. 2, πολιτεία). The church is a sphere of harmonised relationships and responsibilities, just as is the body politic of the state.

The church is thought of as existing in continuous life. Thus the church in Corinth, in the language of Clement, is not merely the company of the faithful, who were living in Corinth at the time he wrote his letter. It is the continuous institution, which from the Apostles' days onwards had preserved its unbroken life. So he speaks of "the very stedfast and ancient church of the

Corinthians" (Clem. 47), where the epithets applied show
that his idea is of an institution, which, as generations
pass, itself remains. The church is one society through
the passing years.

In connection with the phrase "the church of the
Corinthians" (Clem. 47), it should be noticed that we do
not yet find any such phrase as "the church of Corinth."
The church does not yet use a mode of description which
would seem to imply a somewhat complete occupation of
the ground. It is as yet only a "church composed of
Corinthians" or "the church of God which sojourneth in
Corinth" (Clem. inscr.).

The local church is an organic unity, for it can speak
with a single voice. Thus it is in the name of the church
sojourning in Rome that Clement's letter is written to
the church sojourning in Corinth. Clement, as its mouthpiece, voices the thought of the church.

The fundamental unity of the church is derived from
the unity of God, and must find outward expression in
unity of life[1]. "Wherefore are there strifes and wraths
and factions and divisions and war among you? Have
we not one God, and one Christ, and one Spirit of grace,
that was shed upon us? And is there not one calling in
Christ? Wherefore do we tear and rend asunder the
members of Christ and stir up factions against our own
body, and reach such a pitch of folly as to forget that we
are members one of another?" (Clem. 46). The sphere of
divine grace is an organised body, in which the members,
who are "members of Christ," have each their proper
function. This body, which is the church, has a definite
outline. It does not shade off vaguely into the world,
but stands out clear-cut and distinct, in possession of the

[1] Cf. Eph. iv. 4 f.; Ign. Magn. 7 ; Hermas, *Sim.* ix. 13, ix. 18.

"Spirit of grace, that was shed" (ἐκχυθέν) upon each member. The aorist probably points back to a definite moment, the initiatory rite, by which the new member was incorporated in "the body," the church. In baptism a definite step was taken of entrance into a society, a definite gift was received, and from that time the recipient was no longer an irresponsible individual, but under obligation to fulfil his function in the corporate life. The society thus constituted is in touch with the gifts of grace. Thus one local church sends to another its greeting of "grace and peace" (Clem. inscr.).

The figure, which in the thought of Clement best describes the true spirit of this society, is that of brotherhood. Again and again he makes his appeal to his readers as "brothers"; he enforces the obligation which brotherhood entails. Twelve times he addresses them as "brothers"; ten times he appeals to them as "beloved." The community is "the brotherhood" (Clem. 2); its ruling spirit must be "love of the brothers" (Clem. 47, 48); the fact of brotherhood should be reflected in the tone of the society. So indeed it had been at Corinth. "You used to be all lowly in mind and free from arrogance, yielding rather than claiming submission" (Clem. 2). Among other qualities emphasised as a necessity of brotherhood, the readiness to give hospitality is prominent. Examples are cited from the Old Testament. Thus Abraham is an example of hospitality and faith (Clem. 10); Lot of hospitality and goodness (Clem. 11); Rahab of hospitality and faith (Clem. 12). And this indeed had been a distinguishing mark of the church in Corinth. "Who did not publish abroad your magnificent disposition of hospitality?" (Clem. 1). The duty of hospitality occupies a very large place in the life of the

early church, though very soon care had to be taken to
prevent abuse of the claim (cf. *Didaché*, 11).

This strong emphasis of the fact of brotherhood leads
by contrast to a condemnation of the spirit of faction,
as contradictory to brotherhood. It is fatal to that
harmonious working in the body politic, which is only
possible when the members show a due subordination of
self and a recognition of the claims of loyalty. Thus
faction is described as a " detestable and unholy sedition,
so strange and alien to the elect of God " (Clem. 1).
Faction is not only evil but is "strange and foreign "
(Clem. 1). It is foreign to the whole spirit of the church
in that it is subversive of brotherhood. " Let us root
this out quickly." Let us pray to the Master that " He
may restore us to the seemly and pure conduct, which
belongeth to our love of the brethren " (Clem. 48). Each
man " ought to seek the common advantage of all and not
his own." That is a summary of the duties of brotherhood. The root motive of all is love. " Love hath no
divisions, love maketh no seditions, love doeth all things
in concord[1]." This was the principle which the church in
Corinth had so conspicuously violated.

By an ascending climax Clement describes the dis-
astrous results of the neglect of this principle (Clem. 46).
Strife (ἔρεις) issues in outbursts of wrath (θυμοί). Then
comes the growth of party spirit (διχοστασίαι), bearing
its fruit in actual divisions (σχίσματα), and in consequence active enmity (πόλεμος)[2]. The unity that
proceeds from the one God is to be embodied in a united
society, in which each is to strive for the welfare of all.
Divisions are a " tearing and rending asunder of the

---

[1] ἀγάπη σχίσμα οὐκ ἔχει, ἀγάπη οὐ στασιάζει, ἀγάπη πάντα ποιεῖ ἐν
ὁμονοίᾳ (Clem. 49).　　　　[2] See Lightfoot, *ad loc.*

members of Christ." A state of things so contrary to true principle cannot but bear evil fruit. Here then is the result. "Your division (τὸ σχίσμα ὑμῶν) hath perverted many; it hath brought many to despair, many to doubting, and all of us to sorrow" (Clem. 46). In spite of this, those guilty of faction have persisted in their course. "Your sedition continueth."

This violation of principle is further emphasised by reference to a rebuke, which in earlier days St Paul himself had given to this same church in Corinth. There had then been the same tendency, the making of parties. The present sin is indeed far worse. For then the parties were grouped around revered names. In this case there is not even that excuse. "It is shameful, dearly beloved, yes, utterly shameful and unworthy of your conduct that it should be reported that the very stedfast and ancient church of the Corinthians, for the sake of one or two persons, maketh sedition against its presbyters" (Clem. 47). Appeal, further, is made to the leaders of the schism themselves. "They also, who set themselves up as leaders of faction and division, ought to look to the common ground of hope" (Clem. 51). Thus the variety and the earnestness of the appeal show the importance attached to the principle of unity in the local church, which the seditions and schisms had violated.

The schism at Corinth is thought of as division within the church, not as separation from the church. The sectaries are still thought of as members of "the body." Their action has the effect of rending the body, not of separation from it. "Wherefore do we tear and rend asunder the members of Christ, and stir up factions against our own body, and reach such a pitch of folly, as to forget that we are members one of another?"

(Clem. 46). The effect of such action is to destroy the common life (ὁμόνοια, ἀδελφότης) which should mark the church. The correction is given in Clement's exhortation, " Let us be good one towards another according to the compassion and sweetness of Him that made us " (Clem. 14). And, moreover, the peace, which should be found in the church, must be a true peace, proceeding from a heartfelt submission, not a mere outward conformity. " Let us cleave unto them that practise peace with godliness, and not unto them that desire peace with dissimulation " (Clem. 15).

Schism, then, is the destruction of that outward unity and fellowship, which should above all things be shown by those who are in the one church. Sedition is " detestable and unholy, alien and strange to the elect of God " (Clem. 1), because it contradicts so forcibly the essential spirit of the church.

Nor does this element of unity affect only the internal life of the local church. It implies a bond of union subsisting between all the churches, and binding them together into one. This finds expression, for instance, in the greeting which one local church sends to another. Thus " the church of God which sojourneth in Rome " sends greeting to " the church of God which sojourneth in Corinth " (Clem. inscr.). That the local churches are united together in a bond of practical fellowship is further illustrated by the fact, that he, who by a self-denying ordinance leaves the community, in which his presence is a source of discord, will find a welcome in the church in another place. " He that hath done this, shall win for himself great renown in Christ, and every place will receive him " (Clem. 54).

The members of the church are spoken of as " the

elect of God " (Clem. 1). God has made them " an elect
portion unto Himself" (Clem. 29) and they are therefore
" the special portion of a holy God " (Clem. 30). But
election so described does not exclude the possibility of a
subsequent apostasy. So Clement says of the Corinthian
Christians, " Ye had conflict night and day for all the
brotherhood, that the number of His elect might be saved,
with fearfulness and intentness of mind " (Clem. 2).
From this follow two considerations as to the conception
of church membership. On the one side, it is a sacred
privilege, the outcome of a divine "election," the admission
to a sacred society. On the other side, it does not
guarantee salvation. " The elect " may fall away. Salvation is to be the outcome of struggle, in which the
brethren will strive one for another.

Christians then have by active struggle to realise that,
for which by their election they are intended, the perfecting of their relation to God. But the thought of approach
to God introduces the idea of sacrifice, by means of which
that approach may be made possible. The church has its
offerings to make ; the church needs a priesthood. This
need is satisfied in Jesus Christ. He is " the High-priest
of our offerings, the Guardian and Helper of our weakness.
Through Him let us look stedfastly into the heights of
the heavens ; through Him we behold as in a mirror His
faultless and most excellent visage ; through Him the
eyes of our hearts were opened ; through Him our foolish
and darkened mind springeth up into the light ; through
Him the Master willed that we should taste of the knowledge that shall not die " (Clem. 36). In Jesus Christ then
is the perfection of priesthood. Through Him the church
has access to God, with all the high blessings which such
access brings with it. He it is who presents our offerings

(προσφοραί). These, "our offerings and ministrations"
(Clem. 40, τὰς προσφορὰς καὶ λειτουργίας), are an integral
part of Christian worship. But the words have a sacrificial
connotation[1]. Christian worship has a sacrificial aspect.
In these sacrificial acts all Christians, according to their
due order, are to share. They are to "make their
offerings at the appointed seasons" (Clem. 40).

Consistently with this idea the work of the ministry
is spoken of in sacrificial language. It is the work of the
"bishop" to "offer the gifts of his office" (Clem. 44, ὁσίως
προσενεγκόντας τὰ δῶρα τῆς ἐπισκοπῆς). The Christian
ministry has a sacrificial character (Clem. 44, λειτουρ-
γήσαντας...τῷ ποιμνίῳ τοῦ Χριστοῦ, cf. Didaché, 15).

But this sacerdotal character does not separate the
ministry from the laity as by a caste distinction. For, as
we have seen, the laity also have their sacrificial part to
take, each according to "the appointed rule of his service"
(Clem. 41). The nature of this "appointed rule" and
due order is explained by comparison with the Jewish
system, which assigned to priests and people their respective parts in the ritual of sacrifice. "They therefore that
make their offerings at the appointed seasons are acceptable and blessed, for while they follow the institutions of
the Master they cannot go wrong. For unto the high-
priest his proper services have been assigned, and to the

---

[1] The service expressed by λειτουργία is not necessarily sacrificial,
but the fact that the word is here united with προσφοραί under a single
article indicates that the two words together express a single idea, that
of sacrificial service and offering. But, further, Clement seems always to
use the term λειτουργία with a sacrificial colour. He speaks of the Christian
worship as a λειτουργία and then compares it with the Jewish sacrificial
ritual (Clem. 41). He evidently holds that an analogy obtains between
the two. Cf. Heb. x. 11, where λειτουργῶν is used of the ministry of the
Jewish priests in their sacrificial worship.

priests their proper office is appointed, and upon the levites their proper ministration is laid. The layman is bound by the layman's ordinances. Let each of you, brethren, in his own order give thanks unto God, maintaining a good conscience and not transgressing the appointed rule of His service" (Clem. 40, 41). So then the church as a whole is thought of as offering its sacrificial worship to God, while to laity and ministers are assigned the respective parts which each is to take in the orderly offering of the service. This exactly corresponds with the New Testament conception of Christians as a priestly people, with a ministerial priesthood, authoritatively appointed, to give expression to its worship (cf. 1 Pet. ii. 5 ; Rev. v. 10).

SECTION II.

CLEMENT OF ROME (continued).

Organisation of the church.—Public worship, which must be celebrated (1) at the right times ; (2) in the right places ; (3) by the right persons.—The Christian ministry ; (1) Its apostolic origin ; (2) The appointment of ministers ; (3) Its organisation ; (4) Its character.

The church appears in Clement as something very different from a mere aggregate of Christians. It is an organised society, bound by a definite discipline. This is taught by means of two metaphors.

The church is as an army. As there are various grades in an army, and each rank must be in due subordination to its superiors, the soldiers readily obeying their officers, so it must be in the church. This is in accordance with the divine scheme for the church, the "faultless ordinances" of God. The church officers must therefore

receive due submission and obedience. " Let us therefore
enlist ourselves, brethren, with all earnestness in His
faultless ordinances. Let us mark the soldiers that are
enlisted under our rulers, how exactly, how readily,
how submissively, they execute the orders given them.
All are not prefects, nor rulers of thousands, nor rulers of
hundreds, nor rulers of fifties, and so forth ; but each man
in his own rank executeth the orders given by the king
and the governors " (Clem. 37).

This, however, does not exhaust the whole truth as to
relationships in the grades of the church. The church is
as a body ; and this second metaphor expresses a further
truth. It teaches that submission is to be mutual, not
one-sided. Each, whatever be the difference of office, is
necessary to the other. " The head without the feet is
nothing; so likewise the feet without the head are nothing;
even the smallest limbs of our body are necessary and
useful for the whole body ; but all the members conspire
and unite in subjection, that the whole body may be saved.
So in our case let the whole body be saved in Christ
Jesus, and let each man be subject unto his neighbour,
according as also he was appointed with His special grace"
(Clem. 37 f.).

The discipline of this organised society is illustrated
by the conditions regulating public worship. In speaking
of the services of the church, it is the Eucharist, which is
chiefly, though probably not exclusively, in the mind of
Clement. These services are subject to certain disciplinary
rules. " Let each one of you, brethren, in his own order
give thanks unto God[1], maintaining a good conscience and
not transgressing the appointed rule of His service, but
acting with all seemliness " (Clem. 41). The offerings

[1] ἕκαστος ὑμῶν, ἀδελφοί, ἐν τῷ ἰδίῳ τάγματι εὐχαριστείτω Θεῷ.

must be made and the ministrations conducted (1) at the right times, (2) at the right places, (3) by the right persons.

Public worship is among the things which "the Master hath commanded us to perform at their appointed seasons" (Clem. 40). "The offerings and ministrations He commanded to be performed with care, and not to be done rashly or in disorder, but at fixed times and seasons[1]." And so it follows that "they who make their offerings at the appointed seasons are acceptable and blessed" (*ibid.*). So then certain appointed times and seasons are recognised as being set down for the public service of the church, and this arrangement is referred back to the institution of Christ.

But just as the celebration of public worship has its proper times and seasons, so also it has its proper place. "And where...He would have them (*i.e.* the offerings and ministrations) performed, He Himself fixed by His supreme will" (Clem. 40). This discipline of the Christian church is enforced by reference to the Judaic ordinances. "Not in every place are the continual daily sacrifices offered...but in Jerusalem alone. And even there the offering is not made in every place, but before the sanctuary in the court of the altar" (Clem. 41). The employment of this analogy implies that a sacred building had already been set apart for the Christian worship and offerings, and that this appointment of a definite sanctuary for worship was held to be by the command of Christ Himself.

[1] Clem. 40, ὡρισμένοις καιροῖς καὶ ὥραις. Lightfoot points out that καιροί and ὥραι differ only in that the former refers to the *fitness* and the latter to the *appointedness* of the time ; and that ὥραι does not refer to the hour of the day. The point therefore is that certain seasons and occasions have been appointed as proper to the celebration of public worship, and especially of the Eucharist. No doubt Sunday would be regarded as prominent among such ὥραι. Cf. Justin, *Apol.* i. 67.

The church had now passed out of that earlier stage
of worship, when it was accustomed to "break bread at
home" (Acts ii. 46). This had indeed been an inevitable
stage in the process of growth. But now that special
places had been set apart for worship, and special occasions
of service appointed, to depart from these would be a
breach of church order and discipline. The leaders of the
schism had committed this breach of order by their claim
to celebrate the Eucharist and hold the Agapé when and
where they pleased.

Clement, as we have seen, ascribes this principle of a
special sanctuary to the institution of Christ Himself.
Now having regard to Clement's nearness to the apostolic
age and his opportunities of knowing what the Apostles
taught, we may conclude at least that this principle, that
worship should be offered in an appointed sanctuary at an
appointed time, was taught by the Apostles. But when
we look behind the Apostles to the teaching of Christ
Himself, we should probably not be justified in postulating
any such specific directions as having been uttered by
Him. The fact is that a permanent and unchangeable
principle finds embodiment in varying positive ordinances
according to change of circumstances. In this case the
fundamental principle is that of unity in the brotherhood.
This principle will naturally receive a changing expression
with the change of outward conditions. In the first days
of the church the celebration at home of the Agapé
and Eucharist was the only possible course. Afterwards
the communities grew. But in each place the principle of
unity had to be safeguarded. As applied to worship, this
involved the regulation of the service, the setting apart
for it of a special place and a special time.

But in a third respect the worship of the church is

regulated.   Not every one might lead the worship of the
church or celebrate the Eucharist, but only those
authorised to do so.   "By whom He would have" the
public service "performed, He Himself (the Master) fixed
by His supreme will" (Clem. 40).   This principle of an
authorised ministry is enforced by reference to the Judaic
ministry.   The offering at Jerusalem is made "through
the high-priest and the aforesaid ministers" (*i.e.* the
priests and levites) (Clem. 40).   Thus Clement claims
that the appointment of a regular ministry in the church
is in accordance with the will of Christ.   Christ wills to
have "the offerings and service" administered not by any
chance worshipper, but by authorised persons.   The duly
appointed minister is alone entitled to lead the worship of
the church and to present the offerings.

A ministry, authoritatively appointed, with differences
of function assigned according to grade is a necessity in
the Christian church.   This necessity arises from the very
nature of the church as an organism, a "body."   Just as
in the Jewish church (Clem. 40) the high-priest had his
proper functions, and to the priests their proper office was
assigned, and upon the levites their proper ministrations
were laid, while the layman was bound by the layman's
ordinances, so it must be in the Christian church.   There
is no necessary comparison of order with order, Jewish with
Christian.   The essential point has no reference to the
number of orders, whether two or three or many, but in
the fact of an authoritative ministry, representative of the
church (Clem. 44) and acting under discipline (Clem. 40 f.).

The authority of the ministry is traced up to its
fountain-head in God, through Christ and the Apostles.
"The Apostles received the Gospel for us from the Lord
Jesus Christ; Jesus Christ was sent forth from God.   So

then Christ is from God, and the Apostles are from Christ.
Both therefore came of the will of God in the appointed
order.   Having therefore received a charge, and having
been fully assured through the resurrection of our Lord
Jesus Christ, and confirmed in the word of God, with full
assurance of the Holy Ghost, they went forth with the
glad tidings that the kingdom of God should come"
(Clem. 42). The commission thus received is then handed
on to others.   " Preaching everywhere in country and
town, they appointed their firstfruits, when they had
proved them by the Spirit, to be bishops and deacons
unto them that should believe [1]" (Clem. 42). We note that
the guidance of the Holy Spirit is claimed for the Apostles
in making these appointments [2].   Clement claims further
for the Apostles that their action in the appointment of
" bishops and deacons " had Old Testament sanction.
"This they did in no new fashion ; for indeed it had been
written concerning bishops and deacons from very ancient
times ; for thus saith the Scripture in a certain place,
I will appoint their bishops in righteousness and their
deacons in faith " (Clem. 42).   The particular argument
indeed fails ; for Isaiah writes not of " deacons " but of
"rulers[3]." But Clement's desire to find Scriptural precedent
is at least a witness to the importance which he attached
to the apostolic ministry.

The arrangements for the appointment of ministers in
the church, as laid down by the Apostles, were governed
by the desire to avoid unseemly strife, such as might arise
over the office of oversight (Clem. 44).

---

[1] Cf. Acts xiv. 23, "having appointed for them elders in each church."

[2] Cf. 1 Tim. i. 18, " the prophecies that led the way to thee"; Hort's
Ecclesia, p. 180.

[3] Is. lx. 17, LXX. ἄρχοντας...ἐπισκόπους.

So the Apostles made the first appointments themselves. And they further made provision for the next set of appointments in succession. "For this cause, therefore, (*i.e.* for the avoiding of strife), having received complete foreknowledge, they appointed the aforesaid persons, and afterwards they provided a continuance, that, if these should fall asleep, other approved men should succeed to their ministration. Those therefore who were appointed by them, or afterwards by other men of repute with the consent of the whole church, and have ministered unblameably to the flock of Christ in lowliness of mind, peacefully and with all modesty, and for a long time have borne a good report with all—these men we consider to be unjustly thrust out from their ministration " (Clem. 44).

So, then, when those who had been appointed by the Apostles should die, others were to be appointed in their place. The appointment was to be made by "men of repute " (ἐλλόγιμοι ἄνδρες). These men, with whom the appointment rested, are not further defined. But since the object of the mode of appointment was to prevent jealousies, it would seem to follow that they must have been, at least as a rule, men who possessed some official qualification. Sometimes, no doubt, they would be such men as Timothy and Titus, to whom a definite oversight had been authoritatively committed[1]. Sometimes, we may suppose, the body of ἐπίσκοποι would themselves make the selection. In churches, in which episcopacy had become monarchical, it is reasonable to suppose that the appointment would rest with the bishop. At Rome we may suppose that Clement himself would be such an ἐλλόγιμος ἀνήρ as he describes.

It is important to notice that the appointment thus

[1] Titus was charged with this duty. See Tit. i. 5.

D. 2

made required the consent of the church (Clem. 44). It was needful that the entire local community of Christians should ratify it.

So, then, while the object of this mode of appointment by recognised men is to provide a method which will leave no room for disputatious strife, it gives full recognition to the principle that the minister is the representative of the church, in that the consent of the whole local church is required for his appointment.

The ministers so appointed cannot be displaced at will, without a grievous breach of church order, provided that they exercise their ministry aright (Clem. 44)[1]. They are not the mere servants of the community. They occupy a position in a sacred order, which has its place in the church, not by human invention, but by the will of God. For God Himself has appointed the ministry. It exists "by His supreme will" (Clem. 40). It is this fact which constitutes the special heinousness of "sedition against the presbyters" (Clem. 47).

In the mind of Clement, then, the ministry of the church has a divine sanction. It remains for us to consider in what form this ministry was organised. We have already found the use of the term "presbyter" as the title of an office. "It is shameful, dearly beloved, yes, utterly shameful and unworthy of your conduct in Christ, that it should be reported that the very stedfast and ancient church of the Corinthians, for the sake of one or two persons, maketh sedition against its presbyters" (Clem. 47). "Blessed are those presbyters who have gone before, seeing that their departure was fruitful and ripe" (Clem. 44). But on the other hand the term is not yet

[1] Cf. Clem. 54, "Let the flock of Christ be at peace with its duly appointed presbyters."

finally hardened to an exclusively technical meaning. It is still used to express age. "Submitting yourselves to your rulers (τοῖς ἡγουμένοις ὑμῶν) and rendering to the older men among you (τοῖς παρ' ὑμῖν πρεσβυτέροις) the honour which is their due" (Clem. 1). That οἱ πρεσβύτεροι are not here the bearers of office is shown by the phrase standing in contrast to οἱ ἡγούμενοι. For these latter are the church officers, not the civil officers[1], and the form of the sentence shows that the two phrases do not express an identical body of men. But, further, οἱ πρεσβύτεροι stands in contrast with οἱ νέοι. "On the young too ye enjoined modest and seemly thoughts" (Clem. 1). So that while in Clement's use a rank of officers in the ministry of the church is described as "the elders," the same term is still used by him in a non-technical sense, descriptive simply of age.

We have next to consider the use of the term ἐπίσκοπος. Is ἐπίσκοπος a title of office or does it merely describe a function? Does it merely mean "one who has oversight," of whatever kind? Now Hort maintains[2], apparently with success, that in the New Testament ἐπίσκοπος represents not an office but a function. It denotes the function of oversight, which was as a fact committed to the elders, so that οἱ πρεσβύτεροι, the church officers, were ἐπίσκοποι, men charged with the duty of oversight of the church. This is the usage of the Pastoral Epistles.

In Phil. i. 1 ἐπίσκοποι καὶ διάκονοι are "they that have oversight and they that do service." And the thought is not of any particular form of ministry, but simply of a ministry which, in whatever way, provides

---

[1] See Lightfoot, *ad loc.*; cf. Heb. xiii. 7, 17, 24; Hermas, Vis. ii. 2, iii. 9.

[2] See Hort, *Christian Ecclesia*, pp. 190 f., 211—213.

the two fundamental types of oversight and of service, which are necessary in an organised body.

Hort further thinks[1] that the usage is the same in Clement, Hermas and, perhaps, the *Didaché*.

But the following considerations seem to show that with Clement ἐπίσκοπος is the title of an office. It is admitted that διάκονος had already become so. Hort allows that the term is used as the title of an office in the Pastoral Epistles[2]. Hence we need not doubt that it was so used by Clement. But when the phrase ἐπίσκοποι καὶ διάκονοι is used by a writer with whom the second term is the title of an office, it must surely follow that in his thought the first term also denotes an office. When Clement writes " they appointed their firstfruits...to be ἐπισκόπους and deacons unto them that should believe " (Clem. 42), he must mean by ἐπίσκοπος the title of an office which stands in contrast with the office of deacon. It is quite likely, as Hort suggests of the same phrase in the *Didaché*[3], that the phrase is suggested by Phil. i. 1. But it does not follow that the words were used by Clement in the same sense as by St Paul.

That ἐπίσκοπος is with Clement a title of office is further corroborated by his use of ἐπισκοπή. It is true that in the case quoted by Hort, ἐπὶ τοῦ ὀνόματος τῆς ἐπισκοπῆς (Clem. 44), there is no need to infer any other meaning in ἐπισκοπή than " the function of oversight." The dignity attaching to such a function was a source of strife. But in the same paragraph we find those who have been thus appointed to the ministry described as προσενεγκόντας τὰ δῶρα τῆς ἐπισκοπῆς. Now inasmuch as

---

[1] Hort, *Christian Ecclesia*, p. 213.

[2] Hort, *op. cit.* p. 209.

[3] Hort, *op. cit.* p. 213. See *Didaché*, 15.

the aspect of their work, which is in question in this place, is not that of oversight over the flock, but their liturgical action of presentation of the oblations to God, we must assume that the term ἐπισκοπή carried with it another connotation than that of oversight. In other words it had now come to express an office in the church which indeed included the function of oversight over the flock but was of wider significance.

If then it be granted that, with Clement, ἐπίσκοπος is the title of a church officer, we have now to show that his office is the same as that of the πρεσβύτερος, though described under a different aspect. There is no thought of a monarchical episcopate.

This identity appears from Clement's threefold reference to ἐπίσκοποι καὶ διάκονοι (Clem. 42), without any mention of the πρεσβύτεροι. For it is impossible to suppose that the πρεσβύτεροι are omitted from his argument. His whole purpose is to vindicate their position. If we grant that ἐπίσκοπος is the title of an office, it follows that this office is that of the πρεσβύτερος. And this further appears from the fact that the presbyters are clearly identified with those who have the office of ἐπισκοπή. " It will be no light sin for us, if we thrust out those who have offered the gifts proper to ἐπισκοπή unblameably and holily. Blessed are those presbyters who have gone before, seeing that their departure was fruitful and ripe ; for they have no fear lest anyone should remove them from their appointed place" (Clem. 44). If then from the term " bishop " we dissociate the idea of monarchical rule, we may for convenience so translate ἐπίσκοπος, and our conclusion will then be that in the language of Clement, " bishop" and "presbyter" are titles of the same office.

It does not, however, follow that the two titles were used indifferently. The fact that the combination ἐπίσκοποι καὶ διάκονοι occurs three times (Clem. 42) suggests that, when mentioning the diaconate, it was natural to speak of the other ministerial office under that title, the etymology of which suggested its contrast with the lower office. We may therefore conclude that while πρεσβύτερος and ἐπίσκοπος are in Clement both titles of the same office, they are not used indiscriminately; that πρεσβύτερος (Clem. 44) was the ordinary term, but that the title ἐπίσκοπος was given when a particular aspect of the office was in question, notably in emphasising the contrast with the lower office of διάκονος.

Those who are charged with this authority must not use it for personal aggrandisement. They must not "exalt themselves over the flock" (Clem. 16)[1]. They must bear rule "in lowliness of mind." All alike, both pastors and flock, must remember that they are under discipline, under a yoke. "Ye see, dearly beloved, what is the pattern that hath been given to us; for if the Lord was thus lowly in mind, how ought we to behave, who through Him have been brought under the yoke of His grace?" (Clem. 16). So then "humility and submissiveness" (Clem. 19) must mark their lives.

This involves submission to discipline. The lay-folk are under discipline, as Clement shows by analogy with Jewish order. "The layman is bound by the layman's ordinances" (Clem. 40). He has his place in an organised body, the Christian society, and he must therefore fulfil his function in the body. The phrase ὁ λαϊκὸς ἄνθρωπος of course emphasises the fact of a ministry set apart authoritatively, but it is to be noted that the power of

---

[1] Cf. Acts xx. 29.

discipline rests, not with the ministry acting alone, but with the whole church. Thus the penitent disturber of the peace is represented as carrying out his self-denying ordinance in obedience to the whole community. " I do that which is ordered by the people " (Clem. 54). This disciplinary authority, resident in the whole local church, is also illustrated by the fact that the appointment of presbyters required " the consent of the whole church " (Clem. 44).

But, on the other hand, an authority of leadership is vested in the presbyters, who have a claim upon the obedience of the people. This, of course, follows from the very conception of a body politic. It is illustrated by the exhortation to submission addressed to the leaders of the schism. Submission is to be made to the presbyters. " Ye therefore that laid the foundation of the sedition, submit yourselves unto the presbyters and receive chastisement unto repentance " (Clem. 57).

So, then, on the one side we have a view of discipline exercised by the whole local church acting together; and on the other we find that the presbyters, as authoritatively appointed leaders and as representing the church, have a claim to the obedience of those over whom they are placed.

SECTION III.

IGNATIUS.

The ideal and the institutional church.—The universal church.—The local churches.—Their relations and character.—The principle of unity.—The expression of unity : (1) In the Eucharist ; (2) In the Agapé ; (3) In social activities ; (4) In public worship ; (5) In teaching.—The standard of church teaching.—The local church of Rome.—Sacrificial aspect of the church.—The question of salvation outside the church.

Ignatius was bishop of the church in Antioch in Syria at the beginning of the second century. He was taken to Rome for martyrdom in the amphitheatre and it was during his journey thither that his seven Epistles were written. The genuineness of the letters in the shorter Greek form may now be taken as established. Tradition states that Ignatius was martyred during the reign of Trajan and this should probably be accepted as accurate. The date of the letters is about A.D. 110—115, or may possibly be a few years later[1].

The church is, with Ignatius, sometimes an ideal conception, a sphere of which certain attributes are predicated ; sometimes an institution, a society, visible upon earth. The ideal church was foreordained in the counsel of the Father; it will last for ever. It is manifested on earth in the company of Christians, as the empirical or institutional church. Both these senses, the ideal and the empirical, are employed in regard sometimes to the church universal, sometimes to the church in a locality.

The church, then, is not merely the company of the faithful. It has a mystical or ideal existence apart from

[1] Harnack, *Chron.* i. p. 406.

its outward manifestation in the individuals who belong
to it. Thus, as the outward body of believers is associated
with their bishop, so the church, by which is meant the
local church, conceived of as having a mystical existence,
is associated with Jesus Christ. The outward and seen
relationship has its counterpart in the mystical and unseen
relationship. In each case the relationship is one of close
union. "You (the members of the Christian community
at Ephesus) are closely joined with him (the bishop), as
the church (the local church, conceived of ideally) is with
Jesus Christ, and as Jesus Christ is with the Father"
(Ephes. 5).

The local church, then, is not merely the aggregate of
the individuals who compose the Christian community,
but is thought of ideally, and, as such, is addressed almost
in the terms of personality. Thus in the counsel of God,
the local church in Ephesus was "foreordained before the
ages to be for ever unto abiding and unchangeable glory"
(Ephes. inscr.). The same foreordination is predicated of
the local church by Ignatius as of the individual Christian
by St Paul[1]. The thought of Hermas, as we shall see, goes
even beyond this: for he thinks of the church as not
merely foreordained, but as preexisting (Hermas, *Pastor*,
Vis. ii. 4). It should, however, be noticed that, while
Ignatius is referring to a local church, Hermas is speaking
of the universal church.

At the same time this ideal conception is closely
bound up with its concrete manifestation. This church
in Ephesus, thus predetermined, is "united and elect"
(Ephes. inscr.). In both of these terms the thought of the
individual members of the local church is predominant
over the thought of the church itself. It is the members

[1] Eph. i. 4.

who are united; it is the members who are elect. Yet,
at the same time, they are united because they belong to
the church, which is one; they are elect to the church,
which owes its being to the counsel of God.

But, still more, the church universal has an ideal
existence. The ideal church universal is incorruptible.
When the Lord was anointed at Bethany "the house was
filled with the odour of the ointment." Ignatius takes
this as representing mystically the fragrance of incorrup-
tibility with which the church was to be endowed. "For
this cause did the Lord receive ointment upon His head,
that He might breathe incorruption upon the church"
(Ephes. 17).

Ignatius does not, however, often use the term ἐκκλησία
in the sense of the one church universal. The other
instances may be noted.

The church is the final element in the successive stages
of those dealings of God with man which are to find
ultimate fusion in the supreme unity of God. Christ is
"the door of the Father, through whom Abraham and
Isaac and Jacob enter in, and the Prophets and the
Apostles and the whole church; all these things combine
in the unity of God" (Philad. 9).

The church is the object of the Lord's love. "Charge
my brothers in the name of Jesus Christ to love their
wives as the Lord loved the church" (ad Polyc. 5)[1].

The church is a single visible organisation, set up in
the world as a standing witness to the reality of the
Incarnation, as exhibiting in itself the life of the risen
Christ. This "one body of His church" is "set up as an
ensign unto all the ages through His resurrection, for His

---

[1] A reminiscence of Eph. v. 29.

saints and faithful people, whether among Jews or among Gentiles " (Smyrn. 1).

The condition of its existence is the presence of Jesus Christ. "Where Jesus Christ may be, there is the universal church[1]" (Smyrn. 8).

Passing now from the thought of the one church universal to that of the local community, we find that, just as is the case in the New Testament, the Christian body in a particular place is called the church in that place[2]. Thus we may take as typical the expression "the church which is in Ephesus." We also have the phrase " the church of you Ephesians" (Ephes. 8)[3]. And another form may be noted : " The church of God which sojourneth at Philippi " (Ep. Polyc. inscr.). But, on the other hand, no such expression yet occurs as "the church of Ephesus[4]." The significance of this fact would seem to be that the bulk of the population was still heathen. The city of

---

[1] ἡ καθολικὴ ἐκκλησία. The epithet here has not the later technical sense, which appears first in the Muratorian Fragment, meaning the true church as opposed to heretical sects. Here it simply expresses the one universal church. It is the entire church, as opposed to the local churches, the communities in particular places. The word καθολικός was in common use at the time, signifying "universal" as opposed to "individual." It is applied as an epithet to ἐκκλησία in Mart. Polyc. three times (circ. A.D. 155) in the same sense as here. It was only at a later date that, as the Muratorian Fragment shows, a technical sense began to be attached to the phrase " the Catholic church," as descriptive of its character and doctrine.

[2] Instances are as follows: "the church which is in Ephesus" (Eph. inscr.) ; "the church which is in Magnesia on the Meander" (Magn. inscr.) ; "the holy church which is in Tralles of Asia " (Trall. inscr.); "the church of God the Father and of Jesus Christ, which is in Philadelphia of Asia" (Philad. inscr.); "the church which is in Antioch of Syria" (Philad. 10) ; "the church which is in Smyrna of Asia " (Smyrn. inscr.).

[3] Cf. ad Polyc. inscr. "the church of the Smyrnæans."

[4] Cf. Hort, *Christian Ecclesia*, pp. 114 f. on the usage of the N.T.

Ephesus could not yet claim the church as its possession.
The local church was as yet only the church of a relatively
small company, which happened to live in Ephesus.

The local communities, contemplated in groups, are
spoken of as " the churches," a usage which also is that
of the New Testament. Thus we read, " All the other
churches salute you " (Magn. 15)[1].

There is, however, an instance of a form of expression,
which seems at first sight to represent a departure from
the usage of the New Testament. Ignatius four times
speaks of " the church in Syria" (Ephes. 21 ; Magn. 14,
twice ; Rom. 9). Now in the New Testament we find
such a phrase as " the churches in Asia" but not " the
church in Asia "; where we are concerned not with a
single city, but with a region in which several cities, each
with its Christian community, might be found[2]. Ignatius,
however, writes, " Pray for the church in Syria, from whence
I am being led in bonds to Rome " (Ephes. 21); and again
he speaks of " the church in Syria, in which I am not
worthy to be reckoned " (Magn. 14). " I have need," he
says again, " of your united prayer and love in God, that
it may be granted to the church in Syria to be refreshed
by the dew of your earnest prayer " (ibid.).

The question then is whether " the church in Syria "
means that particular local church from which Ignatius

[1] The other instances are: Magn. 1, "I sing the praises of the
churches": here " the churches" were probably those through which or near
which his route lay on his way to martyrdom ; Magn. 15, " all the other
churches," which must mean those churches with which he had in
some way come in contact ; Trall. 12, " the churches of God that are
present with me "; Rom. 4, " I write to all the churches "; Rom. 9,
" the love of the churches"; " those churches which did not lie on my
route"; ad Polyc. 8, "I have not been able to write to all the churches";
" thou shalt write to the churches in front."

[2] Cf. Hort, *Christian Ecclesia*, p. 115.

came, the church namely in Antioch, or whether it refers
to the aggregate of the various Christian communities
scattered throughout the province of Syria.

If we decide on the latter meaning, we have an
example of a new usage for which there is no parallel in
the New Testament. For "the church in Syria" must
then refer not to a singly organised community, but to a
number of communities, each with its own organisation.
For it is reasonable to suppose that each of these communities had its own bishop. The language of Ignatius
on the subject of episcopacy, taken together with his
nearness to these communities, in which his influence
would be strong, makes this supposition reasonable. It is
not likely that he would have allowed his neighbours to
lack that which he himself considered essential.

Nor should we be justified in supposing that the
phrase "the church in Syria" implied an organisation
throughout the province under the rule of a single bishop.
Ignatius indeed is spoken of as ὁ ἐπίσκοπος Συρίας
(Rom. 2), but this phrase must mean merely "the bishop
belonging to Syria[1]." To suppose that, in later phrase,
Syria was his "diocese," is to imagine a condition of things
which did not originate till a later time. Indeed we
may note that the Antiochene Acts say of Ignatius that
"he governed the church of the Antiochenes." They
make no attempt to represent his jurisdiction as any
wider than the limits of the city. The phrase "the
bishop belonging to Syria" is accounted for by the fact
that Syria, of which Antioch was the capital, was much
in his mind. He speaks of himself repeatedly as having
come "from Syria[2]." So too the church over which

---

[1] See Lightfoot, *ad loc.*
[2] Ephes. 1, Rom. 5, Philad. 11, ad Polyc. 7, 8.

he is bishop is " the church which is in Antioch of
Syria[1]."

But the fact that the episcopal authority of Ignatius
was limited to the local church in Antioch supplies
conclusive evidence that his phrase "the church in Syria"
is to be interpreted as meaning that particular local
church in Syria with which Ignatius was connected and
which was so much in his thoughts. " Remember in your
prayers," he writes to the Romans, " the church in Syria,
which hath God for its shepherd in my stead " (Rom. 9).
Here quite clearly the church in Syria means the local
church of Antioch, over which Ignatius had exercised his
pastoral authority. The other passages already quoted,
in which the same phrase occurs, will easily bear the same
interpretation. The phrase therefore does not really
represent any departure from the usage of the New
Testament.

In one place there is one local church. Such an
arrangement as a plurality of churches in the same
place would be quite foreign to the thought of Ignatius.
This is shown by the consistent occurrence of such phrases
as " the church which is in Ephesus," " the church which
is in Magnesia." There is no such phrase as "the churches
in Ephesus."

There is, however, one instance of an anarthrous use
which must be examined. Polycarp is spoken of as
ἐπίσκοπος ἐκκλησίας Σμυρναίων (ad Polyc. inscr.). But
this does not mean "bishop of a church of Smyrnæans" in
the sense of " one out of several churches of Smyrnæans."
The form of the expression (ἐκκλησίας instead of τῆς
ἐκκλησίας) lays stress on the nature of the oversight
exercised by Polycarp as bishop. The sphere of its exercise

[1] Philad. 10, Smyrn. 11, ad Polyc. 7.

is a church, the church, namely, of the Smyrnæans. This church is subject to his oversight, even as he himself is subject to the supreme oversight of God.

So, then, in one place there is one church. The churches of different places preserve harmonious, friendly relations one with another, through mutual intercourse and acts of sympathy, as befits communities that together make up ἡ καθολικὴ ἐκκλησία, the sum of them all.

The local church has its origin in the will of God. It is " elect " (Trall. inscr.). Hence there is stamped upon it a character of holiness. It is " holy," consecrated to God. In so far as this consecration is reflected in its life it is "worthy of God." With divine origin goes divine possession. The local church is "a church of God" (Trall. 2, 12 ; Philad. 10)[1].

The local church is not an amorphous collection of believers, but an organised body under a properly constituted ministry of bishop, presbyters and deacons. Without a regular ministry such as this the community has no claim to be called a church. " Apart from these," says Ignatius, " the title of church is not given (ἐκκλησία οὐ καλεῖται)" (Trall. 3). It is probable that the emphasis should be laid not so much on the exact way in which the orders in the ministry are differentiated one from another, as upon the fact that a regular and properly constituted orderly ministry must exist in order to give the local community a claim to rank as a church. None the less the fact remains that the only form of regular ministry known to Ignatius is the ministry organised in the three-fold ranks of bishop, presbyters and deacons.

[1] The following epithets are used of local churches : προωρισμένη, ἡνωμένη, ἐκλελεγμένη, ἀξιομακάριστος (Ephes. inscr.), εὐλογημένη (Magn. inscr.), ἠγαπημένη, ἐκλεκτή, ἁγία, ἀξιόθεος (Trall. inscr.), ἠλεημένη, πεφωτισμένη, ἀξιοπρεπής, ἀξιέπαινος, ἀξιοεπίτευκτος, ἀξίαγνος, χριστόνομος, πατρώνυμος (Rom. inscr.).

One of the fundamental principles, upon which Ignatius insists most strongly, is that of unity. Unity must mark the life of each local church ; it must find full expression in the church universal.

The local church is " made one" ($\dot{\eta}\nu\omega\mu\acute{e}\nu\eta$), has received the gift of unity (Ephes. inscr.). The bond of union is the Passion of Christ. Its outcome is participation in the life of God. " It is profitable for you to be in blameless unity, that ye may also be partakers of God always" (Ephes. 4). "Let there be nothing among you, which shall have power to divide you" (Magn. 6). Unity will be their defence against the powers of evil. " As children of the light, shun division and wrong doctrines ; and where the shepherd is, there follow ye as sheep. For many specious wolves with baneful delights lead captive the runners in God's race ; but, where ye are at one, they will find no place " (Philad. 2). So those are of God who " enter into the unity of the church " (Philad. 3). And, on the other hand, " If any man followeth one that maketh a schism, he doth not inherit the kingdom of God " (Philad. 3). Disunion is inconsistent with the presence of God in the church. " I therefore did my own part, as a man composed unto union. But where there is division and anger God abideth not. Now the Lord forgiveth all men when they repent, if repenting they return to the unity of God " (Philad. 8). " Shun therefore divisions as the beginning of evils " (Smyrn. 8). In the same spirit Polycarp is bidden to "have a care for unity" (ad Polyc. 1). And this must be no cold formal unity, but a unity warmed by love. " Each of you severally love one another with undivided heart " (Trall. 13). " Assemble yourselves all together with undivided heart " (Philad. 6).

How then is this unity to be secured? Ignatius answers that it is to be secured by obedience to the bishop.

"It is meet for you in every way to glorify Jesus Christ who glorified you ; that being perfectly joined together in one submission, submitting yourselves to your bishop and presbytery, ye may be sanctified in all things" (Ephes. 2). "I congratulate you, who are closely joined with him (your bishop), as the church is with Jesus Christ and as Jesus Christ is with the Father, that all things may be harmonious in unity" (Ephes. 5). "Be ye united with the bishop and with them that preside over you"(Magn. 6). "As the Lord did nothing without the Father, either by Himself or by the Apostles, so neither do ye anything without the bishop and the presbyters. And attempt not to think anything right for yourselves apart from others ; but let there be one prayer in common, one supplication, one mind, one hope, in love and in joy unblameable, which is Jesus Christ, than whom there is nothing better. Hasten to come together all of you, as to one temple, even God ; as to one altar, even to one Jesus Christ, who came forth from one Father and is with One and departed unto One" (Magn. 7). Thus in all matters concerning the church, no action is to be taken contrary to the bishop's will. The Christian must not live his life on a basis of individualism, but as a member of a community. "Do nothing without the bishop...cherish union; shun divisions" (Philad. 7).

But unity should subsist not only in each local church, but also between the churches. The whole church universal must show a bond of union. "I pray that there may be in them (the churches) union of the flesh and of the spirit, which are Jesus Christ's, our never-failing life —an union of faith and love, which is preferred before all things—and, what is more than all, an union with Jesus and with the Father" (Magn. 1). There should be unity, that is, both in external intercourse and in interior life. This unity is supported by faith and love and is derived from the fundamental fact of union with God. Church organisation and discipline, in the mind of Ignatius (Ephes. 3, 4), are instruments for producing a perfect harmonious unity in the far-spreading church. At the head of all is the Eternal Father, whose mind the church must express. Note, then, the chain of agencies through which this result is to be attained. The mind of the Father is revealed by Jesus Christ. "Jesus Christ is the mind of the Father" (Ephes. 3 ; cf. St Joh. xiv. 9). But just as Jesus Christ is the mind of the Father, so the bishops are "in the mind of Christ." In his government, in his teaching, the bishop is to be regarded as setting forth the mind of Christ. So, however widely separated the various bishops may be "in the farthest parts of the earth," a bond of harmony unites them, since all alike express the same mind, the mind of Christ.

The statement of course represents an ideal. It is not to be taken as upholding the infallibility of each individual bishop. But it expresses the principle that a harmonious unity and agreement marks them all, in so far as they express, as express they should, the mind of Christ. So presbyters and people alike are to follow in each case the bishop of their own church. Thus the body of the faithful all over the world will live within a bond of union, which is independent of the distance in space that may separate one community from another. The whole church universal will be united in accordance with the mind of God.

The unity of the church finds characteristic expression in the Eucharist. In the Eucharist all are united in the solemn act of communion, "breaking one loaf" (Ephes. 20), the loaf being a symbol of the oneness of the many (cf. 1 Cor. x. 17). "Be ye careful therefore to observe one Eucharist. For there is one flesh of our Lord Jesus Christ and one cup unto union with His blood; there is one altar, as there is one bishop" (Philad. 4). Here, again, the "one flesh" is, as the "one loaf," the symbol of the unity of the church in the body of Christ. The heretics, on the other hand, destroyed the unity of the church by abstaining from the church's Eucharist and claiming to celebrate a Eucharist of their own (Smyrn. 6, 8).

In close connection with the Eucharist was the Agapé, or Love-feast. In this there was a further emphasis of the unity of the church. For the fact of unity was therein expressed by practical hospitality. The Agapé was a common meal provided by the Christians, so that the poorer brethren might feast with the richer. In accordance with the principle of unity, the Agapé could not be held apart from the bishop's sanction (Smyrn. 8). So then the Eucharist by symbol, and the Agapé by practical kindness, gave expression to the unity of the church.

The social activities of the church have the same significance. There is the treatment of widows. These have a special claim upon the community. "Let not widows be neglected," writes Ignatius to Polycarp. "After the Lord be thou their protector" (ad Polyc. 4). So with regard to slaves. It is clearly contemplated that the Christian community will have a special fund for the purpose of purchasing the freedom of Christian slaves, which however is to be used with due discretion (ibid.). All this illustrates the practical character of the bond, which united the members of the Christian church.

In close connection with this is the question of public worship. For public worship is a necessary outward

expression of the unity of the church. Church membership must show itself in attendance at the church's
worship. "Whosoever cometh not to the congregation
doth thereby show his pride and hath separated himself"
(Ephes. 5). He has, as it were, pronounced against
himself his own sentence of excommunication. "Do your
diligence to meet together more frequently for thanksgiving
to God and for His glory. For when ye meet together
frequently, the powers of Satan are cast down" (Ephes.
13). "Assemble yourselves together in common"
(Ephes. 20). "Assemble yourselves all together with undivided heart" (Philad. 6). There is to be "one prayer
in common, one supplication" (Magn. 7). For all alike
have the same object of worship, all alike the same means
of access to God. "Hasten to come together all of you,
as to one temple, even God; as to one altar, even to one
Jesus Christ" (*ibid.*). The members of the church are to
be summoned by the bishop. He is to call them by name,
that each may come to the exercise of his religious duty.
"Let meetings be held more frequently. Seek out all
men by name" (ad Polyc. 4).

No doubt the worship of the synagogue would
influence in some degree the earliest public worship of the
Christian church[1]. The fact, that the preaching of Apostles
and others in synagogues was the starting point of many
of the churches, would result in a strong influence of
synagogue arrangements upon the primitive form of
worship. Thus a Christian assembly is called a συναγωγή,
not only in the Judaic Epistle of St James (Jas. ii. 2), but
by Ignatius, Hermas and Theophilus[2]. It is indeed

---

[1] Cf. Wordsworth, *Ministry of Grace*, pp. 115 f.
[2] ad Polyc. 4; Hermas, *Mand.* 11; Theophil. ad Autol. II. 14.

noteworthy that this word with Jewish associations should be used by Ignatius, who certainly has no Judaic bias [1].

But whatever may have been the extent of the influence of the synagogue, Ignatius shows at the same time that the Christian worship of his day was modelled on the arrangement of the basilica. In the centre on the dais sat the bishop, as president. On either side of him, and forming a half circle, sat the presbyters. This is the arrangement which underlies the description of the bishop, " with the fitly wreathed spiritual circlet of your presbytery, and with the deacons who walk after God " (Magn. 13).

The church holds firmly to a standard of true doctrine. It is a grievous sin to teach false doctrine. If those guilty of certain sins of the flesh are put to death, " how much more if a man through evil doctrine corrupt the faith of God, for which Jesus Christ was crucified?" (Ephes. 16). So the Philadelphians are bidden to " shun wrong doctrines " (Philad. 2). " If any man walketh in strange doctrine, he hath no fellowship with the passion " (Philad. 3). The organisation of the church is of importance in this connection. For recognition of the bishop's authority has a conservative effect (Ephes. 6). It puts a check upon those who might otherwise have fallen into heresy. Ignatius has heard from their bishop of the good discipline ($\epsilon\dot{v}\tau a\xi\acute{\iota}a$) of the Ephesian Christians, an important element in which is their stedfast adherence to the truth. "Ye all live according to truth and no heresy hath a home among you ; nay, ye do not so much as listen to anyone if he speak of aught else save concerning Jesus Christ in truth " (ibid.).

The standard of truth is subsequently laid down. It

[1] See e.g. Philad. 6 ; Magn. 10.

is the doctrine of the Apostles. The Ephesian Christians are praised for being " ever ot one mind with the Apostles in the power of Jesus Christ " (Ephes. 11). So then the substance of the teaching of the church is the apostolic tradition, "the ordinances of the Lord and of the Apostles" (Magn. 13), and Ignatius looks forward to attaining the final "inheritance " by "taking refuge in the Gospel as the flesh of Jesus and in the Apostles as the presbytery of a church " (Philad. 5). The Gospel is the ground of his hope ; the Apostles are his authoritative teachers and guides.

A church, as such, has duties to other churches, expressive of the ties of unity, which bind them together. This is illustrated by the practice of sending delegates from one church to another to bear greetings or to offer congratulations.

Thus Ignatius points out that it is the duty of the church in Philadelphia to send a representative to the church in Antioch to congratulate it upon once more enjoying peace. "It is becoming for you, as a church of God, to appoint a deacon to go thither as God's ambassador, that he may congratulate them, when they are assembled together" (Philad. 10). These congratulations, it should be noted, are to be delivered in public assembly. The message is not sent to individuals, but from one church to another church. Other churches, says Ignatius, have already recognised this duty. Those nearer to Syria have been able to send a larger number of representatives. "The churches, which are nearest, have sent bishops, and others presbyters and deacons " (Philad. 10). Nor is this duty a mere act of friendship. It is based on principle, the fundamental principle of unity ; and the representatives are therefore "an embassy of God " (*ibid.*). This same duty is incumbent upon the church in Smyrna. It also is bidden to send a representative, who in the same way is described as "an ambassador of God" (Smyrn. 11). Polycarp therefore, as bishop of the church in Smyrna, is addressed on the same subject. "It becometh thee, most blessed Polycarp, to call together a godly council and to elect some one among you, who is very dear to you and zealous also, who shall be fit to bear the name of God's courier—to appoint him, I say, that he may go to Syria" (ad Polyc. 7). Here we have the important point clearly brought out, that the election of the representative rests with the church[1]. It is the bishop's function to summon a council (συμβούλιον) of the church for this purpose. Polycarp is further bidden (ad Polyc. 8) to write to the more distant churches, that they also may send messengers, or at least letters, to the church in Antioch. This series of injunctions throws a strong sidelight upon the close relation which was felt to subsist between the local churches, however distant from one another.

In discussing the relation between the local churches, a word may be added with regard to the church in Rome. To this church a special local preeminence was attaching. It is a church which "has the presidency in the country of the region of the Romans" (Rom. inscr.). This local preeminence was quite natural, not only on account of the prestige of the Imperial City, but also on account of the apostolic foundation of the church there[2]. Ignatius

[1] Cf. Smyrn. 11, "that your church should appoint."

[2] Cf. Tert. de Præscr. 36, "percurre ecclesias apostolicas, apud quas ipsæ adhuc cathedræ apostolorum suis locis president" (quoted by Lightfoot, ad loc. Rom. inscr.). The above interpretation of the phrase descriptive of the church in Rome, ἥτις καὶ προκάθηται ἐν τόπῳ χωρίου Ῥωμαίων, is the only possible one. It is grammatically quite impossible to interpret the clause as ascribing to the church in Rome an absolute,

probably regarded the church in Antioch as having the
same kind of local preeminence in Syria. For he speaks of
himself as "the bishop from Syria" (Rom. 2), as though
a sort of local primacy attached to his office.

We have now to determine the conception, in the mind
of Ignatius, of the work of the church in relation to
sacrifice.

The rationale of sacrifice should be remembered.
The idea underlying it is that man, by sin, has forfeited
the right of access to God; that the death of a victim is
accepted as a propitiation for sin; that by offering to God
the life of a victim, slain in sacrifice, there is opened out
to the offerer a way of access to God.

Under the old covenant, the Temple, with its sacrifices,
provided this means of access.

Under the new covenant, the church is itself an "altar-
precinct" ($\theta\upsilon\sigma\iota\alpha\sigma\tau\eta\rho\iota\upsilon$, Ephes. 5), a sanctuary, a sphere of
sacrifice, so to speak; it is therefore a medium of intercourse
between man and God. The sacrifice offered is the united
prayer of the faithful, "the bishop and the whole church"
(*ibid.*). The church, therefore, which is the sphere of sacrifice
and which, as such, provides the means of access to God, is
the sphere within which God's spiritual gifts are brought
to man. Indeed, outside the church these gifts cannot
be had. "Let no man be deceived. If anyone be not

as distinct from a local, preeminence. If Ignatius had meant "the church
which has the preeminence [over all], the church, that is, in the country
of the region of the Romans," the definite article would be required or some
other indication that the closing words of the clause are in apposition to
the subject of the verb. He must have written $\dot{\eta}$ $\dot{\epsilon}\nu$ $\tau\dot{o}\pi\omega$ or $\dot{\epsilon}\nu$ $\tau\dot{o}\pi\omega$ $o\dot{\upsilon}\sigma\alpha$
χ. 'P. Moreover such an interpretation could not account for the
phrase $\dot{\epsilon}\nu$ $\tau\dot{o}\pi\omega$ $\chi\omega\rho\dot{\iota}o\upsilon$ 'P$\omega\mu\alpha\dot{\iota}\omega\nu$. Why not $\dot{\epsilon}\nu$ 'P$\dot{\omega}\mu\eta$? It is quite safe to
set aside such an interpretation as impossible. The phrase means that
the local church in Rome had a local preeminence in a district vaguely
described as "the region of the Romans."

within the precinct of the altar, he lacketh the bread [of God]. For if the prayer of one and another hath so great force, how much more that of the bishop and of the whole church " (*ibid.*). Thus the reason given for the church's prerogative is that the great spiritual force, which draws these gifts from God, is the force of the united prayer of the church, led by the bishop, a force which is of a sacrificial character. So, coming to the assembly of the church and joining in this united prayer, a man may participate in this spiritual force and thus win God's blessings.

This unique position of the church is further emphasised. "There is one altar, as there is one bishop, together with the presbytery and the deacons, my fellow-servants" (Philad. 4). Here, again, the altar is the whole local church, led by the bishop. The Christian church in any place is the point of contact with God. In the church, as upon an altar, the sacred social meal is celebrated, the "one Eucharist" (*ibid.*). In this the sacrificial power of the blood of Christ is communicated to the worshipper, thus allowing him access to God. "There is one flesh of our Lord Jesus Christ and one cup unto union in His blood" (*ibid.*).

Thus the sustenance of the spiritual life is through the church. But so too is the antecedent gift of cleansing and forgiveness, which must be preparatory to the sound growth of the soul. "He that is within the sanctuary is clean; but he that is without the sanctuary is not clean; that is, he that doeth aught without the bishop and presbytery and deacons, this man is not clean in his conscience" (Trall. 7).

It is important to notice that this sacerdotal character belongs to the entire church. All members of the church, as such, stand in a direct relation to God and exercise a priesthood. They are all "God's stewards, assessors and ministers" (ad Polyc. 6). So then the members of the church are charged with the stores of God's grace for the benefit of their fellows. They have moreover a power of discipline as being "assessors of God."

But though Ignatius uses this exclusive language in speaking of the church as the sole means of access to God, it is to be noted that at least in one case he admits salvation outside the church. The prophets of the Old Testament were saved. "They were saved in the unity of Jesus Christ, being worthy of love and admiration as holy men, approved of Jesus Christ and numbered together in the Gospel of our common hope" (Philad. 5). Ignatius thus suggests that holiness of life brings a man into unity with Jesus Christ, the one source of eternal life. He does indeed, in this case, contemplate salvation outside the church, but not outside Jesus Christ. Christ is "the door of the Father through which Abraham and Isaac and Jacob enter in, and the prophets and the Apostles and the church" (Philad. 9).

SECTION IV.

IGNATIUS (*continued*).

The ministry of the church.—Three orders in the ministry.—Monarchical
episcopacy.—Authority of the ministry.—Apostolic origin of episcopacy.—Appointment to the ministry.—The bishop: his representative
character.—His authority.—His work.—The presbyters: their
obedience to the bishop.—Their authority.—The deacons: their
rank.—Their character.—Their work.

We now come to a subject which fills a large place in
the letters of St Ignatius, and upon which he expresses
very strong and definite opinions.   This subject is that of
the Christian ministry. It is very largely his treatment of
the ministry which has led to the repeated attempts to
disprove the authenticity of the letters.   It is said that the
theory of church order which they disclose is inconsistent
with what actually existed in the church in the first decades
of the second century, and that they are an attempt of a
later period to read into these early days a system which
in fact did not then exist. Now we are not as yet concerned
with the problem as to how the Ignatian statements in
regard to church order are to be fitted into that fragmentary
picture of the church of the sub-apostolic days, which we
are able to piece together by a study of contemporary
writings.   Our present object is merely to examine the
Ignatian writings themselves and to ascertain the exact
teaching which they give.

We have already seen that a local church, in the
mind of Ignatius, is not a mere aggregate of believers, but
an organised society, with its ministry consisting of
bishop, presbyters and deacons, and that unless the local

society possesses a regular ministry it cannot claim to be
called a "church" (Trall. 3).

That all the churches of Asia, to which Ignatius
wrote, had in fact their bishop, presbyters and deacons,
appears from the letters. At Ephesus we have mention
of Onesimus, the bishop (Ephes. 1, 2, 4, etc.), of the
presbytery (Ephes. 2, 4, 20) and of Burrhus, the deacon
(Ephes. 2). To the Magnesians Ignatius writes of "Damas
your godly bishop and your worthy presbyters Bassus and
Apollonius and my fellow-servant the deacon Zotion"
(Magn. 2). It will be noted that in both these letters
only a single deacon is mentioned. This does not however
mean that the diaconate had only one representative in
each of these two churches but that only one deacon was
included among the representatives sent to meet Ignatius.
Doubtless each church had its body of deacons just as it
had its body of presbyters, but a single deacon would be
quite sufficient to fulfil the duties of service which the
embassy required. In all the other Asiatic letters we
have allusions to a body of deacons, as well as to the
bishop and the presbyters. "Do nothing without the
bishop. Be obedient to the presbytery...Those who are
deacons of the mysteries of Jesus Christ must please all
men in all ways" (Trall. 2). The Philadelphians are
bidden to "be at one with the bishop and the presbyters
who are with him and with the deacons that have been
appointed according to the mind of Jesus Christ" (Philad.
inscr.; cf. Philad. 4, 7, 10). The Smyrnæans are to follow
their bishop, as Jesus Christ followed the Father, and the
presbytery as the Apostles, and to the deacons they are
to pay respect (Smyrn. 8; cf. Smyrn. 12 and ad Polyc. 6).

In all these Asiatic churches the episcopacy is what
we may conveniently call monarchical. That is, a single

bishop stands at the head of the local church. At
Ephesus there is Onesimus (Ephes. 1), at Magnesia
Damas (Magn. 2), at Tralles Polybius (Trall. 1), at Smyrna
Polycarp (ad Polyc. inscr.). Philadelphia too has its
bishop, who is unnamed (Philad. 1). It is to be noted, on
the other hand, that no mention is made of a bishop at
Rome in the letter to the Romans. But this omission has
little significance, for no mention of any kind is made of
the ministry in the church in Rome. There is equal
silence as to its presbyters and deacons. And moreover
there can be little doubt that, whatever may have been
the precise facts, Ignatius at least believed that the
Christian society there possessed its full organisation of
bishop, presbyters and deacons. For he not only accords
to that society the title of a church, but describes it as a
church which is enlightened, worthy of God, worthy of
honour, worthy of praise (Rom. inscr.).

Now is it conceivable, having regard to the uncompromising words to the Trallians (Trall. 3), that Ignatius
would have bestowed upon the Christian community in
Rome these and other laudatory epithets, if he had
believed that community to be lacking in an element
which he regarded as essential to the proper constitution
of a church? It is of course a further question how far
Ignatius had accurate knowledge of the local conditions
at Rome. But at least the mere fact of omitting to
mention a bishop in that church cannot be regarded as
having any significance. The positive fact emerging from
the letters is that in the first decade of the second
century monarchical episcopacy was not only established
from Syria to the Hellespont but was regarded by
Ignatius as essential to the full life of the church. He
speaks indeed of " the bishops that are settled in the

farthest parts of the earth" (Ephes. 3). The expression
is of course vague and rhetorical. It may imply the
existence of bishops as far distant as Gaul in the one
direction and Mesopotamia in the other. At the very
least it must cover the wide range of the personal
experience of Ignatius himself. From Antioch to Troas,
at least, monarchical episcopacy was the rule.

The ministry so constituted has divine authority. It
is "a ministry of God" (Smyrn. 12). The analogy of the
courts of heaven is taken to illustrate the authority
committed to the ministry, "the bishop presiding after
the likeness of God and the presbyters after the likeness
of the council of the Apostles, with the deacons also who are
most dear to me, having been entrusted with the diaconate
of Jesus Christ" (Magn. 6). "Let all men respect the
deacons as Jesus Christ, even as they should respect the
bishop as being a type of the Father and the presbyters
as the council of God and as the college of Apostles"
(Trall. 3). We may note here that, while all three orders
of the ministry, bishop, presbyters and deacons, are entitled
to respect, obedience is due to two, the bishop and the
presbyters. It therefore follows that "he who doeth
aught without the bishop and presbytery and deacons, is
not clean in his conscience" (Trall. 7).

Nor is this precept of merely local application. It is
not given in view of special local conditions, but is of
universal obligation. Ignatius insists on this in writing
to the Philadelphians. He had said to them, "Give heed
to the bishop and the presbytery and deacons" (Philad. 7).
But the effect of his words had been minimised because it
was said that they were only addressed to special local
circumstances. "There were some who suspected me of
saying this, because I knew beforehand of the division of

certain persons" (*ibid.*). Ignatius therefore asserts emphatically that such is not the case. This duty of obedience to the bishop and of union with the threefold ministry is not merely one which special local conditions imposed, but is the expression of a universal principle. His precept is "God's own voice" and "the preaching of the Spirit" (*ibid.*). The authority of the threefold ministry is therefore based on divine sanction.

Consistently with this doctrine that the ministry rests upon divine authority, we find that the institution of monarchical episcopacy is referred by Ignatius to the Apostles. He speaks of "the ordinances of the Apostles" (Trall. 7, τὰ διατάγματα τῶν ἀποστόλων), where clearly the ruling thought in his mind is that of an episcopal ministry[1]. The brethren must be "inseparable from Jesus Christ and from the bishop and from the ordinances of the Apostles." For "he that doeth aught without the bishop and presbytery and deacons, is not clean in his conscience" (*ibid.*).

In accordance with this character of the ministry, as having a divine sanction, we find that appointment to it rests upon a double basis. On the one hand the presbyters and deacons receive their appointment through human agency. They are "designated for office" (Philad. inscr. ἀποδεδειγμένοι), whether by the whole local church or by the church officers. And, on the other hand, the appointment so made receives the ratification of Jesus Christ (*ibid.* ἐν γνώμῃ Ἰησοῦ Χριστοῦ), while the men so appointed receive a special gift of divine grace. They are "confirmed and established by His Holy Spirit" (*ibid.*). Thus the two sides of the ministry find expression in the

[1] Cf. Lightfoot, *Apostolic Fathers*, Part II. vol. II. sect. 1, p. 169, *ad loc.*, "The reference is doubtless to the institution of episcopacy."

appointment to office.   On the one side the presbyters
and deacons are the servants of the church and so receive
their appointment from those to whom they are to
minister. On the other side they have a divine commission
and exercise their ministry under the authority of God.

We have already seen that the threefold ministry,
possessing such a charter, has a claim upon the respect of
the brethren (Trall. 3). But this lays upon the possessors
of such an office the responsibility to show themselves
worthy of the respect they claim. So Ignatius gives
charge to Polycarp: "Vindicate thine office" (ad Polyc. 1).
He is to give open proof of the greatness of his office by
the earnestness with which he discharges its duties. But
the thought of high authority must not lead him to pride.
"Let not office puff up any man" (Smyrn. 6). The words
indeed are general, but Ignatius is probably thinking
especially of office in the church. Such office must be
held in such a way as to show due regard for its dignity,
but there must be no personal pride.

We have now to consider more in detail the Ignatian
conception of the function of the bishop and of the place
he occupies in the life of the church.

The bishop is the representative of the local church
and is also its centre of unity. "I have received your whole
multitude in the person of Onesimus, who is your bishop"
(Ephes. 1), writes Ignatius to the church in Ephesus. So
also to meet Damas, the bishop of the Magnesians, is to
meet the whole church (Magn. 2). In Polybius, bishop in
Tralles, Ignatius sees the whole of the Trallian church.
So he describes the various local churches as being present
with him, in that their representatives are in his company.
"I salute you from Smyrna, together with the churches of
God that are present with me" (Trall. 12). "Those

churches, which did not lie on my route, after the flesh, went before me from city to city " (Rom. 9).

Since the bishop is the representative of the church and its centre of unity, it follows that at the characteristic acts of the church the bishop must himself be present, either in person or by commission. " Let no man do aught of things pertaining to the church apart from the bishop. Let that be held a valid (βεβαία) Eucharist, which is under the bishop or one to whom he shall have committed it. Wheresoever the bishop shall appear, there let the people be; even as where Jesus Christ may be, there is the universal church. It is not lawful apart from the bishop either to baptize or to hold a love-feast; but whatsoever he shall approve, this is well-pleasing to God; that everything which ye do may be sure and valid" (Smyrn. 8). Jesus Christ stands in relation to the universal church as its Head. An analogy to this headship is found in the relation of the bishop to the local church. Just as the one universal church is gathered up in the person of Jesus Christ, so in the person of the bishop is centred the life of the local institutional church. For this reason, Baptism, the rite of entry into the church, must of necessity be performed in union with the bishop, that is either by the bishop himself or by one who holds the bishop's commission. The Eucharist, with its accompanying Agapé, symbolising as it does the unity of the church, must be celebrated under the same conditions. It was the custom of the heretics, as this passage shows (cf. Philad. 4), to celebrate their own Eucharist separately. A Eucharist, so celebrated, was not valid. That, which was designed to be an act expressive of unity, became in the hands of heretics a badge of division.

But, further than this, " he that doeth aught without

the knowledge of the bishop rendereth service ($\lambda \alpha \tau \rho \epsilon \acute{\upsilon} \epsilon \iota$) to the devil" (Smyrn. 9). His ministry is not merely invalid, but is even a ritual service offered not to God but to the devil. So fundamental is the principle of unity, of which the bishop is the visible centre in the local church.

"Let nothing be done without thy consent" is therefore the injunction to Polycarp (ad Polyc. 4). Polycarp is to assert his claim to control the church, but for his own part he is to see that his life is in accordance with the will of God. "Neither do thou anything without the consent of God, as indeed thou dost not" (*ibid.*).

An exhortation to obey the bishop is based on the character of the church as an altar-precinct ($\theta \upsilon \sigma \iota \alpha \sigma \tau \acute{\eta} \rho \iota o \nu$), through which man has access to God, and whereby he receives God's spiritual gifts. "Let us therefore be careful not to resist the bishop, that by our submission we may give ourselves to God" (Ephes. 5). For he who stands apart from the bishop is outside that sacrificial sphere, through which God is approached and through the medium of which His great gifts are bestowed. Obedience therefore is enforced, as a duty following from the sacrificial aspect of the church.

The metaphor then changes and the church is thought of not as an altar-precinct but as a household. The bishop occupies the position of steward over the house. He is the representative of Christ. And obedience to Christ involves obedience to those to whom Christ has committed authority (cf. St Joh. xiii. 20, St Matt. x. 40). "Every one whom the Master of the household sendeth to be steward over His own house, we ought so to receive as Him that sent him. Plainly therefore we ought to regard the bishop as the Lord Himself" (Ephes. 6). The meaning of the closing words is that the bishop is to be regarded as representing Christ, the unseen Head of the household. In a line with this, are words written to the Trallians. " When ye are obedient to the bishop as to Jesus Christ, it is evident to me that ye are living not after men, but after Jesus Christ " (Trall. 2). " Fare ye well in Jesus Christ, submitting yourselves to the bishop as to the commandment" (Trall. 13). The comparison of the bishop to Jesus Christ is not made absolutely, but from the point of view of representative character. As Jesus Christ is the supreme Head, so His visible representative is the bishop. The comparison therefore does not mean that the duty of obedience to the bishop is without limit or condition. Indeed the very fact of reference to Jesus Christ implies a limit. His is the supreme authority, and the bishop can claim obedience only in so far as he is truly representing Jesus Christ. But within such limits church order and discipline require loyal obedience to be offered to the bishop's commands. There is of course no claim of infallibility made on behalf of the bishop. He may issue unworthy commands, in which case there could be no claim upon the obedience of the brethren. Indeed the limit of obedience is indicated. Submission is to be yielded to the bishop "as to the commandment " (Trall. 13), by which is meant the supreme law of God.

Ignatius is concerned not with particular cases but with general principles. His general principle is that the local church is the channel of divine gifts; that the bishop is its official head, that as such he claims obedience. Ignatius uses various similes to express the duty of obedience to constituted authority. Elsewhere (Magn. 6, Trall. 3) there is a comparison with the basilican arrangement, claiming for the ministry of the church a limited

judicial authority, even as such an authority belongs
supremely to the court of heaven.

There must therefore be loyal cooperation with the
bishop. The brethren must work in harmony with him,
supporting him in what he undertakes. This loyalty
must especially find expression in attendance at that
lawful assembly for public worship, which is under the
authority and direction of the bishop. The tendency to
act apart from the bishop and to set up other assemblies
for worship was already showing itself. "Some persons
have the bishop's name on their lips, but in everything
act apart from him. Such men appear to me not to keep a
good conscience, forasmuch as they do not assemble themselves together according to commandment" (Magn. 4).
Again and again exhortations to the same effect are
repeated. "Be obedient to the bishop" (Magn. 13). "It
is necessary, even as your wont is, that ye should do
nothing without the bishop" (Trall. 2). "He that doeth
aught without the bishop and presbytery and deacons, this
man is not clean in his conscience" (Trall. 7). "Do ye
all follow your bishop....Let no man do aught of things pertaining to the church apart from the bishop" (Smyrn. 8).
"He that honoureth the bishop is honoured of God"
(Smyrn. 9). "Give ye heed to the bishop that God also may
give heed to you. I am devoted to those who are subject
to the bishop, the presbyters, the deacons" (ad Polyc. 6).

The reason for these earnest exhortations is to be
found in the source of the bishop's authority. For his
authority is derived from God, whose representative he is.
So in giving allegiance to their bishop, the presbyters in
Magnesia are paying reverence "not to him but to the
Father of Jesus Christ, even to the Bishop of all"
(Magn. 3). And to deal deceitfully with the bishop is to

deal deceitfully with God. "A man doth not so much deceive this bishop who is seen, as cheat that other who is invisible" (*ibid.*). So too the bishop of the church in Philadelphia holds his office "not of himself or through men" (Philad. 1). His commission is from above.

However strong the expressions which Ignatius uses in regard to the obedience due to the bishop, however exalted his teaching as to episcopal authority, he yet makes it clear that this authority is exercised and this obedience claimed, only subject to the supreme authority of God. So while obeying the bishop the brethren are to "abide in the unity and supervision (ἐπισκοπή) of God" (ad Polyc. 8). God is the supreme Bishop (cf. Magn. 3). The expressions of Ignatius, therefore, however unqualified, must yet be interpreted in the light of this fundamental presupposition. Remembering this, we shall see that the charge of extravagance in his teaching disappears. His mode of expression belongs to his own fervid nature. He does not trouble always to balance his statements. He leaves something to the common sense of his readers.

The bishop's authority, limited thus by conformity to God's supreme ἐπισκοπή, has also a local limitation. The bishop has authority only within his own local church. Thus Ignatius claims no authority over the Ephesians. "I do not command you, as though I were somewhat" (Ephes. 3). We need not doubt that Ignatius, who lays stress on submission to the bishop, himself claimed submission at Antioch. So his words to the Ephesians indicate the local limit of the claim of obedience. And indeed such a limitation is to be expected. For if a bishop could everywhere claim obedience this would at once destroy the unifying force in the local church, which

obedience to a single bishop was calculated to produce. A
leading purpose of monarchical episcopacy was to secure
unity in each local church by obedience to a single head,
"that being perfectly joined together in one submission
submitting yourselves to your bishop and presbytery, ye
may be sanctified in all things" (Ephes. 2).

This local limit to a bishop's jurisdiction is further
emphasised by contrast with the universal authority of
Apostles. Thus to the Trallians: "I did not think
myself competent for this, that being a convict I should
order you as though I were an Apostle" (Trall. 3). And
again to the Romans: "I do not enjoin you, as Peter and
Paul did. They were Apostles, I am a convict" (Rom. 4).
While then in the view of Ignatius an Apostle rightly
claimed obedience from all the churches[1], a bishop
possesses authority over his own church only.

The bishop, as we have seen, is placed in a position of
authority over the local church. It is important however
to remember that this authority is not arbitrary but
constitutional. We have already noted that it is limited
by the condition that the bishop's commands must be in
accordance with the commandments of God. We should
now note that he is to act, at least on occasion, in
conjunction with a council of the whole church. It is the
bishop's function to summon a council of the local church
from time to time. Thus Polycarp is bidden to summon
a council of the church in Smyrna for the purpose of
electing a representative to go to Antioch. "It becometh
thee, most blessed Polycarp, to call together a godly

[1] This claim is illustrated by St Paul's letters. He claims the right
to give commands to the church of Corinth (1 Cor. xvi. 1), to the churches
of Galatia (*ibid.*), to all the churches (1 Cor. vii. 17), to Titus (Tit. i. 5)
and to Philemon (Philem. 8).

council and to elect some one among you who is very
dear to you and zealous also, who shall be fit to bear the
name of God's courier—to appoint him, I say, that he
may go to Syria" (ad Polyc. 7). The election, then, of the
representative lies with the church in council. It is the
bishop, however, who gives to the elected representative
his commission. "I salute him that shall be appointed
(*i.e.* by the church) to go to Syria. Grace be with
him always and with Polycarp, who sendeth him"
(ad Polyc. 8).

The directions given to Polycarp show the spirit in
which the bishop should do his work and exercise his
authority. "Let not widows be neglected. After the
Lord be thou their protector. Let nothing be done
without thy consent; neither do thou anything without
the consent of God, as indeed thou doest not. Be stedfast.
Let meetings be held more frequently. Seek out all men
by name. Despise not slaves, whether men or women.
Yet let not these again be puffed up, but let them serve
the more faithfully to the glory of God, that they may
obtain a better freedom from God" (ad Polyc. 4). The
bishop, then, is to be careful to maintain his authority,
not however out of any spirit of vainglory, but for the sake
of his office. The weak and the oppressed are to be his
special care. Indeed we may best sum up his position by
saying that he is to be the elder brother in the brotherhood
of the church.

One word must be added as to the function of the
bishop in relation to marriage. The exaltation of the
celibate life at the expense of the married state has
already begun to appear. St Paul hardly goes beyond the
position of advising celibacy for the sake of the parties
concerned, in the special circumstances of the times,

" because of the present distress " (1 Cor. vii. 26). But in Ignatius, ἁγνεία, in its new technical sense of " virginity," is evidently exalted as the higher ideal. He, who of set purpose, with a view to the carrying out of an ideal, embraces the celibate life, may communicate his purpose to the bishop, but must beware of making it a subject of public boasting. " If anyone is able to abide in chastity to the honour of the flesh of the Lord, let him so abide without boasting. If he boast, he is lost; and if it be known beyond the bishop he is polluted " (ad Polyc. 5). Marriage, on the other hand, is a sacred institution, which requires the sanction of the church. So the consent of the bishop as representative of the church must be obtained. " It becometh men and women too, when they marry, to unite themselves with the consent of the bishop, that the marriage may be after the Lord and not after concupiscence. Let all things be done to the honour of God" (*ibid.*). So the church, through the bishop, gives its blessing to the married life of its members.

From the bishop we turn to the presbyters. These, on the one hand, must obey the bishop, but on the other hand they can claim obedience both from the deacons and from the people.

They must obey the bishop. Ignatius notices with approval that the presbyters of Magnesia have not taken advantage of the youth of their bishop to withhold from him the deference which is his due. " They give place to him as to one prudent in God " (Magn. 3). They are to work in harmony with the bishop. So the presbytery at Ephesus is praised because "it is attuned to the bishop, even as its strings to a lyre" (Ephes. 4). It is a true instinct of human nature, which leads Ignatius to describe further the relation that should subsist between the bishop and the presbyters. "It becometh you severally and more especially the presbyters to cheer the soul of your bishop unto the honour of the Father, of Jesus Christ and of the Apostles" (Trall. 12). The burden of office should command the affectionate and effective sympathy of those over whom the bishop bears rule. The presbyters especially should do their best to lighten his burden. Indeed to some extent they do share the bishop's burden, as being his assessors in council, "the bishop presiding after the likeness of God and the presbyters after the likeness of the council of the Apostles" (Magn. 6). The responsibility of decision rests with the bishop, but he has the advantage of the deliberations and advice of the presbyters.

Such then are the relations of the presbyters to their bishop. But they are themselves in a position of authority. They claim the obedience both of the deacons and of the people. Ignatius rejoices in the deacon Zotion, because "he is subject...to the presbytery as unto the law of Jesus Christ" (Magn. 2). The terms of comparison show that in this case, just as in the case of the bishop, obedience to authority is limited by the fundamental claim of obedience to "the law of Jesus Christ." The presbyters are spoken of as presiding over the local church (Magn. 6). The people must therefore submit themselves to the presbytery (Ephes. 4, Trall. 13); they must "obey the presbytery without distraction of mind" (Ephes. 20); they must "be obedient to the presbytery, as to the Apostles of Jesus Christ our hope" (Trall. 2).

An analogy holds between the position of the Apostles in the church universal and that of the presbyters in a local church. Ignatius speaks of "taking refuge in the Apostles as in the presbytery of a church" (Philad. 5). This shows that the conception of the presbytery is that of an institution for the purpose of helping and protecting those over whom authority is exercised. The presbytery exists for the people.

The deacons owe obedience both to the bishop and to the presbyters (Magn. 2). But on the other hand they have a right to the respect of the people. "Let all men respect the deacons as Jesus Christ" (Trall. 3). "To the deacons pay respect, as to God's commandment" (Smyrn. 8). Pay respect, that is, to the messenger and the message alike. The deacon, as the title of his office implies, is a servant. Nor is he a servant only of his superiors in the ministry, the bishop and presbyters, but also of the people. "Those who are deacons of the mysteries of Jesus Christ must please all men in all ways. For they are not deacons of meats and drinks but servants of the church of God" (Trall. 2). So then, while the obedience of the people is claimed for the bishop and the presbyters, respect and not obedience is as a rule claimed for the deacons. There is however a possible exception to this distinction. Ignatius says, "I am devoted to those who are subject to the bishop, the presbyters, the deacons" (ad Polyc. 6). It may be contended that this only implies obedience to the ministry generally, not specifically to the deacons, towards whom the proper attitude is one of heedful respect. We may note however that Polycarp himself urges submission "to the presbyters and deacons as to God and Christ" (Polyc. ad Phil. 5). In this case the terms of comparison show that submission is to be rendered to both ranks of the ministry severally.

The deacons must be of good character, as befits their office. They are "servants of a church of God. It is right therefore that they should beware of blame as of fire" (Trall. 2).

The work of the deacons is no mere ministry of meat and drink. They have indeed this lower function. They occupy a position to which that of the Seven largely corresponds. They have the serving of tables, the distribution of alms, the arrangement of the Agapé. But this lower side of their work is overshadowed by their spiritual duties. They are " deacons of the mysteries of Jesus Christ," not merely " deacons of meats and drinks " (Trall. 2). The contrast here implied shows that the leading idea in " the mysteries " is that of the Eucharist. The act in which the deacons find their characteristic service is no mere earthly meal of " meats and drinks," but has a mystical significance.

Further, they are " deacons of a church of God" (*ibid.*), servants of a definite local community, which has a sacred existence as belonging to God.

SECTION V.

POLYCARP.

Disciplinary authority of the local church.—Its sacrificial character.— Relations between the local churches; permitting divergence of custom, but not divergence of doctrine.—The ministry.—Episcopacy. —Divine authority of the ministry.—Qualifications for (1) the presbyterate, (2) the diaconate.—The order of widows.

Polycarp, bishop of the church in Smyrna, was the younger contemporary of Ignatius. To him, as we have seen, one of the Ignatian letters was written. The Epistle of Polycarp was written to the Philippian church soon after the martyrdom of Ignatius.

Polycarp uses the same phraseology as Ignatius of the local Christian communities. The body of Christians in

Philippi is "the church of God which sojourneth at
Philippi" (Polyc. Phil. inscr.). The various communities
are "the churches." "He boasteth of you in all those
churches, which alone at that time knew God" (Polyc.
Phil. 11).

It is hinted that the local church possesses a disciplinary authority. This power of discipline is to be
exercised with mercy. "Frail and erring members," such
as Valens and his wife, are not to be held as enemies, but
are to be restored to their position (Polyc. Phil. 11).

We have an indication of a sacrificial conception of
the church, similar to that displayed by Ignatius. In the
church there are means of access to God. Thus for instance
the order of widows provides a means of offering the sacrifice of alms to God. The widows therefore are described
as "God's altar," since through them the sacrifice is made.
They are reminded that "all sacrifices are carefully inspected, and nothing escapeth Him either of their thoughts
or intents or any of the secret things of the heart" (Polyc.
Phil. 4).

Polycarp encourages harmonious relations between the
churches, both by writing letters to other churches himself and by forwarding to them copies of the letters of
Ignatius. He also warmly takes up the suggestion of
Ignatius that delegates should be sent from his own
church to Syria. Indeed he contemplates going himself
(Polyc. Phil. 13).

Very instructive on the subject of inter-communion
between local churches is the account of his intercourse
with Anicetus, bishop of the church in Rome. "When
the blessed Polycarp was sojourning in Rome in the time
of Anicetus, although a slight controversy had arisen
between them as to certain other points, they were at

once reconciled, not being willing that any quarrel should arise between them on this subject (*i.e.* the mode of observance of Easter). For neither could Anicetus persuade Polycarp to forego his own method of observance, inasmuch as these things had been always so observed by John the disciple of our Lord, and by the other Apostles with whom he had been conversant; nor, on the other hand, could Polycarp persuade Anicetus to follow his observance, for he maintained that he was bound to adhere to the usage of the presbyters who preceded him. And under these conditions they held fellowship with each other; and Anicetus conceded to Polycarp in the church the celebration of the Eucharist, by way of showing him respect; so that they parted in peace one from the other, and those alike who observed and who did not observe the custom were at peace with the whole church" (Iren. *ad Vict.*). This narrative of Polycarp's intercourse with Anicetus at Rome is a vivid illustration of the fellowship that existed between local churches, however widely separated. The local churches are bound together in the higher unity of the one church universal. The fact of this unity is further emphasised by the agreement to admit a difference of use. For this agreement shows that the bond of union was held to rest upon a deeper foundation than anything that could be affected by such divergences of custom. Polycarp's own use was sacred to himself on account of the long tradition that lay behind it in his own church. He feels that it would not be right for him to abandon it. But Anicetus has his own use as well, which rests upon old-established custom. Each therefore agreed that the other should adhere to the use in which he had been trained, and this agreement was a striking witness to the deep-seated sense of fellowship which united these representatives of an eastern and a western church. No difference of custom could be allowed to impair their essential unity. It is important to notice that the celebration of the Eucharist is the symbol of unity. As a ratification of the compact, Polycarp receives permission from Anicetus to celebrate the Eucharist in his church in Rome.

But while difference of custom is thus tolerated, as having no power to weaken real union, there is on the other hand no toleration of heresy. The attitude of Polycarp towards heresy is illustrated by the story of his encounter with Marcion. "Dost thou not know me?" was Marcion's question to Polycarp. "I do know thee, the firstborn of Satan," was the uncompromising reply (Iren. *Hær.* III. iii. 4).

We come now to the question of Polycarp's view as to the constitution of the Christian ministry. We find that he himself writes as a bishop, in the monarchical sense of the word. The salutation to the Philippians is from "Polycarp and the presbyters that are with him" (Polyc. Phil. inscr.). He is distinguished from the presbyters. He is a bishop surrounded by his presbyteral council, though the actual title of office does not occur. He is of course so represented in the Ignatian letters (Magn. 15, Smyrn. 12, ad Polyc. inscr.). The question however arises as to how the ministry at Philippi was constituted at the time of Polycarp's letter. He makes no mention of a bishop. The ministers he refers to are the presbyters and the deacons (Polyc. Phil. 5, 6). It is interesting to compare this with the salutation in St Paul's Epistle to the Philippians. St Paul does not particularise any offices, but speaks of the ministry as represented by two classes, those charged with oversight and those charged with service[1].

[1] See Hort, *Christian Ecclesia*, pp. 211 f.

It would seem then that whatever ministers may have been designated by St Paul under these descriptions, the ministry at Philippi had in Polycarp's time attained definition in at least two ranks. There were the presbyters, who may be said to have had an office of supervision, and there were the deacons, whose ministry had, for its characteristic, service.

Now if these sections, in which Polycarp speaks of presbyters and deacons in Philippi stood alone, the inference might be drawn that the absence of any allusion to a bishop meant that monarchical episcopacy had not yet been established at Philippi. But the argument from silence is notoriously precarious. And indeed another passage has a direct bearing upon the question of the character of the ministry at Philippi. Polycarp is sending to the Philippians the letters of Ignatius (Polyc. Phil. 13). And he sends them without any hint that they will find in them a grave element of divergence from their own practice, something, in fact, which is to unchurch them. For Ignatius denies the very title of church to those communities which have not the three orders of bishop, presbyters and deacons in their ministry (Trall. 3). But Polycarp, instead of warning them on this point, unreservedly commends the letters to them. " They comprise faith and endurance and every kind of edification, which pertaineth unto our Lord " (Polyc. Phil. 13). Now it is inconceivable that Polycarp should have written so, if he had been cognisant of conflicting practice in a matter upon which he knew that Ignatius laid such stress. There must in that case have been some allusion to the matter, some apology for sending letters, which on the present supposition would be felt so emphatically to condemn them. Nor can we suppose that Polycarp was ignorant of the circumstances of the Philippian church.

He shows accurate local knowledge. His allusion to Valens shows that he knew what was going on in the church at Philippi. We are thus driven to conclude that Polycarp recognised no essential difference between the church government at Philippi and that insisted on by Ignatius. It is therefore natural to suppose that the process had been at work at Philippi, which gave to the body of presbyters a leader or president, by whatever title of office described. Whenever a body of presbyters had been formed in a local church, it was almost inevitable that the body should receive a head, and such a head would correspond, in the view of Polycarp and of the Philippians themselves, to the Ignatian bishop. Probably, however, in the church order in Philippi at that date the head of the presbyteral council did not stand out so conspicuously as did the bishop in the churches in Asia. This would account for his not being specifically mentioned by Polycarp.

The officers of the church are the visible representatives of the divine Lord of the church. As such they have a claim to obedience. The Philippians are to submit themselves "to the presbyters and deacons as to God and Christ" (Polyc. Phil. 5). Of course the comparison, which gives the ground of obedience, implies also a limit of the range within which obedience is due. Since the ministry claims obedience, on the ground of being representative "of God and Christ," its authority must be exercised in harmony with the will of God. It is no obedience to an arbitrary or capricious individual will that is required.

The presbyterate requires definite qualifications both of character and capacity. Presbyters must be "compassionate, merciful towards all men, turning back the sheep that are gone astray, visiting all the infirm, not neglecting a widow or an orphan or a poor man; but providing always for that which is honourable in the sight of God and of men, abstaining from all anger, respect of persons, unrighteous judgment, being far from all love of money, not quick to believe anything against any man, not hasty in judgment, knowing that we are all debtors of sin" (Polyc. Phil. 6). It will be noted that Polycarp's list of qualifications is practically covered by those set down in the Pastoral Epistles, as necessary for one who has the function of an ἐπίσκοπος (1 Tim. iii. 2 ff., Tit. i. 7 ff.). The vocabulary indeed is quite different, but the ideas are parallel. Polycarp gives a larger amount of detail, especially in relation to works of love and charity, upon which in the Christian community much stress was laid. The position of judge also occupies a prominent place in the mind of Polycarp. The presbyter is to execute judicial functions, and must therefore possess all the qualities which are essential for a good judge. The necessity of good character for the presbyterate is emphasised by the fall of Valens. "I was exceedingly grieved for Valens," says Polycarp, "who aforetime was a presbyter among you, because he is so ignorant of the office which was given him" (Polyc. Phil. 11). It is an office which requires high character. For how shall a man impress upon others virtues, which he does not aim at himself? "He who cannot govern himself in these things, how doth he enjoin this upon another?" (ibid.).

We turn now to the qualifications required for the diaconate. "Deacons should be blameless in the presence of His righteousness, as deacons of God and Christ and not of men; not calumniators, not double-tongued, not lovers of money, temperate in all things, compassionate, diligent, walking according to the truth of the Lord, who

became a minister (διάκονος) of all" (Polyc. Phil. 5).
Here again the qualifications required differ little from
those set down in the Pastoral Epistles (1 Tim. iii. 8—10,
12 f.). Emphasis is laid upon the sacred character of the
office. Those who hold it are "deacons of God and Christ
and not of men." Their character therefore must be such
as is consonant with such a charge.

We have already noted that Polycarp appears to differ
from Ignatius in that he definitely teaches that submission
is to be yielded to the deacons. "Submitting yourselves
to the presbyters and deacons as to God and Christ"
(Polyc. Phil. 5). The usual attitude towards the deacons,
inculcated by Ignatius, is one of heedful respect, though
it is possible that in one passage he goes beyond this and
requires submission to them (Ign. Polyc. 6).

The language of Polycarp strongly suggests that he
contemplates an order of widows. "Our widows must be
sober-minded as touching the faith of the Lord, making
intercession without ceasing for all men, abstaining from
all calumny, evil speaking, false witness, love of money, and
every evil thing, knowing that they are God's altar, and
that all sacrifices are carefully inspected, and that nothing
escapeth Him either of their thoughts or intents or any
of the secret things of the heart" (Polyc. Phil. 4). Now
the Pastoral Epistles have already revealed the existence
of an order of widows (1 Tim. v. 9), so that it is a fair
inference that Polycarp in speaking here of "our widows"
means those who have been enrolled as widows in the
order, and who in return for this privilege must perform
certain duties. Their character must be good. Their
central duty is that of intercessory prayer. They are
"God's altar," the medium, that is, through which the
sacrifice of alms is offered to God.

The following table will show how far the qualifications required by Polycarp correspond with those of the Pastoral Epistles.

THE PRESBYTERS.

Polycarp § 6.	The Pastorals (referring to ὁ ἐπίσκοπος).
εὔσπλαγχνοι	ἐπιεικής. 1 Tim. iii. 3.
	μὴ αὐθάδης. Tit. i. 7.
ἐλεήμονες ἐπισκεπτόμενοι πάντας ἀσθενεῖς	φιλόξενος. 1 Tim. iii. 2.
ἐπιστρέφοντες τὰ ἀποπεπλανημένα	διδακτικός. 1 Tim. iii. 2.
	δυνατὸς...τοὺς ἀντιλέγοντας ἐλέγχειν. Tit. i. 9.
ἀπεχόμενοι πάσης ὀργῆς	ἄμαχος. 1 Tim. iii. 3.
	μὴ πλήκτης. 1 Tim. iii. 3; Tit. i. 8.
	μὴ ὀργίλος. Tit. i. 7.
ἀπεχόμενοι προσωπολημψίας, κρίσεως ἀδίκου μὴ ταχέως πιστεύοντες κατά τινος μὴ ἀπότομοι ἐν κρίσει	δίκαιος. Tit. i. 8.
μακρὰν ὄντες πάσης φιλαργυρίας	ἀφιλάργυρος. 1 Tim. iii. 3.
	μὴ αἰσχροκερδής. Tit. i. 8.

This list, though exhaustive of Polycarp, is by no means so of the Pastorals.

THE DEACONS.

Polycarp § 5.	The Pastorals.
ἄμεμπτοι	ἀνέγκλητοι. 1 Tim. iii. 10.
μὴ διάβολοι	σεμνοί. 1 Tim. iii. 8.
μὴ δίλογοι	μὴ δίλογοι. 1 Tim. iii. 8.
ἀφιλάργυροι	μὴ αἰσχροκερδεῖς. 1 Tim. iii. 8.
ἐγκρατεῖς περὶ πάντα	μὴ οἴνῳ πολλῷ προσέχοντες. 1 Tim. iii. 8.
εὔσπλαγχνοι	wanting
ἐπιμελεῖς	wanting
πορευόμενοι κατὰ τὴν ἀλήθειαν	ἔχοντες τὸ μυστήριον τῆς πίστεως ἐν καθαρᾷ συνειδήσει. 1 Tim. iii. 9.

In addition to the above, we find in the Pastorals the qualifications relating to family life, μιᾶς γυναικὸς ἄνδρες, τέκνων καλῶς προϊστάμενοι καὶ τῶν ἰδίων οἴκων. There is nothing corresponding to these in Polycarp.

CHAPTER II.

FURTHER WITNESS: THE DIDACHÉ—BARNABAS—HERMAS.

SECTION I.

THE DIDACHÉ.

Two conceptions of the church.—Entrance into the church (1) effected by Baptism; (2) conferring a new relation towards God.—Qualities of the church: (1) Its mystical character: (2) Its holiness: (3) Its brotherhood.—Issuing in a new conception of social relationships.—And in a special exercise of hospitality.—Unity of the church.—Finding social expression.—But not yet in formal organisation.—Recognised however in reciprocal intercourse.—And preeminently in the Eucharist.—But only to be perfected hereafter.—Discipline in the church: exercised by the whole community.—(1) The discipline of entry: (2) The discipline of fasting: (3) Discipline in general.—Public Worship in the church.

The *Didaché* or *Teaching of the Twelve Apostles* is a document of which it is difficult to fix either the date or the place of writing. On the whole the conditions of the problem are best satisfied by placing it between the years A.D. 110 and 130. It has features which indicate that it emanated from a rural district, but more than this can hardly be said. The manual must have been held in high repute, for it seems to have become the basis of other books of church order[1].

---

[1] Cf. Stanton, *Gospels*, i. pp. 29—31.

A dual conception underlies the idea of the church in the *Didaché*. From one point of view the church is regarded as an aggregate of persons, who have been admitted by Baptism to the company of the faithful. From another side, it is defined with reference not to its contents but to its nature. It is thought of as the sphere within which subsists a special relation to God. The two ideas are necessarily interwoven, and now one is dominant, now the other. In each case the thought is implicit rather than explicit.

Entrance into the church is by Baptism, the Sacrament of inclusion (*Did.* 7 and 9, εἰς τὸ ὄνομα). Thus Baptism brings the recipient into that sphere, within which he may claim the spiritual blessings of the kingdom and wherein he is placed in a special relation to God.

The nature of this special relation to God is expressed in the Eucharistic thanksgiving. " We give Thee thanks, Holy Father, for Thy holy name, which Thou hast made to tabernacle in our hearts, and for the knowledge and faith and immortality, which Thou hast made known unto us through Thy Son Jesus " (*Did.* 10). None may join in this Eucharistic thanksgiving but those who have been " baptized into the name of the Lord " (*Did.* 9), and so have entered into the privileges of the new relationship. The words therefore of the thanksgiving, thus confined to those who by the gate of Baptism have entered the church, will, so far as they go, express the privileges which the church bestows upon its members. The new federal relation in the church is expressed by the indwelling of " the holy name "; the characteristic title of relationship, that namely of " Father," is given to God; the gifts bestowed are "knowledge, faith and immortality." In this triad is expressed the proper development of the

Christian life. The knowledge of God must issue in a personal realisation of this knowledge in faith, and thence will flow eternal life. And so, on the side of divine agency, the initiation into this new relationship (*Did.* 10, " Thy holy name, which Thou hast made to tabernacle in our hearts ") is followed by its maintenance through spiritual gifts (*ibid.* " Thou didst bestow upon us spiritual food and drink and eternal life through Thy Son "). This spiritual maintenance is thus expressed by the gifts in the Eucharist, which therefore becomes the characteristic expression of the life of the church.

The church therefore is thought of as the sphere within which a new federal relationship to God obtains and in which are bestowed spiritual gifts for the maintenance of the spiritual life. And these privileges, which belong to the church, are further emphasised by contrasting its members with those who are outside its pale. Upon all men, indeed, God has bestowed temporal blessings (*Did.* 10, "Thou didst give food and drink unto men for enjoyment "), but upon those who are in the church (*ibid.* ἡμῖν δέ—in emphatic contrast) He has bestowed "spiritual food and drink and eternal life." And in accordance with this same emphatic contrast is the condition that those only who have been "baptized into the name of the Lord" (*Did.* 9) may partake of the Eucharist. For only those within the Christian society are competent to receive the spiritual food associated with the Eucharist.

This mystical conception of the church as the sphere of a special relation to God is corroborated by a difficult sentence. " Every prophet approved and found true, if he doeth aught as an outward mystery typical of the church (ποιῶν εἰς μυστήριον κοσμικὸν ἐκκλησίας), and yet teacheth you not to do all that he himself doeth, shall

not be judged before you " (*Did.* 11). Now the interpretation of this sentence is confessedly obscure, and
possibly the text may be corrupt. But taking the text
as it stands, the interpretation, which seems most to
commend itself, is that which regards the prophet as
voluntarily practising celibacy for the sake of exhibiting,
by his own betrothal to the church, that mystical relation
of Christ to the church, which is expressed under the figure
of bride and bridegroom. But whether this be the true
interpretation or not, it remains clear that a certain
mystical character is associated with the idea of the
church.

The church, thus related to God, has the attribute of
holiness. Here, as in the New Testament, the members of
the church are "saints," holy, consecrated to God. Thus it
is said, "Thou shalt seek out day by day the persons of the
saints, that thou mayest find rest in their words" (*Did.* 4).
The church, composed of those who have been baptized
into the holy name (*Did.* 9) and who are sustained by
holy gifts (see *Did.* 9, " Give not that which is holy
unto the dogs"), must itself grow in holiness towards
"perfection." Hence the burden of the Eucharistic prayer.
" Remember, Lord, Thy church to deliver it from all evil
and to perfect it in Thy love ; and gather it together from
the four winds, even Thy church which has been made
holy (τὴν ἁγιασθεῖσαν), unto Thy kingdom which Thou
hast prepared for it" (*Did.* 10). Holiness is the goal
which the church, already consecrated and ideally holy, is
to reach through conflict in the world. The kingdom of
the Father, the sphere within which perfect obedience is
offered to the Father and His will perfectly kept, is the
eternal spiritual realm, into which the church is to be
finally gathered, when the process of sanctification is

complete. Not only does inclusion in this kingdom
represent the final condition of the church, but it is for
the church that the kingdom has its being. God prepared
it for the church (*Did.* 10, βασιλείαν, ἣν ἡτοίμασας
αὐτῇ).

The ruling characteristic of the church, as a sacred
society in the world, is that of brotherhood. This spirit
of brotherhood must find definite and varied expression.

Thus the fact of brotherhood in the church will
control the question of almsgiving. "Thou shalt not
turn away from him that is in want, but shalt make thy
brother partake in all things, and shalt not say that anything is thine own" (οὐκ ἐρεῖς ἴδια εἶναι, *Did.* 4; cf.
Acts iv. 32). Here indeed we have a reminiscence of the
original communism of the church in Jerusalem. It is
clear however that the writer of the *Didaché* is not urging
a literal perpetuation of such conditions. For his directions
presuppose the possession of private property. But the
spirit, which animated the first company of believers, is to
be retained. The possessor of goods is to sit loosely to his
possessions; he is to regard himself rather as a steward
than as an owner. He is to recognise the dominant claims
of brotherhood in the community.

This bond between Christians in the church is a
fellowship (κοινωνία), which finds its deepest basis in the
joint partaking of spiritual gifts and which also will be
expressed in the care of the brethren, one for another,
in the things of this world. "If ye are fellow-partakers
(κοινωνοί) in that which is imperishable, how much rather
in the things which are perishable?" (*Did.* 4).

Further, this sacred fellowship in the community must
transform social relationships. Thus parental duty is
emphasised. "Thou shalt not withhold thy hand from thy

son or from thy daughter, but from their youth thou shalt teach them the fear of God " (*Did.* 4). A new considerateness is required at the hand of masters towards their slaves. For God's call is irrespective of social standing and is based on a spiritual qualification. This bond of union, even between master and slave, is emphasised by the thought that it is the same God who is over both and whom both alike worship. "Thou shalt not command thy bondservant or thine handmaid in thy bitterness, who trust in the same God as thyself, lest haply they should cease to fear the God who is over both of you ; for He cometh, not to call men with respect of persons, but He cometh to those whom the Spirit hath prepared " (*Did.* 4). Thus the church is thought of as a brotherhood, in which a sacred bond binds men together and in which the distinctive force is that of the Holy Spirit.

But again the thought of brotherhood in the church underlies the directions given as to the discipline to be exercised by the community. The only offences which are mentioned as calling for disciplinary action on the part of the Christian community are those against society. No other offences are mentioned in this connection. One who " has fallen foul of his neighbour " is to be cut off from all social intercourse, " until he repent " (*Did.* 15). This singling out of social offences for special notice illustrates the strong sense of brotherhood by showing the enormity of an offence against the community.

Nor was the sense of brotherhood confined to the local community. It was as wide as the universal church. The brother arriving from a distant church was sure of a welcome and of food and shelter (*Did.* 12). True, such hospitality might easily be abused ; and it was necessary therefore to lay down regulations as to its exercise. A traveller may and should receive hospitality as he passes through. But if he intends to remain more than at the most three days, he must work for his living. The hospitality rightly shown by brother to brother must not be abused by the idle, in order to save the necessity of work.

So then the church at large, and the local community in its smaller sphere, is a brotherhood. The local church is to live, so far as possible, a corporate life. "Thou shalt seek out, day by day, the persons of the saints, that thou mayest find rest in their words" (*Did.* 4). The member of a local church therefore must not be self-willed and obstinate. He must show a readiness to accept the counsels of the brethren and to "find rest in their words." In the same spirit there is added the injunction from "The Two Ways," which is also found in Barnabas. "Thou shalt not make a schism, but shalt pacify them that contend" (*Did.* 4). It is incumbent upon the Christian to do what he can to prevent discord ; he must show a spirit of conciliation in dealing with the contentious. In this way he is to strengthen the bonds of unity within the church.

This thought of unity underlies the teaching of the *Didaché* as to the church. The mere use of the term "the church" (*Did.* 9 and 11) to express the universal Christian society is an assumption of unity. The church universal is a fellowship in which all the local communities are united. Its unity is that of a brotherhood, which, as we have already seen, must find expression in acts of fraternal kindness.

It is not as yet embodied in any centralised or monarchical system of organisation, but is content with its spiritual and mystical basis. Its organs are apostles and prophets (*Did.* 11). These go from place to place as witnesses of one and the same evangelical tradition, and are everywhere welcomed by the local church, which in thus yielding allegiance to the visitor from a distance recognises the larger life, of which itself forms a part, the life of the church universal.

This unity finds a special expression in the Eucharist, where the many are blended into one, through participation of the one sacred food. "As this bread was scattered upon the mountains and being gathered together became one, so may Thy church be gathered together from the ends of the earth into Thy kingdom" (*Did.* 9). The sacred rite is the symbol of a unity, as yet but partially realised, and is the occasion of prayer for the consummation of that upon which under present conditions human infirmity stamps its imperfection.

So then in all parts of the world the church has its members. Though so widely scattered, they still form a single body, "Thy church" (*Did.* 9).

This unity will be perfected in God's kingdom, which is the final goal of the church. When this consummation is reached, all those, who in all parts of the world have been "baptized into the name of the Lord," and have been faithful to their profession, will be gathered together into one, and the one society will be united in "the kingdom." That the condition of faithfulness is necessary for the attainment of this consummation, and that partial apostasy is possible, is of course implied by the fact that the desired end is made the subject of prayer. "May Thy church be gathered together from the ends of the earth into Thy kingdom" (*Did.* 9). "Gather it together from the four winds, even the church which has been sanctified, into Thy kingdom which Thou hast prepared for it" (*Did.* 10).

The church then is characterised by unity. This unity, considered in relation to God, is based upon the unity of allegiance due from those who all alike have been baptized into one name, "the name of the Lord," and who thus have accepted the one divine rule. At the same time, considered in relation to man, this unity finds expression in the spirit of brotherhood.

Now the fact of brotherhood must show itself, not only in the giving of hospitality, but also in the exercise of discipline. Thus the earliest discipline is fraternal, not official. It is exercised not by the ministry acting judicially by itself, but by the brotherhood. The authority of discipline resides in the church as a whole. And this authority is both real and peremptory.

So, in the first place, discipline is exercised in imposing the conditions of entrance into the church by Baptism. Now the section relating to Baptism (*Did.* 7) may perhaps contain interpolations. It will be noticed that in some of the sentences the address changes from the plural of the community to the singular of the officiating minister[1], a subtle indication that the clauses in which the singular occurs were inserted at a time when the thought of the congregational character of Christian discipline was receding into the background, and the authority of the minister was becoming more prominent. The sentences so marked contain certain detailed directions as to the ceremonial of Baptism. "If thou hast not running water, then baptize in other water; and if thou art not able in cold, then in warm. But if thou hast neither, then pour water on the head thrice in the name of the Father and of the Son and of the Holy Spirit......And thou shalt order him that is baptized to

[1] Cf. Hastings, *D. B.*, art. "Didaché," vol. v. p. 447.

fast a day or two before " (*Did.* 7). This attention to ceremonial detail seems rather to reflect the tone of the Canons of Hippolytus, and the sentences here quoted may perhaps be best referred to the last quarter of the second century. If we accept this theory of interpolation as accurate, the original form of the section will then read as follows:—" Now concerning Baptism, thus shall ye baptize. Having first recited all these things, baptize into the name of the Father and of the Son and of the Holy Spirit in running water. But before the Baptism let him that baptizeth and him that is baptized fast, and any others also, who are able " (*ibid.*).

Now we note here that Baptism is preceded by a recitation of the characteristics of the Two Ways of Life and of Death. (" Having first recited all these things," *Did.* 7.) The candidate must be reminded of the obligations which he will have as a member of the church. Entry into the church must be marked by renunciation of the Way of Death and by embracing the Way of Life.

The force and reality of this obligation is further shown by the preparation which precedes Baptism. " Let him that baptizeth and him that is baptized fast, and any others also, who are able." A sharp line, the undertaking of a definite moral obligation, is to mark off those who are within the church from those who are without. So a definite discipline is to precede Baptism, in order that this distinction may be impressed upon the candidate.

But in this discipline the candidate is not to stand in isolation. He is entering a brotherhood, and the inclusion of a new brother is not a matter of indifference to the community. The brethren—so many, at least, as can do so—will fast with him. So the fact will be brought home to the candidate, that he is entering a society, in which no individual is isolated and in which none stands alone, but the welfare and the interests of each are the object of all.

Again in the matter of fasting, we find the exercise of discipline by the church. The church claims the right to lay down certain regulations with regard to fasting.

It should be noticed here that fasting is not thought of as an end in itself, but as assisting spiritual growth. Thus it is placed in close connection with prayer (*Did.* 8). It is of value as tuning the mind to spiritual thoughts and so assisting prayer. We have seen, above, its disciplinary connection with Baptism. In that case, no doubt, it would be thought of as illustrating the great renunciation, required by entrance into the church and emphasised at Baptism by the recitation of the opposing characteristics of the Way of Life and the Way of Death.

The disciplinary authority of the church is illustrated by the regulations laid down in the matter of fasting. In form these regulations are governed by consideration of Jewish usage. The compiler of the *Didaché* here shows a marked unwillingness to appear to copy Jewish practice.

The Christian church must not follow the example of "the hypocrites," as the non-Christian Jews are called (*Did.* 8). These have two weekly fasts, the second and the fifth days of the week. Let the Christians then fast on the fourth day and on "the preparation day," that is the sixth day. No doubt the sixth day would be chosen in memory of the Lord's Crucifixion on that day; the fourth day, perhaps, because with the sixth a convenient division of the week would be obtained. The fact that concerns us, for our present purpose, is that the compiler of the *Didaché* assumes the right of the church to lay down this more or less arbitrary rule of discipline.

But discipline, in general, rests in the hands of the church. The admonition as to the Lord's Day is addressed to the community, who are to see that it is duly observed. "On the Lord's own day gather yourselves together and break bread and give thanks, first confessing your transgressions, that your sacrifice may be pure" (*Did.* 14). The church is to receive the open confession of sins. For from the regulation that the confession is to be made when the congregation are gathered together (συναχθέν-τες), the clear inference is that it is to be a public confession. But beyond this discipline of confession, there is also the duty of admonition. "Reprove one another, not in anger but in peace, as ye find in the Gospel" (*Did.* 15). And beyond this again, a discipline of practical excommunication, or exclusion from the brotherhood. "Let no one speak to any that has gone wrong towards his neighbour, neither let him hear a word from you, until he repent" (*ibid.*).

The local church has authority to choose its own local ministers, "bishops and deacons." "Appoint for yourselves therefore bishops and deacons worthy of the Lord, men who are meek and not lovers of money, and true and approved; for unto you they perform the service of the prophets and teachers" (*Did.* 15). It will appear, from what we have seen as to the authority residing in the church as a whole, that these local officers do not possess authority apart from the local church, but are its executive officers, the official organisation which voices the decisions of the church.

Once more, the church has authority to lay down regulations as to prayer and to fix liturgical forms. Thus the Lord's Prayer has attached to it a liturgical ending and is to be recited three times a day (*Did.* 8). A form of Eucharistic thanksgiving is drawn up, which is to be binding ordinarily, though not upon the prophets. "Permit the prophets to offer thanksgiving as much as they desire" (*Did.* 10). It may be noted that a liturgical ending, similar to that which the church has given to the Lord's Prayer, is twice repeated in the Eucharistic thanksgiving (*Did.* 9 and 10).

These liturgical regulations lead us next to consider the necessary place of Public Worship in the life of the church. The church must needs express its corporate relation to God by Public Worship. "On the Lord's Day gather yourselves together and break bread and give thanks" (*Did.* 14). In this public assembly the thought of brotherhood must still be prominent. No element can be permitted which interferes with the spirit of brotherhood. Hence if anyone is at enmity with his fellow, he must be reconciled before he comes to Public Worship. "Let no man, having his dispute with his fellow, join your assembly (μὴ συνελθέτω ὑμῖν) until they have been reconciled, that your sacrifice may not be defiled" (*Did.* 14). And on the other hand, the man must put himself right with God before joining in the worship of the church. He must therefore first make confession of his sins (*ibid.*).

SECTION II.

THE DIDACHÉ (*continued*).

The teaching of the church : the apostolic tradition.—Sacerdotal character of the church : the Eucharist.—The ministry of the church : two types recognised.—(1) The charismatic ministry.— The prophets.—The apostles.—The teachers.—(2) The local ministry : the bishops and deacons.—They hold definitely constituted offices.—Their appointment.—Their work.—The treatment to which they are entitled.—Significance of the *Didaché*.

The church in its teaching holds to and delivers the teaching of the Apostles. From this body of truth, handed down by tradition, nothing may be taken away ; to it nothing may be added. "Thou shalt keep those things which thou hast received, neither adding to them nor taking from them " (*Did.* 4). That the standard of truth here laid down is the teaching of the Apostles appears from the character of the *Didaché* itself. For, as appears both from its title and from uniform tradition regarding it, the book purports to be written in the name of the Apostles and claims that its teaching is theirs. So " the Apostles' teaching " (cf. Acts ii. 42) is to be the constant standard, to which the teaching of the church must conform. The church has no authority to depart from this traditional faith.

The very existence of this treatise is an evidence of the importance which was attached to the apostolic tradition. For the book is written in the name of the Apostles. It claims to put their teaching into a written form, so that this teaching might be handed down intact in the church, after the Apostles themselves had been withdrawn. Now it is a significant fact that our manual

D. 6

should, in spite of its manifest deficiencies, have attained
so wide a popularity. For we need not doubt that its
wide circulation, as evidenced by patristic allusions to it,
was due to its claim to embody the teaching of the
Apostles. The high value set upon this book shows the
desire of the church to rest both teaching and usage
upon apostolic sanction. From the very beginning the
church appealed to tradition. The Twelve had passed
into silence; but " the Apostles' doctrine " was still, as in
the first days (Acts ii. 42), the standard by which the
church sought to model its teaching.

To the church belongs the right of sacrifice. The
Eucharist is a sacrificial action. " On the Lord's own
day...break bread and give thanks...confessing your sins
that your sacrifice may be pure...for this sacrifice it was
that was spoken of by the Lord " (*Did.* 14). This
injunction is followed by a quotation of Malachi's prophecy of " the pure offering," which should be offered in
every place (Mal. i. 11, 14). Thus the "pure offering" of
Malachi is interpreted of the Eucharist. In accordance
with this conception is the application to the Christian
prophets of the title "chief priests" ($\dot{a}\rho\chi\iota\epsilon\rho\epsilon\hat{\iota}s$). " They,"
it is said, "are your chief priests " (*Did.* 13), an expression
which clearly implies a sacrificial conception of their work.
The Christian prophets then are endowed with a power of
priesthood, which finds a central occasion for its exercise
in the offering of the Eucharist.

Two distinct types of ministry stand out clearly in
the *Didaché*. That occupying the foremost place is the
ministry of " prophets, apostles and teachers." This
ministry was largely unlocalised : it was distinguished
by strongly marked gifts of the Spirit, and so may be
conveniently described as the " charismatic ministry." In

addition to this ministry, which as a rule was itinerant
or missionary, there was also the fixed local ministry of
" bishops and deacons."

But though, for the sake of convenience, we may use
the term "charismatic" to describe the itinerant ministry,
of which the " prophets " formed the leading feature, it
must not be supposed that the local ministry of " bishops
and deacons " was wanting in spiritual endowment. For
in the local church, the " bishops and deacons " " perform
the service of the prophets and teachers" (*Did.* 15).
And an office, to which was committed such a service,
must be held to have carried with it a special gift of the
Spirit, though not that of enthusiastic prophecy. It is
true, no doubt, that the local ministry of "bishops and
deacons " occupied a lower place in estimation than did
the prophets, but both alike did their work under the
sanction of the Holy Spirit, though the gifts bestowed
were of different kinds.

It will be necessary then for us to consider separately
these different functions. Let us first take the " charismatic ministry " of "prophets, apostles and teachers."

Prophecy was a prime mark of the apostolic age.
" Your sons and your daughters shall prophesy " (Acts
ii. 17). The words are quoted by St Peter, as expressing
the leading characteristic of the dispensation which
Pentecost inaugurated. The prophets possess a divine
afflatus. They speak " in spirit " (ἐν πνεύματι, *Did.* 11).
This must mean that the prophet's own spirit is in an
exalted condition. The phrase cannot be interpreted of
the Holy Spirit. For we are warned that " not every one
that speaketh in spirit is a prophet " (*Did.* 11). The
ecstatic utterance may present the same outward pheno-
mena both in true and false prophets. And so the

prophets must be otherwise tested (cf. 1 St John iv. 1).
A test of character is to be applied. " From his ways the
false prophet and the [true] prophet shall be recognised "
(*Did.* 11). It would be felt, on the one hand, that the
gift of " enthusiasm " was liable to abuse, and that it
required to be very carefully watched, lest it should
degenerate into a disorderly fanaticism. And on the
other hand the claim to hospitality, made by these
itinerants, who would probably not be personally known
to the local church, to which they had come, would supply
an obvious motive to make a false claim to the possession
of the prophetic gift. The simple tests imposed would be
sufficient to test the man's motives. He must not
be able to trade upon his prophetic gift: and moreover
his character must be in accordance with his profession.
" Not every one that speaketh in spirit[1] is a prophet, but
only if he have the ways of the Lord. From his ways
therefore the false prophet and the [true] prophet shall
be recognised. And no prophet, when he ordereth a table
in spirit, shall eat of it ; otherwise he is a false prophet.
And every prophet teaching the truth, if he doeth not
what he teacheth, is a false prophet" (*Did.* 11). Thus
to the prophet the only tests applied are those of motive
and example. There is no doctrinal test. That test we
shall find is applied to the "teacher," though not to the
prophet.

The prophet is not necessarily and always itinerant.
He may settle in some particular place. And in such
a case he is worthy of support. So to the prophets
the firstfruits are assigned. For their position in the
Christian community is analogous to that of the chief
priests in the Jewish community. " Every true prophet

---

[1] Not " in the Spirit," as Harmer, *Apostolic Fathers*, p. 233.

desiring to settle among you is worthy of his food....Every firstfruit then of the produce of the wine-vat and of the threshing-floor, of thy oxen and of thy sheep, thou shalt take and give as the firstfruit to the prophets; for they are your chief priests. But if ye have not a prophet, give them to the poor. If thou makest bread, take the first-fruit and give according to the commandment. In like manner, when thou openest a jar of wine or of oil, take the firstfruit and give to the prophets; yea, and of money and raiment and every possession take the first-fruit as shall seem good to thee, and give according to the commandment" (*Did.* 13).

It is the special prerogative of the prophets to offer the Eucharistic thanksgiving. Owing to the superiority of their gift, they are allowed a special freedom. The liturgical forms which are normally used in the worship of the church (*Did.* 9, 10) are not to bind the prophets. They may offer thanksgiving "as much as they desire" (*Did.* 10).

The service of the prophets is a λειτουργία (*Did.* 15). This, it may be noted, is the word used in connection with the prophets in the New Testament (cf. Acts xiii. 2, λειτουργούντων).

It may happen that the prophets follow certain practices, which yet they do not teach as of universal obligation. We have already (pp. 70 f.) alluded to the difficult sentence in which this is conveyed. "Every prophet approved and found true, if he doeth aught as an outward mystery typical of the church, and yet teacheth you not to do all that he himself doeth, shall not be judged before you; he hath his judgment in the presence of God." Having regard to the language of St Paul, it would appear that the practice alluded to is that of voluntary celibacy. The prophet regards the church as his bride. Thus he symbolises "the mystical union between Christ and His church." His practice is an acted parable.

So then the age of "enthusiasm" is not over in the days of the *Didaché* (cf. Jude 12, 19, 2 Pet. ii. 1 f., 13). Prophetic utterance plays an important part in the life of the church. Its dangers are felt, and care therefore is taken to guard against them.

Next, associated with the prophets, are "apostles." The apostles, or men with a mission, are such in virtue of a divine commission, however conveyed. They are not envoys of particular local churches (as in 2 Cor. viii. 23, Phil. ii. 25), but are envoys of God, divinely prompted missionaries. Their work is to break new ground, to found new churches. But in order to reach their mission field, they may have to pass through existing churches. There they may rest on their journey, and, "in accordance with the rule of the gospel" (κατὰ τὸ δόγμα τοῦ εὐαγγελίου, *Did*. 11), they may claim hospitality. Yet they must not delay on their journey, nor may they ask for anything beyond the bare necessaries of bread and shelter. "Let every apostle, when he cometh to you, be received as the Lord: but he shall not abide more than a single day, or, if there be need, a second likewise; but if he abide three days, he is a false prophet. And when he departeth let the apostle receive nothing save bread, until he find shelter; but if he ask money, he is a false prophet" (*Did*. 11)[1].

The application of the term "false prophet" to those apostles whose acts belie their commission, would seem

[1] For the hospitality shown to these travelling missionaries, we may compare 3 Jn. 5—8.

to imply that the gifts of a true prophet are among those with which an apostle should be endowed. A prophet indeed was not of necessity an apostle ; he need not be distinctively a missionary. But on the other hand an apostle should be a prophet : he should have those gifts of enthusiastic utterance which would give emphasis to his message.

It may be noticed that the circumstances contemplated by the *Didaché* are those of rural life. Thus the firstfruits, to which the prophets have a claim, consist of country produce, such as oxen, sheep, wine and oil (*Did.* 13). This has a bearing upon the prominence given to itinerant teachers. For in a country district the communities of Christians would be widely scattered, and they would necessarily be largely dependent for their ministrations upon men who were able to journey from place to place. It would not be a fair conclusion that the prominence, which the *Didaché* gives to itinerants, is to be taken as representing the normal church life of the time.

From apostles we pass to those who are called distinctively "teachers." It would appear that the term "teacher" is the title of an office, and not merely the description of a function ; that the word does not simply refer to the ministers of the church in general, in their exercise of a particular duty, but that it designates a set of men, whose characteristic work was teaching. For on the one hand the "teachers" are distinguished from the prophets. "Every true prophet desiring to settle among you is worthy of his food. In like manner a true teacher is also worthy, like the workman, of his food" (*Did.* 13). And on the other hand the "teachers" are distinguished from the local ministry. "Appoint for

yourselves bishops and deacons worthy of the Lord....
They are your honourable men along with the prophets
and teachers" (*Did.* 15). We note however that while
the teachers are distinguished both from the prophets
and from the local ministry of bishops and deacons,
there is no such distinction made between apostles and
teachers. Thus we find the conjunction "apostles and
prophets" (*Did.* 11) and also "prophets and teachers"
(*Did.* 15), but the phrase "apostles and teachers" does
not occur. Now we cannot regard as identical the two
bodies of men, apostles and teachers. For it would
appear (*Did.* 13) that a teacher, like a prophet, might
accept a settled local charge, while the commission of the
apostles was in all cases a roving one. They had to break
new ground, to found new churches. But just as we
have seen reason to suppose that an apostle was also in
general a prophet, so he might be a teacher as well. So
that while a teacher was not necessarily an apostle, an
apostle must almost of necessity be a teacher.

There is a definite standard of doctrine to which the
teacher must conform. It is the standard set up by the
earlier chapters of the *Didaché* (ταῦτα πάντα τὰ προειρη-
μένα). "Whosoever shall come and teach you all these
things that have been said before, receive him; but if the
teacher himself be perverted and teach a different doctrine
to the destruction thereof, hear him not; but if to the
increase of righteousness and the knowledge of the Lord,
receive him as the Lord" (*Did.* 11). Remembering that
the purpose of the book is to hand on the teaching of the
Apostles, the standard of teaching here laid down is seen to
be that of the apostolic tradition. The teacher must deliver
that same doctrine which has been handed down from the
Apostles.

From the charismatic ministry we pass to a consideration of the local ministry of "bishops and deacons." A lower position is clearly assigned to these than that which belonged to the more gifted prophets. Yet they too are to be treated with honour. For they have a share in the sacred service, which belongs primarily to the prophets and teachers. "They perform the service of the prophets and teachers. Therefore despise them not; for they are your honourable men along with the prophets and teachers" (*Did.* 15).

They are to be appointed to their office by the local church, and care is to be taken in their selection. They must be men of approved character, to fit the sacredness of their office. "Appoint for yourselves bishops and deacons worthy of the Lord, men who are meek and not lovers of money, and true and approved; for unto you also they perform the service of the prophets and teachers" (τὴν λειτουργίαν τῶν προφητῶν καὶ διδασκάλων, *Did.* 15).

The definite article with προφητῶν καὶ διδασκάλων shows that the bishops and deacons are not regarded as acting as prophets and teachers, but as replacing the prophets and teachers. For though the local ministers are able to perform the service (λειτουργία) which a prophet would have performed, if he had been present, they do not necessarily possess that inspiration, which gave a special character to the ministrations of the prophet.

No doubt the command to appoint settled local ministers (*Did.* 15) would be carried out in every community. So in every place there would be "bishops and deacons" to "break bread and give thanks" (*Did.* 14), where there were no prophets to undertake these functions.

These men might be possessed of no prophetic afflatus, but yet they rightly exercised their ministry in the community which had appointed them.

The terms "bishop" and "deacon," as used in the *Didaché*, are the titles of definite offices. In the New Testament ἐπίσκοπος expresses not an office, but a function, that of oversight[1]. But the terms of allusion, in our manual, to ἐπίσκοποι καὶ διάκονοι, in which they are spoken of in relation to prophets and teachers (*Did.* 15), show that by this time the words express not merely those who have respectively the duties of oversight and of service in the ministry of the church, but specifically the bearers of definite offices. Hence we may conveniently describe them as bishops and deacons, though in doing so we must be careful not to import later ideas into these words.

We find therefore in the local community two distinct offices, making up the local ministry, the bishops and the deacons. There does not appear to be any limitation of number in the case of either office. We may suppose that there would be one or more according to the needs of the community. There is, at least, no hint as yet of rule by a single officer. Nor do we learn from the *Didaché* how the functions of bishop and deacon were differentiated. All that we are told is that together they performed, in the absence of a prophet, that service which would have fallen upon the prophet had one been present (*Did.* 15).

---

[1] See Hort, *Christian Ecclesia*, pp. 211 ff. Dr Hort points out that in speaking of ἐπίσκοποι καὶ διάκονοι in Phil. i. 1, St Paul had in view, not two different and specific offices, but two contrasted functions. The ministry at Philippi, however organised, consisted of men whose duty was oversight (ἐπίσκοποι) and others whose place it was to serve (διάκονοι).

The reason given for the appointment of a local ministry of bishops and deacons (note the οὖν, *Did.* 15) is that provision may be made for the celebration of the Eucharist. The fact that such a reason is given shows the importance attached to this central service of the church. The celebration of the Eucharist is seen, at the same time, to be the characteristic work of the local ministry.

It is noteworthy, that, in the absence of a prophet, the tithes were to be given not to the local ministry but to the poor. How then were the bishops and deacons to be supported ? The inference would seem to be that they were to follow their trade or otherwise earn their bread by their own exertions. It might be held that, though this was impossible for the itinerant prophets, apostles and teachers, it was right and natural for the settled ministry.

The ministry is to be held in honour. "Thou shalt remember him that speaketh unto thee the word of God night and day, and shalt honour him as the Lord ; for whence-soever the Lordship speaketh, there is the Lord" (*Did.* 4). Continuous contact might produce a tendency to despise the local ministry, which moreover might be overshadowed by the more striking gifts of the itinerant prophets. So a special exhortation is added, that the community should pay due honour to those whom they have themselves appointed for their own ministry. "Despise them not ; for they are your honourable men along with the prophets and teachers " (*Did.* 15).

We must not part with the *Didaché* without considering how far we may rely upon its evidence for the conception of the church at the time at which it was written. Does it belong to the true stream of church life or does it represent the teaching only of a sect or of some imperfectly instructed community ? Now it is perfectly true that the doctrine of the *Didaché* is incomplete. It does not, for instance, give the full Pauline doctrine of the Eucharist. But on the other hand there is nothing in its positive teaching inconsistent with the New Testament, and it is highly precarious to judge a document by its omissions. No doubt its omissions in respect of Eucharistic doctrine are great. But this need not surprise us, for the manual does not give a full liturgy, but only the people's thanksgiving. The prayer of consecration is not given, but it by no means follows that there was no consecration of the elements. There is indeed no profession of completeness. Only such teaching is given as suited the particular purpose of the writer. We are not to infer that, if he had given us his full Eucharistic belief, we should have found it meagre. All we can say is that he has given us only a partial account of the nature of the Eucharistic gift. But even so thanksgiving is offered, in connection with the sacred meal, for spiritual food and drink and eternal life through the Son of God (*Did.* 10).

It is clear, again, that a social meal is described, a meal for the satisfying of hunger (*Did.* 10), and not only the partaking of a Sacrament. But it would not be fair to deduce that this meal is confounded with the Sacrament, though indeed it would seem that the title Eucharist (*Did.* 9), here used technically, is applied to the whole feast including the Agapé. In the same way apparently Ignatius (Smyrn. 8) uses the title Agapé to include the celebration of the Sacrament (perh. cf. 2 Pet. ii. 13). So then the Agapé proper and the Eucharist proper are celebrated in conjunction, and either title may be loosely used of the whole celebration. But as no one would suggest that Ignatius confounded the two, so neither is it fair to assume that the writer of the *Didaché* has lost sight of the distinction between them.

The omissions of the *Didaché* therefore do not make it necessary for us to attribute it to an impoverished type of Christianity. And on the other hand the wideness of its reception in early times makes it clear that the early church did not so regard it. The reverence paid to it in early days shows that it was held to be in harmony with the full faith of the church. This does not mean that the faith finds complete expression in it, but that such teaching as it gives is so far in harmony with the central stream of tradition. Its teaching could be fitted into the full faith of the church. So then reliance may be placed upon the *Didaché* as giving us a true though incomplete picture of early Christian life in the true stream of Christian tradition.

SECTION III.

THE EPISTLE OF BARNABAS.

The Christian church as (1) the recipient of the Old Testament promises, (2) the means of access to God.—Qualities of the church : (1) its unity : (2) its brotherhood : (3) its holiness.

The Epistle that bears by tradition the name of Barnabas should probably be dated about the year A.D. 130. Its early reception and internal character alike point to Alexandria as its place of origin. In the antagonism which it shows to Judaism, we may recognise a reflection of the bitter feeling which existed between Jews and Christians in that important Jewish colony. The writer was himself probably a Gentile Christian.

In the mind of Barnabas, the Christian church is the sphere within which are bestowed the blessings of the new dispensation. The church, described absolutely (Barn. 7), as representing the entire Christian society, the universal church, is the recipient of the divine promises. To it are transferred bodily the promises of the Old Testament. The church is "the good land" (Barn. 6), "the land of Jacob" (Barn. 11), "the vessel of His Spirit" (*ibid.*). Thus the Old Testament receives a spiritual interpretation. The true Israel is the Christian community. The promised land, in which this community finds its goal and fulfils its destiny, is the Christian church. The church moreover, as "the vessel of His Spirit," is the depository of spiritual gifts, the organ of the Spirit's manifestation in the world.

The Christian church, thus conceived of, has its local manifestation in the assembly of the faithful. The ecclesia of the Septuagint is interpreted as meaning a Christian ecclesia, the assembly of a local Christian church; and the church, so understood, is stated to be the means whereby the worshipper may enter into God's presence. "Wherein shall I appear unto the Lord my God and be glorified? I will make confession unto Thee in an ecclesia of my brethren and I will sing unto Thee in the midst of an ecclesia of saints" (Barn. 6)[1]. The church then is the means of access to God and the source whence the blessings of God are to be received.

Now the local assembly, the local church, represents in its own locality the one church universal, which, as we have seen, Barnabas speaks of absolutely as "the church" (Barn. 7). And it is this fact that gives the local assembly its spiritual power. For the fundamental idea is that

[1] Pss. xlii. 3 and xxii. 23, LXX.

" the church" is the sphere of divine blessing, the possessor of the promises.

So the church is one. Unity is to mark its life, and schism therefore is condemned. " Thou shalt not make a schism " (Barn. 19). There does not indeed seem to be any thought here of a definitely organised schismatic body. The writer has in view a quarrel between members of one and the same local church, causing a breach in the harmony of local life ; he is not contemplating the setting up of a rival organisation. By schism he means division within the church rather than separation from it. This appears from the way in which the evil is to be remedied. "Thou shalt pacify them that contend by bringing them together" (Barn. 19). There must be harmony of life within the local church. The words quoted, we may notice, do not originate with Barnabas himself. They are taken from the earlier document of " The Two Ways," which is here incorporated in part in the Epistle, as we also find that it occurs in fuller form at the opening of the *Didaché*. The point then that is insisted upon is that a harmonious spirit of unity is of the essence of church life.

The same truth underlies the conception of the church as a brotherhood. The church is " a church of brothers " (Barn. 6). The sense of brotherhood is strong in Barnabas. He addresses his readers under the title of " my brothers " (Barn. 3). Other forms of address which occur are noteworthy : " sons and daughters " (Barn. 1), " children " (Barn. 15), " children of gladness " (Barn. 7), " children of love " (Barn. 9), " children of peace and love " (Barn. 21). Such expressions vividly suggest the authority of the teacher, exercised not by constraint, but as a father's loving influence, in the brotherhood of the church. "I," says Barnabas, "not as though I were a teacher, but as one of yourselves, will show forth a few things, whereby ye shall be gladdened" (Barn. 1). Such is the spirit of brotherhood in which he writes.

The local church is marked by consecration to God. It is "a church of saints" (Barn. 6), an assembly of men, who are dedicated to holiness, and who through the struggles of life are to attain their destiny.

The church therefore receives divine instruction, in order that this destiny may be attained by its members. A curious illustration is given of this. The Rabbinic additions to the story of the scape-goat are said by Barnabas to be for the instruction of the church (Barn. 7). The scarlet wool, representing the blood or atoning power of the sacrifice of Christ, is taken from the head of the scape-goat and placed on a thorn-bush. Thence, and only with pain, so terrible are the thorns, it can be plucked by him who desires it. "Thus, He saith, they that desire to see Me and to attain unto My kingdom must lay hold on Me through tribulation and affliction" (*ibid.*). This ritual of the scape-goat is said by Barnabas to be "a type of Jesus set forth for the church" (*ibid.*). The ritual is regarded as of divine authority, and its purpose is stated to be the instruction of the church. Thus Jewish ritual finds its interpretation, not in any efficacy of its own, but in the edifying of the Christian church.

The Christian church, then, in the thought of Barnabas, is that to which the whole scheme of the old dispensation ministers. In the church men are to live as brothers, in loving unity, as dedicated to a life of holiness and receiving through the church those gifts of the Spirit which will enable them to realise their destiny.

SECTION IV.

THE SHEPHERD OF HERMAS.

Divine origin of the church.—Its pre-existence.—Its consummation.—
Its union with the Son of God.—Character of the church : (1) Its
holiness. (2) Its catholicity. (3) Its unity. (4) Its poverty.
(5) Its growth.—The spiritual and the institutional church.—
Condition of entrance into the spiritual church.—Probation in the
church.—Possibility of the forgiveness of post-baptismal sin.—
Perfecting of the spiritual church.—The spiritual church and the
kingdom of God.

The *Shepherd* of Hermas is a document of a mystical
character, emanating from the church in Rome.   Early
tradition places it in the middle of the second century.
The Muratorian Fragment states that Hermas wrote it
" while his brother Pius, the bishop, was sitting in the
chair of the church of the city of Rome " (Murat. Frag.
ll. 75—77).   The Visions however contain an allusion to
a Clement, who is contemporary with Hermas, and who
is spoken of in terms which raise a presumption that the
author of the letter to the Corinthians is referred to.
Hermas is to send a copy of his book to Clement.   " So
Clement shall send to the foreign cities, for this is his
duty" (Vis. ii. 4).   And further the references to the
Christian ministry in the *Shepherd* are hardly reconcile-
able with so late a date as the episcopate of Pius (circ.
A.D. 140—155).   They fit in much more naturally with a
period nearer to the date of Clement's letter.   We should
moreover note two points in connection with the evidence
of the Muratorian Fragment.   The writer betrays a desire
to disparage the authority of the *Shepherd*, and so lays
stress upon its having been written "recently."   But also

D.   7

we only possess the Fragment in a very illiterate Latin translation, and it is possible that the Greek original did not definitely state that the book was written while Pius was bishop. It may well be that Hermas was the brother of Pius, but that he wrote his book some time before his brother became bishop. He might easily have been also a contemporary of Clement, and have placed the ideal date of the vision in Clement's lifetime, while not actually writing his book till the second or third decade of the century. We may with most probability suppose that the book was written between A.D. 110 and 125.

Hermas vividly enforces his doctrine of the church by means of elaborate similes, conveyed in the form of visions and parables. Thus he sees a tower, which he is told represents the church. The tower is in building and the process of building is fully described, all its details being so constructed as to convey teaching about the church.

The church, then, is of divine origin. It owes its foundation to God, and from God is derived its strength. " The tower has been founded by the word of the Almighty and Glorious Name, and is strengthened by the unseen power of the Master " (Vis. iii. 3).

By another vision Hermas is taught the pre-existence of the church. An aged woman appears to him, whom he takes to be the Cumæan Sibyl, but who in fact is the church. He asks why she should appear as aged. " Because," replies his guide, " she was created before all things ; therefore is she aged ; and for her sake the world was framed " (Vis. ii. 4)[1]. From this it appears that Hermas' conception of the church is not exhausted

[1] Cf. 2 Clem. 14.

by the empirical or institutional church, but that behind
the outward organisation he conceives of an ideal church
brought into existence by divine agency before all created
being. And, further, the world was then created for the
sake of the church. The church is the final cause of
creation. "God...created out of nothing the things
which are, and increased and multiplied them for His
holy church's sake" (Vis. i. 1). The world therefore will
only exist so long as it is required for the building up of
the church. "Whensoever therefore the building of the
tower shall be finished, the end cometh; but it shall be
built up quickly" (Vis. iii. 8). When, that is, the church is
complete, the world shall pass away. We may note that
there is still, in the days of Hermas, an expectation of a
rapid consummation of the church and a swift coming of
the end. Indeed it would seem that Hermas expected
this two-fold consummation in the actual lifetime of his
readers. For in his warning to the rich (Vis. iii. 9), the
opportunity of entering the tower is limited, not by the
lifetime of those whom he addresses, but by the com-
pletion of the building, the consummation of the church.
And, further, they are contemplated as still in possession
of the good things of this life, when they are finally "shut
outside the door of the tower" (*ibid.*).

But while the tower represents the church, the rock,
upon which it is built, represents the Son of God. Indeed
not only is the tower built upon the rock, but so closely
united is it with the rock, that it seems to be one with
the rock itself. In this way is represented the close and
intimate union of the church with the Son of God. The
tower "was builded, as it were, of a single stone, being
fitted together into one. And the stonework appeared as
if hewn out of the rock; for it seemed to me to be all

7—2

a single stone " (Sim. ix. 9). The church then is one with the Son of God. "For this cause thou seest that the tower has become a single stone with the rock " (Sim. ix. 13).

In the ancient rock a new gateway is hewn, representing the Incarnation of the Son of God. " How, Sir," asks Hermas of the Shepherd, " is the rock ancient, but the gate recent ? " " The Son of God," replies the Shepherd, " is older than all His creation, so that He became the Father's adviser in His creation. Therefore also He is ancient." " But the gate, why is it recent, Sir ? " asks Hermas again. "Because He was made manifest in the last days of the consummation ; therefore the gate was made recent, that they which are saved may enter through it into the kingdom of God " (Sim. ix. 12). Through this gateway, and through this alone, the stones must be brought to be built into the tower. Stones brought in by some other way are found to be " unsightly in the building of the tower" (Sim. ix. 4), and so have to be removed. The meaning is that only through the incarnate Christ can entrance be had to the living spiritual church. " No one shall enter into the kingdom of God except by the name of His Son " (Sim. ix. 12). " This gate is the Son of God ; there is this one entrance only to the Lord. No one shall enter in unto Him otherwise than through His Son " (Sim. ix. 12).

In accordance with this close connection with the Son of God, the attribute of holiness is ascribed to the church. God has created all things " for His holy church's sake " (Vis. i. 1). The God of Hosts " by His own wisdom and providence formed His holy church, which also He blessed " (Vis. i. 3). Visions and revelations were shown to Hermas by the Lord " through His holy church " (Vis. iv. 1). The character of the church as requiring and

promoting holiness is further illustrated by the seven
women round the tower representing the virtues, Faith,
Continence, Simplicity, Knowledge, Guilelessness, Reverence, Love. By them the tower is supported. They
illustrate the progress of moral and spiritual growth in
the church, for each, we are told, is the daughter of the
preceding. "From Faith is born Continence, from Continence Simplicity, from Simplicity Guilelessness, from
Guilelessness Reverence, from Reverence Knowledge, from
Knowledge Love. Whosoever therefore shall serve these
women and shall have strength to master their works,
shall have his dwelling on the tower with the saints of
God" (Vis. iii. 8).

The church is catholic, in the sense of being for all the
world. It rises superior to distinctions of nationality. It
is gathered from all nations alike. Twelve mountains
standing around the plain, from which rises the rock,
upon which the tower is built, represent the nations of the
world. The diversity of the nations is represented by the
varied characters of the several mountains. "The twelve
tribes which inhabit the whole world are twelve nations;
and they are various in understanding and in mind. As
various, then, as thou sawest these mountains to be, such
also are the varieties in the mind of these nations, and
such their understanding" (Sim. ix. 17). But national
types so distinct from one another each contribute to the
fulness of the church, and find their harmony in a higher
existence, in which national distinctions fade away. So
the stones, in great diversity, brought from all these
different mountains to a place in the tower became "all
of one colour." "The six men ordered the multitude of
the people to bring in stones from the mountains for the
building of the tower. They were brought in accordingly

from all the mountains, of various colours, shaped by the men, and were handed to the virgins ; and the virgins carried them right through the gate and handed them in for the building of the tower. And when the various stones were placed in the building, they became all alike and white, and they lost their various colours " (Sim. ix. 4). Hermas therefore asks the Shepherd the meaning of this symbolism. " First, Sir," he says, " show me this, why, the mountains being so various, yet their stones became bright and of one colour when set into the building." "Because," so answers the Shepherd, "all the nations that dwell under heaven, when they heard and believed, were called by the one name of the Son of God. So having received the seal, they had one understanding and one mind, and one faith became theirs and one love, and they bore the spirits of the virgins along with the name ; therefore the building of the tower became of one colour, even bright as the sun " (Sim. ix. 17). There could not be any clearer enunciation than this of the catholicity of the church, in respect of its capacity to embrace all types of nationality, and to weld them into unity. Jew and Gentile, Greek and Roman, have their specific national traits, but " all are one in Christ Jesus."

So then, closely connected with the catholicity which marks the church, is the fundamental principle of unity, which binds its members closely to one another and to Christ, upon whom the church is built. " The tower has become a single stone with the rock. So also they that have believed in the Lord through His Son and clothe themselves in these spirits[1], shall become one spirit and one body and their garments all of one colour " (Sim. ix. 13). " When they had received these spirits, they were

[1] *i.e.* the Virtues above enumerated. See Sim. ix. 15.

strengthened and were with the servants of God, and they had one spirit and one body ; for they had the same mind and wrought righteousness " (Sim. ix. 13). This unity, however, represents an ideal, which is not yet fully attained. Hermas seems to imply that in the present imperfect stage, disunion will be the accompaniment of imperfection. Not till the end, when the process of purification of the church is complete, will true unity be achieved. " There shall be one body of them that are purified, just as the tower after it had been purified, became made as it were of one stone. Thus shall it be with the church of God also, after it hath been purified, and the wicked and hypocrites and blasphemers and double-minded and they that commit various kinds of wickedness have been cast out. When these have been cast out, the church of God shall be one body, one understanding, one mind, one faith, one love " (Sim. ix. 18). This ideal unity described as that of " one body " must mean an organic unity, which ought to find expression in outward unity of organisation. This glorious condition of harmonious unity is, however, promised, not as a present possession, but as a final achievement. It represents the true ideal of the church, the goal at which it is to aim. No lower ideal is to be accepted, as the goal of effort, than that of the " one body," one outward organisation, giving expression to the one life of the one church, founded on the one faith and indwelt by the one Spirit.

Nor is it only in the church universal that a general unity is to be observed. This unity must also find expression in the harmonious life of each local church. " Be at peace among yourselves and have regard one to another and assist one another " (Vis. iii. 9). Divisions, however, had appeared in the local church of Rome, which is here the object of address, and so warning is given as to what the result of such conduct must be. " Look ye, children, lest these divisions of yours deprive you of your life " (*ibid.*).

With Hermas, the ascetic side of Christianity is emphasised. He seems at times to adopt uncompromisingly the position that riches are a fatal barrier to entrance into the church. Certain white and round stones, which could not fit into the building of the tower, are interpreted as representing the rich, who, so long as they retained their riches, could find no place in the church. " When their wealth, which leadeth their souls astray, shall be cut off, then will they be useful for God. For just as the round stone, unless it be cut away, and lose some portion of itself, cannot become square, so also they that are rich in this world, unless their riches be cut away, cannot become useful to the Lord." " Learn first from thyself" is the admonition to Hermas. " When thou hadst riches, thou wast useless ; but now thou art useful and profitable unto life " (Vis. iii. 6). Just as the round stone must be squared, in order to fit into the building, so the encumbrance of riches must be cut off[1].

This view, stated so strongly by Hermas, may be regarded as the outcome of his experience of Roman social life. For the most part the Christian community was poor and uneducated ; many were slaves. The gulf between these and the rich would seem too wide to be bridged, making it impossible for a rich man, retaining his riches, to enter into the full Christian life. For the social aspects of Christianity were accentuated by the strong sense of brotherhood in the early church. The central

[1] See also Sim. ix. 30 f

rite, comprising Eucharist and Agapé, was essentially an
expression of brotherhood. If then, under the conditions of
the time, the possession of riches interposed a social barrier,
we can understand the vigour with which Hermas denounced them. His words are to be regarded, not as
the expression of a fundamental principle, but as having
reference to the special circumstances of time and place.

But on this point, as on others, Hermas is not always
consistent. From his teaching elsewhere it is clear that
there were people of wealth in the local church in Rome
at this time. For they receive an admonition against
superfluous worldly expenditure. " Thou, who hast fields
and dwellings and many other possessions, when thou art
cast out, what wilt thou do with thy field and thy
house and all the other things that thou preparedst for
thyself?" (Sim. i.). And, indeed, private possessions have
their value if rightly used. They afford an opportunity
for a special service. " Instead of fields buy ye souls that
are in trouble, as each is able, and visit widows and
orphans, and neglect them not ; and spend your riches
and all your displays, which ye received from God, on
fields and houses of this kind " (*ibid.*).

But in the parable of the Elm and the Vine, Hermas
goes even beyond this. The rich man and the poor man
are necessary, each to the other, in the life of the church.
The vine climbs up the elm and, owing to the support
thus given, is enabled to bear its fruit, which else would
rot upon the ground. So " the poor man being supplied
by the rich maketh intercession for him, thanking God
for him that gave to him. And the other is still more
zealous to assist the poor man, for he knoweth that the
intercession of the poor man is acceptable and rich before
God. They both then accomplish their work " (Sim. ii.).

It remains true, however, that riches constitute a temptation. " As it is difficult to walk on briars with bare feet, so
also it is difficult for the rich to enter into the kingdom
of God " (Sim. ix. 20).

The church grows not only by outward expansion
but also in deepening vitality. Its outward growth is
illustrated by the building of the tower. Its vital growth
is symbolised by the vision of the lady, who first
appears to Hermas, and who, as he learns, is the
church. She appears three times, in three different
forms : the first time, as an aged lady, seated, as be-
seems her age ; the second, with youthful features,
though aged in form, and now standing, so as to
represent added strength ; the third, with all the spring
of youth and exceeding great beauty, save only that the
hair still retains its marks of age. So the splendour of
the Christian hope has given fresh life and vigour to the
church. There was the early period of weakness, when
difficulties seemed overwhelming. " Your spirit was
broken and ye were aged by your sorrows " (Vis. iii. 11).
Then came the renewal of strength, as the result of the
Christian message, " when ye heard the revelation which
the Lord revealed to you " (Vis. iii. 12). Then comes
the third period where the lady of the vision is once
again represented as seated, no longer in weakness, but
now in the dignity of conscious strength. The church is
planted firmly in the world. This process of growing
vigour in the church seems to be viewed by Hermas in
special reference to the actual circumstances of the local
church in Rome, for the process is stated as the actual
experience of those to whom he is writing (ὑμεῖς, Vis. iii.).
But no doubt he would wish his words to receive a wider
than merely local application. His fundamental thought

is of the vital growth of the church, as the result of divine protection and in the face of worldly assaults.

We have already seen that Hermas' conception of the church is not exhausted by the outward institution which bears that name. His deeper thought in regard to the church is of a spiritual sphere, which lies behind the institutional form. This is the " first church " or " living church " of the Pseudo-Clement (2 Clem. 14). It is this spiritual church, not the institutional church as such, which is represented by the tower.

That entrance into the spiritual church is subject to fitness for the privilege is shown by the choice of stones for the tower. There are first " the stones that are squared and white, and that fit together in their joints. These are the apostles and bishops and teachers and deacons, who walked after the holiness of God, and exercised their office of bishop and teacher and deacon in purity and sanctity for the elect of God " (Vis. iii. 5). Then there are the stones that were "dragged from the deep," representing " those that suffered in the name of the Lord " (*ibid.*). Those, again, brought from the dry land and placed in the building, unhewn, are they who " walked in the uprightness of the Lord and rightly performed His commandments " (*ibid.*).

Repentance is required as a condition of entrance. Those who repent, while the tower is in building, that is during this world's period of probation, may be brought into the church. " They that shall repent shall be strong in the faith, if they repent now while the tower is in building " (*ibid.*). Thus entrance to the spiritual church implies the satisfying of a searching test. Some there are, who remain outside, because they cannot bring themselves to make the renunciation, which entrance into the church demands. "The others, which fall near the waters, and yet cannot roll into the water, wouldst thou know who they are ? These are they that heard the word, and would be baptized into the name of the Lord. Then when they call to their remembrance the purity of the truth, they change their minds and go back again after their evil desires" (Vis. iii. 7).

We have said that the tower represents, not the institutional or empirical church, but the spiritual church, which lies behind the outward form. This appears clearly from the parable of the Willow (Sim. viii.). Branches from a great willow tree are given to a multitude of people, who have come under its shadow. "The tree is the law of God, which was given to the whole world ; and this law is the Son of God, preached unto the ends of the earth" (Sim. viii. 3). The law referred to is, therefore, not the law of natural religion, but the law of the Gospel of Christ, which is for the whole world. And, moreover, the multitude, to whom the rods are given are "those who are called by the name of the Lord" (Sim. viii. 1), *i.e.* baptized Christians. That they are thought of as members of the church is shown by the fact that those, who have proved unworthy of their position, are described as "renegades and traitors to the church, that blasphemed the Lord in their sins, and still further were ashamed of the name of the Lord, which was invoked upon them" (Sim. viii. 6).

Here then we have a picture of the institutional church, which is figured by those to whom the willow rods are delivered. The parable represents the probation of those who make up the church upon earth. They live in possession of the Gospel, symbolised by the willow rod committed to each. Their lives are tested by the condition of their rods, which may be found to be green or withered, fruitful or barren. Those whose rods are fruitful are admitted to the tower (Sim. viii. 2); they win a place in the spiritual church. A further opportunity is given to the rest, and three different states are described as resulting from this further probation. "As many of them as have repented, have their abode within the tower; but as many of them, as have repented tardily, abide within the walls; and as many as repent not, but continue in their doings, shall die the death" (Sim. viii. 7). The penitent, therefore, shall find a place in the spiritual church, but tardy repentance leads only to a condition of lower privilege, described as "within the walls." Final impenitence ends in spiritual death.

A special warning is given to the rulers of the institutional church, which brings out emphatically its probationary character. "Now therefore I say unto you, who are rulers of the church and who occupy the chief seats; be ye not like unto the sorcerers. The sorcerers indeed carry their drugs in boxes, but ye carry your drug and your poison in your heart. Ye are case-hardened, and ye will not cleanse your hearts and mix your wisdom together in a clean heart, that ye may obtain mercy from the Great King. Look ye therefore, children, lest these divisions of yours deprive you of your life" (Vis. iii. 9). Those who in the institutional church fail to cleanse their hearts, will be excluded from the spiritual church and will be deprived of life. Incidentally this passage shows that the institutional church, at all events in the local church in Rome, was far from realising its true ideals.

It is to be noted that entrance even into the spiritual church is not equivalent to final salvation. The position of privilege is still one of probation, and may be forfeited.

" If any one shall turn again to dissension, he shall be cast
out of the tower and shall lose his life " (Sim. viii. 7).
The early days of the spiritual life must especially be
guarded.   " They that are brought and placed in the
building, who are they ? " asks Hermas.   " They are
young in the faith and faithful," is the answer ; "but they
are warned of the angels to do good, because wickedness
was found in them " (Vis. iii. 5).   Life in the spiritual
church is to be a period of growth.   Those who are still
" young in the faith," whose spiritual life is but beginning,
must put away evil and grow in holiness.

This continued probation in the spiritual church is
further illustrated by the careful testing to which the
stones, already built into the tower, are subjected by the
Master.   " He inspected the building so carefully, that he
felt each single stone ; and he held a rod in his hand and
struck each single stone that was built in.   And when he
smote them, some of the stones became black as soot,
others mildewed, others cracked, others broke off short,
others became neither white nor black, others rough and
not fitting in with the rest of the stones, and others with
many spots ; these were the varied aspects of the stones,
which were found unfit for the building.   So he ordered
all these to be removed from the tower, and to be
placed by the side of the tower, and other stones to be
brought and put into their place " (Sim. ix. 6).

From this teaching emerges the serious character of
post-baptismal sin, which in producing its full effect
results in separation from the spiritual church.   But can
post-baptismal sin receive forgiveness ?   At first sight it
would appear that Hermas would answer this question in
the affirmative.   For those just described as removed from
the tower may be reinstated, if they repent.   " For this

is the reason why there was also a cessation in the building, that, if these repent, they may go into the building of the tower; but if they repent not, then others will go and these shall be finally cast away " (Sim. ix. 14).

A comparison with other passages shows, however, that Hermas regarded this possibility as belonging only to the time already past. In time past by God's mercy repentance might win the forgiveness of sins committed after baptism. But for the future this could not be. Henceforward there could be no other remission of sins than the forgiveness granted in baptism.

The stern doctrine is clearly laid down that post-baptismal sin can no longer be forgiven. " I have heard, Sir," says Hermas, " from certain teachers, that there is no other repentance save that which took place when we went down into the water and obtained remission of our former sins." " Thou hast well heard," replies the Shepherd, " for so it is. For he that hath received remission of sins ought no longer to sin, but to dwell in purity. But, since thou enquirest all things accurately, I will declare unto thee this also, so as to give no excuse to those who shall hereafter believe, or those who have already believed on the Lord. For they that have already believed, or shall hereafter believe, have not repentance for sins, but have only remission of their former sins. To those then that were called before these days the Lord hath appointed repentance. For the Lord, being a discerner of hearts and foreknowing all things, perceived the weakness of men and the manifold wiles of the devil, how that he will be doing some mischief to the servants of God, and will deal wickedly with them. The Lord then, being very compassionate, had pity on His handiwork and appointed this repentance, and to me was given the

authority over this repentance.   But I say unto you, if
after this great and holy calling any one, being tempted
of the devil, shall commit sin, he hath only one repentance " (Mand. iv. 3).   The same doctrine, that for the
future there can be no forgiveness of post-baptismal sin,
appears in the Visions.   In the little book, which is given
to Hermas by the aged lady, the church, are found these
words : " After thou hast made known unto them all these
sayings, which the Master commanded me that they
should be revealed to thee, then all their sins which they
sinned aforetime are forgiven to them ; yea, and to all the
saints that have sinned unto this day, if they repent with
their whole heart and remove double-mindedness from
their heart.   For the Master sware by His own glory, as
concerning His elect ; that if, now that this day has been
set as a limit, sin shall hereafter be committed, they
shall not find salvation ; for repentance for the righteous
hath an end ; the days of repentance are fulfilled for all
the saints ; whereas for the Gentiles there is repentance
until the last day " (Vis. ii. 2).   Hermas therefore regards
his own time as a critical moment in the history of the
church.   Till then the full working of what he seems to
regard as a fundamental principle had, by the mercy of
God, been suspended.   He feels constrained to admit that
God had up till then granted forgiveness to penitents
subsequently to baptism.   Perhaps actual experience and
the evidence of facts made it impossible to deny this.
But for the future, so he teaches, this cannot be.

Hermas, it should be noted, does not claim for this
teaching any wide authority.   It is only the teaching of
the few (παρά τινων διδασκάλων, Mand. iv. 3), and in spite
of the emphasis which Hermas lays upon it, he seems
conscious that it is something new.

There is then in the church a process of probation, and through this process the church is to be purified by the expulsion of those who prove unworthy. " In this way therefore shall the church of God be purified. And as thou sawest the stones removed from the tower and delivered over to the evil spirits, they too shall be cast out ; and there shall be one body of them that are purified, just as the tower, after it had been purified, became as it were of one stone " (Sim. ix. 18). Through the casting out of the wicked the spiritual church shall gradually advance towards its final purification, when its unity shall be consummated and it shall be as " of one stone " and one with the rock (Sim. ix. 9). We should note its title, " the church of God." When the wicked have been cast out, " the church of God shall be one body, one understanding, one mind, one faith, one love " (Sim. ix. 18).

So Hermas watches the church advancing towards its consummation. And we shall not fail to note that this consummation is characterised by the perfect realisation of unity. The divisions, which belong to partial view and imperfect life, will all have passed away.

It will be well, before passing on, to summarise what has appeared from the above as to Hermas' conception of the character and function of the church. Though he does not specifically define the distinction, he clearly assumes throughout a double idea of an outward or institutional church and an inward or spiritual church. A man may be a member of the institutional church, and yet not be in the spiritual church, the " living church " of the Pseudo-Clement. In order to make his outward condition of church membership a living fact, he must bear the good fruit of a life of obedience to the commandments of the Gospel. In this way he will make effective his spiritual privileges, and will secure his position in the spiritual church. But even so, he is still under probation. If he fall back into sin, he will lose his privilege and his position can only be regained by true repentance. The church, whether in its outward or in its spiritual aspect, is the sphere of probation, the way to the attainment of salvation.

The spiritual church leads to the kingdom of God. The kingdom of God may be defined as the sphere within which God's sovereignty is acknowledged and God's law obeyed. The relation therefore between the spiritual church and the kingdom of God is not one of simple identity.

But through the spiritual church inheritance in the kingdom of God is won by the believer. " The stones which came through the gate have gone to the building of the tower....Thus no one shall enter into the kingdom of God, except he receive the name of His Son " (Sim. ix. 12). "The tower...is the church....No man can otherwise be found in the kingdom of God, unless these (*i.e.* the virgins, representing the virtues) shall clothe him with their garment " (Sim. ix. 13). " He that beareth these names (*i.e.* of the virtues) shall be able to enter the kingdom of God " (Sim. ix. 15). Thus entering the spiritual church through the gate of the Incarnation, and endowed with the heavenly virtues, the believer may win that perfect harmony with the will of God, in which life in the kingdom consists. The attainment of the kingdom is the goal of the church.

SECTION V.

THE SHEPHERD OF HERMAS (continued).

Entrance into the church is the subject of divine election.—And is
effected by Baptism.—The church includes the righteous of pre-
Christian days.—A measure of salvation is possible outside the
church.—Authority of the church: (1) In teaching. (2) In discipline.—Sacrificial aspect of the church.—The ministry of the
church.—Deacons.—"Bishops."—Presbyters.—Prophets.—A female
ministry.—Position of Hermas in the church.

The members of the "holy church" are spoken of as
"the elect." "By His own wisdom and providence, He
formed His holy church, which also He blessed. Behold
He removeth the heavens and the mountains and the
hills and the seas, and all things are made level for His
elect, that He may fulfil to them the promise, which He
gave them, with exceeding joy and glory, if so be that
they shall keep the ordinances of God, which they
received with great faith" (Vis. i. 3). Thus the privilege
of church membership is the outcome of a divine
election. Those to whom Hermas is to make known
the revelation which he has received are "the elect of
God" (Vis. ii. 1). The divine election brings a man into
the church, but it then rests with the man himself how
far he will use the opportunities thus given. It is clearly
laid down in the passage quoted above that the fulfilment
of the promises to "the elect" is conditional upon their
obedience to "the ordinances of God."

The gate of entrance into the church is Baptism.
The tower, which is seen in the process of building and
which represents the spiritual church, is built "upon the
waters" (Vis. iii. 2). Hermas asks the reason of this, and

receives the answer : " Because your life is saved and shall
be saved by water " (Vis. iii. 3). As then the stones used
for the building had to pass through the water, to reach
the tower, so Baptism is the means of entry into the
church, and is a preliminary to salvation. It is therefore
recognised as a decisive action, which must be accompanied by a change of life. Hermas, as we have already
seen, is told of some who shrank from Baptism, because
they were not able to face the renunciation required
(Vis. iii. 7).

The stones in the lower ranges of the tower represent
the righteous who died before the coming of Christ. The
first and second courses in the foundation of the tower
are the first and second generations of righteous men
(Sim. ix. 15). Then come "God's prophets and ministers"
of the old dispensation. All these are strangely represented as being rescued from their position by the Apostles
and others, who preached the Gospel to them in the under-
world and brought them, as though by Baptism, into the
spiritual church. " The Apostles and the teachers, who
preached the name of the Son of God, after they had
fallen asleep in the power and faith of the Son of God,
preached also to those who had fallen asleep before them,
and themselves gave unto them the seal of the preaching.
Therefore they went down with them into the water and
came up again. But these went down alive and again
came up alive ; whereas the others that had fallen asleep
before them went down dead and came up alive " (Sim.
ix. 16) [1]. So then, as by Baptism in some mystical

---

[1] Cf. Gebhardt and Harnack, *ad loc.* p. 233. It would appear that,
with the exception of Clement of Alexandria, who has transcribed this
passage (*Strom.* ii. ix. 44), Hermas stands alone in teaching that the
Apostles descended into the place of departed spirits to administer
Baptism to the righteous. Later patristic writers speak only of the

sense, the pre-Christian righteous dead receive spiritual life and are brought into the church[1].

We have already seen that the church is regarded as the true sphere of salvation. The tower is the place of safety, into which those may enter who accept its conditions. " Whosoever shall serve these women (*i.e.* the virtues) and shall have strength to master their works, shall have his dwelling in the tower with the saints of God" (Vis. iii. 8). But a measure of salvation, though of an altogether lower degree, is possible outside the church. Certain stones are shown to Hermas, which represent those who " have sinned and desire to repent." These lie in a position of privilege "near the tower." If they repent "while the tower is building," they will have a place in the tower. But if they do not repent during this period of probation, they will remain outside, and still " this privilege only they have, that they lie near the tower" (Vis. iii. 5). There is no indication what spiritual condition this is intended to represent.

A further possibility is however contemplated. There may be repentance after death. "Still importunate," says Hermas, " I asked further, whether for all those stones that were rejected and would not fit into the building of the tower, there was repentance and they had a place in the tower." "They can repent," was the answer, "but they cannot be fitted into the tower. Yet

descent of Christ. We may note, however, that Hippolytus, in the early part of the third century, writes of St John the Baptist that " he was the first to preach the Gospel to those in Hades, becoming a forerunner there when he was put to death by Herod, that there too he might signify that the Saviour would descend to ransom the souls of the saints from the hand of death " (Hippol. *de Antichristo*, 45).

[1] This may be compared and contrasted with the teaching of Justin (*Apol.* i. 46), who gives the name of Christian to men who, before the time of Christ, lived upright lives, such as Socrates or Abraham.

they shall be fitted into another place much more humble, but not until they have undergone torments, and have fulfilled the days of their sins " (Vis. iii. 7). That repentance after death is meant by this passage appears from a consideration of the consequences. For the reward of repentance during life is inclusion in the tower (Vis. iii. 5), but the repentance here contemplated avails only to secure "a place much more humble." The purgatory here contemplated by Hermas is, it may be noted, quite different from that of the Augustinian doctrine. Its purpose is not the cleansing of imperfect souls with a view to their final complete salvation in the glorified church. It is a period of torment for those whose repentance has come too late to admit of their finding a place in the spiritual church. When they have thus done penance for their sins, " then shall it befall them to be relieved from their torments." But they do not then win full salvation. They cannot find a place in the church. Theirs is a condition "much more humble." So then while the church and the church alone is the sphere of full and complete salvation, Hermas contemplates a kind of secondary salvation, but of a much lower degree, as possible outside the church.

The authority of the church is illustrated by its position as the divinely commissioned teacher. The aged lady, who appears to Hermas as his teacher, is made known to him as the church. She is seated in a brilliant throne of snow-white wool, and holds a book in her hands. Thus she appears with the emblems of authority, as commissioned to teach (Vis. i. 2). Hermas is bidden to take the book from her and to deliver its teaching to the people. Here then we have a view of the authority of the church. The church is the divinely appointed teacher and it is through the church that God's revelation is made known. Thus Hermas speaks of " the revelations and visions, which He showed me through His holy church " (Vis. iv. 1). Further, the Holy Spirit (strangely identified with the Son of God) speaks to Hermas by means of the church. The church is the medium through which His teaching is conveyed. " I wish to show thee," says the Shepherd to Hermas, " all things that the Holy Spirit, which spake with thee in the form of the church, showed unto thee. For that Spirit is the Son of God. For when thou wast weaker in the flesh, it was not declared unto thee through an angel; but when thou wast enabled through the Spirit, and didst grow mighty in thy strength, so that thou couldest even see an angel, then at length was manifested unto thee, through the church, the building of the tower " (Sim. ix. 1). So then the church, inspired by the Holy Spirit, is the divinely commissioned teacher, to make known to man the revelation of God.

It is therefore to the church that Hermas turns for encouragement. A terrible vision has been shown to him, which proves to be a figure of a coming persecution. Then appears to him in glorious beauty the lady of his earlier vision. " I knew," says Hermas, " from the former visions that it was the church, and I became more cheerful " (Vis. iv. 2). She bids him then be courageous and hold firmly to his faith in the evil days that are to come.

The church, in addition to its authority as teacher, possesses also a power of discipline. We may perhaps infer, from a curious dialogue which takes place between Hermas and the Shepherd, that the local church in Rome had recently been exercising this disciplinary authority,

in appointing certain days as days of fasting. " As I was
fasting and seated on a certain mountain and giving
thanks to the Lord for all that He had done unto me,
I see the Shepherd seated by me and saying : 'Why hast
thou come hither in the early morning ? ' 'Because, Sir,'
say I, ' I am keeping a station.' ' What,' saith he, ' is
a station ? ' 'I am fasting, Sir,' say I" (Sim. v. 1).
Now a "station," or stationary day ($\sigma\tau\alpha\tau\iota\omega\nu$, Lat. *statio*)
meant a day of fasting, and was so called because there
was a cessation of ordinary occupations, in order that the
time might be spent quietly in prayer[1]. The idea of
a "station" seems to have been a new one in Rome. For
otherwise Hermas would hardly represent the Shepherd
as asking what was meant by a station. It is probable,
therefore, that we have here the beginning of the
disciplinary regulation of fast days by the church. It
would appear that the purpose of the parable is to
utter a warning against these prescribed fasts becoming
formal and unreal. " Fast thou unto God such a fast
as this; do no wickedness in thy life, and serve the
Lord with a pure heart; observe His commandments
and walk in His ordinances and let no evil desire rise
up in thy heart ; but believe God. Then, if thou shalt
do these things and fear Him, and control thyself from
every evil deed, thou shalt live unto God; and if thou
do these things, thou shalt accomplish a great fast, and
one acceptable unto God " (Sim. v. 1).

In the church there rests a power of sacrifice, a means
of sacrificial approach to God. Thus prayer has a sacrificial character, and so is said to be offered at " the altar
of God." " The intercession of a gloomy man hath never

---

[1] See Bingham, *Antiq.* Bk. xxi. Chap. iii.

at any time power to ascend to the altar of God"
(Mand. x. 3).

We have now to enquire what system of church
government is implied by Hermas. The allusions to
church officers are of a somewhat vague character.
They are called "the rulers of the church" (Vis. ii. 2
and iii. 9, οἱ προηγούμενοι τῆς ἐκκλησίας), a phrase
which recalls Heb. xiii. 7 : "Remember them that had
the rule over you" (οἱ ἡγούμενοι ὑμῶν). A more
definite expression, however, occurs : "the presbyters
that preside over the church" (οἱ πρεσβύτεροι οἱ
προϊστάμενοι τῆς ἐκκλησίας, Vis. ii. 4). Hermas recognises therefore an order of presbyters, whose function it
is to preside over the church.

In the building of the tower, the stones squared and
white represent "the Apostles and bishops and teachers
and deacons, who walked after the holiness of God and
exercised their office of bishop and teacher and deacon
(ἐπισκοπήσαντες καὶ διδάξαντες καὶ διακονήσαντες) in
purity and sanctity for the elect of God, some of them
already fallen on sleep and others still living" (Vis. iii. 5).
It would appear that Hermas here combines the ministry
of the past age with that of his own, adding the unique
order of Apostles to the permanent ministry of bishops,
teachers and deacons.

That the Apostles to whom Hermas refers are those
missionary preachers of the first age, whom the New
Testament represents as bearing a special commission,
appears from other allusions to them. The first in
Christian times to find a place in the tower, following
upon the "prophets and ministers" of the Old Testament,
are the "Apostles and teachers of the preaching of the
Son of God" (Sim. ix. 15). These, clearly, are the first

generation of missionary preachers of the Gospel, "Apostles and teachers, who preached unto the whole world" (Sim. ix. 25).

The Apostles, then, may be set aside in our attempt to reconstruct the Christian ministry as implied by Hermas. But in addition to the Apostles there are the "bishops, teachers and deacons" (Vis. iii. 5, ἐπίσκοποι καὶ διδάσκαλοι καὶ διάκονοι). The question, then, first arises whether we have here titles of offices or merely distinctions of function.

That the term διάκονοι is the title of an office is apparent from another passage. Hermas speaks of "deacons who ill performed their service and plundered the livelihood of widows and orphans, and made gain for themselves from the service, which they had received to perform" (ἐκ τῆς διακονίας ἧς ἔλαβον διακονῆσαι, Sim. ix. 26). Thus the διάκονος is one who has been commissioned to hold a definite office; he is a recognised church official, with definite duties, which expose him to certain temptations, against which he must be warned; he is not merely generally a servant, but specifically a deacon. He exercises a stewardship of the material resources of the church. The widows and orphans are under his care. His ministry therefore affords an opportunity for wrongful gain. He must be on his guard against this. He must not make a traffic of his ministry (Sim. ix. 26, ἑαυτοῖς περιποιησάμενοι ἐκ τῆς διακονίας). The work of the deacons is closely akin to that of the Seven in the Acts of the Apostles, whose duty it was to relieve the Twelve of "the serving of tables" (Acts vi. 2).

The close association of the terms ἐπίσκοποι and διάκονοι makes it probable that as the one is used as the title of an office, so also is the other. The evidence is of a similar character to that which we have already considered in Clement's letter to the Corinthians.

The building of the tower gives occasion for a reference to the work of the " bishops." " From the tenth mountain, where were trees sheltering certain sheep, they that believed are such as these ; bishops, hospitable persons, who gladly received into their houses at all times the servants of God without hypocrisy. These bishops at all times without ceasing sheltered the needy and the widows in their ministration, and conducted themselves in purity at all times " (Sim. ix. 27). The trees sheltering the sheep upon the mountain side are doubtless in reference to the pastoral character of the " bishops' " work. As the trees shelter the sheep, so the " bishops " must shelter the needy and widows. The specific reference here is to the duty of hospitality. This duty was ot special prominence and importance in the early Christian society, and it was natural that the leaders of the community should be more particularly charged with this duty. The Pastoral Epistles had already laid it down that the ἐπίσκοπος must be ready to offer hospitality to strangers[1].

But if we grant that ἐπίσκοπος is in Hermas the title of an office, the further question arises as to the nature of the office. Now we have already noted that the Muratorian Fragment assigns the *Shepherd* to the middle of the second century. " The *Shepherd* was written quite lately in our times by Hermas, while his brother Pius, the bishop, was sitting in the chair of the church of the city of Rome " (ll. 73—77). If this testimony be accepted as accurate, the title ἐπίσκοπος must express the office of a monarchical bishop. For by that time

[1] Titus i. 7 f., δεῖ γὰρ τὸν ἐπίσκοπον...εἶναι...φιλόξενον.

monarchical episcopacy was established in Rome, Pius, according to the almost contemporary witness of the Muratorian Fragment, then being bishop. The references to the ministry in Hermas can no doubt be reconciled with these conditions, but, taken apart from this external evidence as to date, they would undoubtedly suggest a more primitive stage of development. They seem in fact to correspond with the ministry implied in Clement's letter to the Corinthians. There are the two offices of ἐπίσκοποι and διάκονοι, mentioned in close conjunction, as in Clement. There are the πρεσβύτεροι, who, again as in Clement, are never mentioned at the same time as the ἐπίσκοποι. All this fits in with the situation, which we were led to infer as existing in the church in Rome at the close of the first century, a ministry of presbyters and deacons, with the title of ἐπίσκοπος used as an alternative to that of presbyter, when it was desired to emphasise the contrast of functions belonging to the two offices. Moreover we recognised that in Clement himself the local Roman church of that date had, if not a monarchical head, at least one who occupied a position of primacy, and who was authorised to write to other churches as the representative of his own. Now Hermas speaks of a Clement as occupying a similar position in the local Roman church of his own day (Vis. ii. 4). This raises a strong presumption that the two Clements are the same ; that we have here a document not later than the first quarter of the second century, witnessing to an organisation of the ministry in the Roman church, which, if it cannot be described as monarchical episcopacy, was yet its immediate precursor, since it shows, in addition to a body of presbyters and deacons, one man occupying a unique position of leadership.

To the presbyters, as a body, is committed the office of ruling. They "preside over the church" (Vis. ii. 4). Prominent among their duties is the work of teaching. For this work they, as "rulers of the church" (Vis. iii. 9), must carefully prepare themselves. "How is it that ye wish to instruct the elect of the Lord, while ye yourselves have no instruction ? Instruct one another therefore, and have peace among yourselves" (*ibid.*). The book of instructions given to Hermas is to be read by him and by the presbyters to the church in the city (Vis. ii. 4). The instruction of the people is to be their care.

The prophets are evidently regarded by Hermas as playing an important part in the worship of the church. They are men who possess in a special degree the inspiration of the Holy Spirit. The divine afflatus will come upon the prophet from time to time in the assembly for public worship, in answer to the united prayer of the congregation ; and under this influence he will then speak in the power of the Holy Spirit. "When the man who hath the divine Spirit cometh into an assembly (συναγωγή) of righteous men, who have faith in a divine Spirit, and intercession is made to God by the gathering of those men, then the angel of the prophetic spirit, who is attached to him, filleth the man, and the man, being filled with the Holy Spirit, speaketh to the multitude according as the Lord willeth. In this way then the Spirit of deity shall be manifest. This then is the greatness of the power as touching the Spirit of the deity of the Lord" (Mand. xi.). It will be noticed from this that the prophet is not regarded as being continuously under the influence of the Holy Spirit. He cannot utter prophecy at pleasure or whenever it may be asked of him, but only when the afflatus is upon him. This affords a means of distinguishing between the true prophet and the false. For the false prophet will always be ready with a pretended prophecy when enquiry is made of him. A curious passage describes the way in which the false prophet meets his enquirers. "The doubtful-minded come to him as to a soothsayer, and enquire of him what shall befall them. And he, the false prophet, having no power of a divine Spirit in himself, speaketh with them according to their enquiries and filleth their souls as they themselves wish. For being empty himself, he giveth empty answers to empty enquirers ; for whatever enquiry may be made of him, he answereth according to the emptiness of the man. So many therefore as are strong in the faith of the Lord, clothed with the truth, cleave not to such spirits, but hold aloof from them ; but as many as are doubters and frequently change their minds, practise soothsaying like the Gentiles, and bring upon themselves greater sin by their idolatries. For he that consulteth a false prophet on any matter is an idolater and emptied of the truth and senseless. For no Spirit given of God needeth to be consulted, but having the power of deity, speaketh all things of itself, because it is from above, even the power of the divine Spirit. But the spirit, which is consulted, and speaketh according to the desires of men, is earthly and fickle, having no power ; and it speaketh not at all, unless it be consulted" (*ibid.*). This passage shows the danger which existed in the early church in the recognition of the gift of prophecy. Men, trading upon a pretended gift of prophecy, might, for the sake of reward like the heathen soothsayers, deceive and lead astray those who superstitiously consulted them. At the same time the true gift of prophecy is shown as standing in vivid contrast to that gift, to which the soothsayers pretended.

It is not the speaking of oracles at the demand of individuals, but the utterance of inspired words in the public assembly of the church in response to the power of corporate intercession. In other words, the special power of the prophet stands in close connection with the corporate life of the church.

The position here occupied by prophecy in the church is much the same as that which is disclosed by the *Didaché*. In each case the danger of imposture is dwelt upon, and directions are given for the testing of the prophets. In each case the final test is the test of character. "How, then, Sir," asks Hermas, "shall a man know, who of them is a prophet, and who a false prophet ?" "Hear," replies the Shepherd, "concerning both the prophets ; and, as I shall tell thee, so shalt thou test the prophet and the false prophet. By his life test the man that hath the divine Spirit. In the first place, he that hath the Spirit, which is from above, is gentle and tranquil and humble-minded, and abstaineth from all wickedness and vain desire of this present world, and holdeth himself inferior to all men, and giveth no answer to any man when enquired of, nor speaketh in solitude, for neither doth the Holy Spirit speak when a man wisheth Him to speak ; but the man speaketh then, when God wisheth him to speak " (*ibid.*). On the other hand the false prophet is thus characterised : " The man who seemeth to have a spirit exalteth himself and desireth to have a chief place, and straightway he is impudent and shameless and talkative and conversant in many luxuries and in many other deceits and receiveth money for his prophesying and, if he receiveth it not, prophesieth not. Now can a divine Spirit receive money and prophesy ? It is not possible for a prophet of God to

do this, but the spirit of such prophets is earthly " (*ibid.*).
Further emphasis is then laid upon the test supplied by the
supposed prophet's relation to the corporate life of the
church. The false prophet " never approacheth an assembly
of righteous men ; but avoideth them and cleaveth to the
doubtful-minded and empty, and prophesieth to them in
corners and deceiveth them, speaking all things in emptiness to gratify their desires ; for they too are empty, whom
he answereth. For the empty vessel, placed together with
the empty, is not broken, but they agree one with the
other. But when he cometh into an assembly full of
righteous men, who have a Spirit of deity, and intercession is made from them, that man is emptied, and the
earthly spirit fleeth from him in fear, and the man is
struck dumb and is altogether broken in pieces, being
unable to utter a word " (*ibid.*).

We find then that the enthusiastic utterance of
prophecy is still recognised and reverenced in the church.
The fact that prophecy plays this important part in the
life of the church supplies an argument in favour of an
early date for the *Shepherd, i.e.* some time during the first
quarter of the second century. This reverence for prophetic
utterance had its place side by side with the normal
" teaching," such as was given by Hermas himself and by
those whom he describes specifically as " teachers "
(Vis. iii. 5). The situation therefore is much the same
as that which we find in the *Didaché.*

There is an indication of an official ministry of women.
A woman, by name Grapté, evidently occupies an official
position in the local church. She has a definite ministry
of teaching. " Grapté shall instruct the widows and
orphans " (Vis. ii. 4).

It is interesting to enquire what office Hermas himself held in the local church in Rome. He is not a mere apocalyptist, charged simply to write down the visions which he receives. But there is committed to him a ministry of teaching. He is a recognised teacher. " I declare to every man the mighty works of the Lord " are his words to the angel (Sim. x. 2). " Continue therefore in this ministry (*in hoc ministerio*) and complete it unto the Lord " is the angel's reply. And further, " Quit you like a man in this ministry ; declare to every man the mighty works of the Lord, and thou shalt have favour in this ministry " (Sim. x. 4). What office then is here implied ? *In hoc ministerio* is doubtless a translation of ἐν ταυτῇ τῇ διακονίᾳ, but we are not to infer from this that Hermas was only a διάκονος, for διακονία is predicated also of the ἐπίσκοποι (Sim. ix. 27). The authoritative tone, in which he speaks of his work, leads us to conclude that Hermas himself was one of those who held the office of " oversight," that in other words he was an ἐπίσκοπος and therefore, if our identification of these terms be correct, a πρεσβύτερος of the local church.

CHAPTER III.

FROM THE AGE OF THE APOLOGISTS TO IRENÆUS.

SECTION I.

ARISTIDES.

The church a spiritual brotherhood.

The *Apology* of Aristides may on the authority of Eusebius be dated about the year 125 A.D. It contains little that touches our subject. We may note, however, that the character of the Christian church as a spiritual brotherhood finds clear expression. " When they (*i.e.* the slaves) have become Christians, they are without hesitation called brethren...for they are not called brethren according to the flesh, but according to the spirit and in God " (Arist. *Apol.* 15). In the church, as the family of God, there subsists a spiritual relationship. This relationship is independent of distinctions of worldly rank and is freely acknowledged by all its members. The ties of brotherhood unite all alike who bear the name of Christ.

SECTION II.

PAPIAS.

Mystical conception of the church.—Monarchical episcopacy.

The fragments of Papias that have come down to us have little that bears upon our present investigation.

We see, however, that he must have had a mystical conception of the church, considered ideally as a spiritual entity. " Papias and [others] interpreted spiritually of the church of Christ the things which were written of Paradise[1]." " Papias [and others after him] considered that the whole Hexahemeron referred to Christ and the church[2]." Behind the empirical or institutional church is the ideal church, which owes its being to God, the Creator, and is in close union with Christ.

Another passage has some bearing upon the question of the position occupied by St James in the church at Jerusalem. Papias speaks of St James as " bishop and Apostle[3]." Now by the term " bishop " he no doubt understood monarchical office. For he was himself bishop in Hierapolis near the middle of the second century, and, as we know from the letters of Ignatius, monarchical episcopacy had then existed in Asia for at least four decades. It does not however follow that Papias was accurate in using the title " bishop " to express the office held by St James. This question will be further considered in connection with Hegesippus.

---

[1] *Anastasius of Sinai*, quoted by Routh, *Rel. Sacr.* vol. i. p. 16.

[2] Ditto, p. 15.

[3] Frag. Papiæ ex cod. MS. 2397 Bodl., quoted by Routh, *Rel. Sacr.* vol. i. p. 16.

SECTION III.

THE SECOND EPISTLE OF CLEMENT.

Ideal conception of the church.—Its pre-existence.—Relation of the church to the kingdom of God.—Brotherhood in the church.—The Christian ministry.—Public worship.

The document which traditionally bears the title of "The Second Epistle of Clement" has in point of fact no claim to Clementine authorship. Its authorship is entirely unknown to us. The document is a homily rather than an epistle. Its place of writing is uncertain, but its allusion to the games (2 Clem. 7) may perhaps be taken as an indication of Corinthian origin. This would account for its being afterwards ascribed to Clement. For Clement's letter, or a copy of it, was kept at Corinth as a treasured possession, and this homily would lie by its side in the same chest of church documents. These two then, the letter to the Corinthians and an anonymous homily, might well come to be copied, one after the other, upon the same parchment. So by an easy step the same authorship might afterwards be ascribed to both. Our homily may probably be assigned to circ. A.D. 140.

The church is pre-existent in heaven, an ideal spiritual conception, created indeed, but yet existing " before the sun and moon." This ideal conception is described as " the first church," " the living church," " the church of life." It is a glorious, spiritual sphere, within which the highest spiritual blessings are bestowed. " If we do the will of God our Father, we shall be of the first church, which is spiritual, which was created before the sun and moon ; but if we do not the will of the Lord, we shall be of the

Scripture that saith, My house was made a den of robbers. So therefore let us choose rather to be of the church of life, that we may be saved. And I do not suppose ye are ignorant that the living church is the body of Christ ; for the Scripture saith, God made man male and female. The male is Christ and the female is the church.   And the Books and the Apostles plainly declare that the church existeth not now for the first time, but hath been from the beginning : for she was spiritual as our Jesus also was spiritual, but was manifested in the last days that He might save us " (2 Clem. 14).

It will be noted that the writer bases his doctrine of the pre-existence of the church upon the Scriptures.   It is said to be the teaching of " the Books and the Apostles." And this is stated, not as matter of controversy, but as something universally accepted and beyond dispute. This idea of the pre-existence of the church answers to the New Testament conception of the eternal purpose of God, who " chose us before the foundation of the world " (Eph. i. 4). It is essentially different from the eternal æon " Ecclesia " of the Valentinian scheme. For this æon, as being eternal, must be a rival of God, whereas the pre-existent church is God's creation for the fulfilment of His eternal purpose.

This ideal spiritual conception, the church, of which pre-existence is predicated, is the body of Christ. " The living church is Christ's body " (2 Clem. 14 ἐκκλησία ζῶσα σῶμά ἐστιν Χριστοῦ). Here, indeed, ἐκκλησία is anarthrous. But it would be quite foreign to the context to take the word as meaning " a living church," in the sense of a local Christian community. It may be that the words are a reminiscence of 1 Cor. xii. 27 (ὑμεῖς δέ ἐστε σῶμα Χριστοῦ), which Hort interprets as meaning that each local church is "a body of Christ[1]." But there is no thought in this case of the local community. The meaning is, that the unique spiritual entity, known as the church, is "Christ's body," the organ through which He manifests His presence and His power.

Under another figure the relation of Christ to the ideal church is expressed as that of male and female. "The male is Christ and the female is the church." This may be compared with St Paul's analogy of the relation of husband and wife, as parallel to that of Christ and the church (Eph. v. 23 ff.). It enforces the twofold doctrine of union and subjection.

Now the ideal church, being spiritual, is in itself invisible. But it has received an embodiment upon earth, and that in the incarnate life of the Son of God. For it is Christ's body; and therefore Christ's earthly life was an exhibition to men of the spiritual church. "The church, being spiritual, was manifested in the flesh of Christ, thereby showing us that, if any of us guard her in the flesh and defile her not, he shall receive her again in the Holy Spirit" (2 Clem. 14). But these words imply not only that the incarnate life of Christ had been a visible representation of the spiritual church, but that also the spiritual church had still an earthly embodiment. In other words the institutional church is the embodiment in outward form of the spiritual church, and is its visible representative. This outward organisation, to which also the name of church is given by the Pseudo-Clement, is related to its spiritual archetype as flesh to spirit. "This flesh is the counterpart and copy of the spirit" (*ibid.*).

[1] Hort, *Christian Ecclesia*, p. 145: "Here evidently it is the Corinthian community by itself that is called 'a body of Christ': this depends not merely on the absence of an article but on ὑμεῖς, which cannot naturally mean 'all ye Christians.'"

So then the spiritual life of the Christian begins in the institutional church.   He receives the church " in the flesh." This " flesh " he must guard.   " Guard ye the flesh, that ye may partake of the spirit" (*ibid.*).   In other words, he must live worthily of his outward church member- ship, and will then win possession of the spiritual church.

This exhortation is further enforced by a somewhat confusing change of metaphor.   For at the close of this same paragraph the contrast between flesh and spirit, instead of standing for the institutional church and the spiritual church, stands now for the institutional church and Christ Himself.   " But if (*i.e.* changing the metaphor) we say that the flesh is the church, and the spirit is Christ, then he that hath dealt wantonly with the flesh hath dealt wantonly with the church.   Such a one shall not partake of the spirit, which is Christ " (*ibid.*).

It must not be supposed that the phrase " the first church " implies the existence of two distinct churches. The institutional church is the manifestation under conditions of earth, in the necessary clothing of outward organisation, of the ideal church, pre-existent in heaven. Through membership of this outward organisation, men are intended to receive the spiritual blessings, which are in Christ.   But it is possible to be a member of this outward organisation without being in contact with the spiritual life, which it enshrines.   If a man lives un- worthily, then, though outwardly he may be a member of the church, yet its life will not be his.   He will stand apart from " the living church."

This same idea of the pre-existence of the church occurs in Hermas (Vis. ii. 4).   It was also taught by Papias, Justin Martyr and Pantænus, who interpreted the

narrative of creation as referring allegorically to Christ
and the church[1].

The kingdom of God is the goal of the Christian life: it
is not a present possession but a future reward. Baptism,
which gives admission to the church, is the starting point
of the Christian life. Life in the church is therefore
disciplinary and probationary. Upon the faithfulness
shown will depend the final admission to the kingdom
of God. "If we keep not our Baptism pure and undefiled,
what confidence can we have of entering into the kingdom
of God?" (2 Clem. 6). In particular, there must be love,
as the characteristic atmosphere of the church. "Let us
therefore love one another, that we may all come unto the
kingdom of God" (2 Clem. 9). "If we shall have wrought
righteousness in the sight of God, we shall enter into
His kingdom" (2 Clem. 11). "Let us await the kingdom
of God betimes in love and righteousness" (2 Clem. 12).
Thus the institutional church, which is the company of
the baptized, is a sphere of probation. It serves the purpose of preparing men for the attainment at last of the
kingdom of God. The attainment of the kingdom is the
crown of human destiny.

Our writer lays stress upon the character of the church
as a brotherhood. His exhortation to mutual love points
to this. So too he repeatedly addresses his hearers as
"brothers," "my brothers," or "brothers and sisters."
The disciplinary life of the church is largely concerned
with the discharge of the duties of brotherhood[2].

It may be noted that the Gentile Christians are spoken

[1] See *Anastasius of Sinai*, quoted by Routh, *Rel. Sacr.* vol. i. pp. 15 f.
Also pp. 98 f., 131 *supra*.

[2] The address ἀδελφοί or ἀδελφοί μου occurs twelve times (2 Clem. 1,
4, 5 twice, 7, 8, 10, 11, 13, 14 twice, 16). The address ἀδελφοί καί
ἀδελφαί occurs twice (2 Clem. 19, 20).

of as forming a church. " Our church was barren before that children were given to her " (2 Clem. 2). The writer contrasts " our church," *i.e.* " the church of us Gentiles," with the other constituent element of the complete body of Christians, the Jewish communities. Thus he sets the Gentile church over against the Jewish church. This is a use of the word ἐκκλησία not found in the New Testament[1]. Below, he speaks of the Gentile church as " our people " (ὁ λαὸς ἡμῶν). " In that He saith, The children of the desolate are more than of her that hath the husband, He so spake, because our people seemed desolate and forsaken of God, whereas now, having believed, we have become more than those who seemed to know God " (2 Clem. 2). So the old theocratic title of the Jews is transferred to the Christian church, and here specifically by the addition of ἡμῶν it is used to denote the sum of the Gentile communities, the Gentile church.

There is very little to be gathered from our homily as to the work and character of the Christian ministry. We do indeed hear of the presbyters. It is their duty to preach in public worship, and to admonish the people. The people therefore are warned to put into practice what the presbyters tell them. " Let us not think to give heed and believe now only, while we are admonished by the presbyters ; but likewise, when we have departed home, let us remember the commandments of the Lord " (2 Clem. 17). Those who have rejected the Gospel will in the day of judgment bewail their disobedience to the presbyters. " We obeyed not the presbyters, when they told us of our salvation " (2 Clem. 17).

Is the writer of the homily dissociating himself from

---

[1] Hort, *Christian Ecclesia*, pp. 116 ff.

the presbyters in this section ? Are we to suppose that he is a layman, and that consequently we here have an example of a layman delivering a homily ? The form of expression does not require us to take this view. It is quite easy to regard him as using a common rhetorical figure, by which he puts himself into the position of his hearers and speaks from their point of view. " Let us not think to give heed and believe now only, while we are admonished by the presbyters." There is nothing in this form of speech, which excludes the speaker from being himself a presbyter. And on the other hand the idea that a layman is delivering the homily, finds no corroboration in what we know of the customs of the early church[1].

We may gather the importance attached to public worship. The writing itself is a homily, and its purpose delivery in public worship. The hearers are exhorted not merely to listen to the homilies, but to keep in remembrance at home what they have heard, when assembled together (2 Clem. 17). They must also be more frequent in their attendance at public worship, which is an expression of the corporate life of the community and a means of strengthening the sense of union one with another. " Coming hither more frequently, let us strive to go forward in the commands of the Lord, that we all having the same mind may be gathered together unto life " (*ibid.*).

---

[1] Cf. Bingham, *Antiq.* xiv. iv. 2.

SECTION IV.

JUSTIN MARTYR.

The church in relation to Christ.—The church as the people of God.—
Condition of entry into the church.—Its spiritual life.—Its
authority.—Its unity.—This unity is as that of a household.—Or
of a brotherhood.—And finds expression in public worship.—It
extends throughout the universal church.—It excludes heretics.—
But is consistent with a certain variation of opinion.—Sacrificial
aspect of the church.—Its organisation : (1) The president. (2) The
deacons. (3) The reader. (4) The laity.

Justin Martyr combines in himself an experience both
of eastern and western Christianity in the first half of the
second century. He was born near the beginning of the
century, and resided both at Ephesus and at Rome. It was
at Rome that he suffered martyrdom in the reign probably
of Antoninus Pius. His *First Apology* was written circ.
A.D. 150. The *Second Apology* was written not long
after. The *Dialogue with Trypho* is to be dated a few
years later. It is our task now to gather from his
writings his conception of the church.

Christ is the source of the church's being. In
contrast with the Jewish synagogue, the Christian
church has its origin in Christ, whose name it bears.
It "has sprung from His name and partakes of His
name" (*Tryph.* 63). Very intimate therefore is the
relation between Christ and the church. This relationship is represented under the figure of marriage. An
Old Testament narrative is taken to illustrate this.
" The marriages of Jacob were types of that which Christ
was about to accomplish. For it was not lawful for Jacob
to marry two sisters at once. And he serves Laban for

his daughters; and being deceived over the younger, he
again served seven years.   Now Leah is your people and
synagogue ; but Rachel is our church.   And for these and
for the servants of both, Christ is even now serving "
(*Tryph.* 134).   It will be noticed that the marriage of
Christ with the church is not regarded as consummated
as yet.   This is the end to which the present work of
Christ is directed.

The church, which thus owes its being to Christ and
whose union with Christ is in the end to be made
complete, is in the meantime the people of God.   The
term λαός, which in the Old Testament is given to the
chosen people to denote their sacred character as a nation
and their relation to God, is appropriated by Justin
to the Christian church.   " We are not only a people
(λαός) but also a holy people " (*Tryph.* 119).   And in
this sense he quotes Is. lxii. 12 : " They shall call them
the holy people, redeemed by the Lord."   The thought
indeed is much in his mind, for he speaks again of
Christians as " having been deemed worthy to be called
a people " (*Tryph.* 123).   And the contrast between
Israel and the Christian church in respect of its relation
to God is further emphasised: " As from the one man
Jacob, who was surnamed Israel, all your nation has been
called Jacob and Israel ; so we from Christ, who begat us
unto God, like Jacob and Israel and Judah and Joseph
and David, are called and are the true sons of God "
(*Tryph.* 123).   Hort has pointed out[1] that, in the New
Testament, the term λαός is applied to the Christian
church, only where there is a direct reference to the Old
Testament.   The above examples show that the same
is true of Justin.   For the term is used of the Christian

[1] Hort, *Christian Ecclesia*, pp. 12 f.

church, not as expressing an idea proper to the term λαός itself, but an idea associated with the term λαός as used in the Old Testament of the people of Israel, a people belonging to God. The appropriateness of the term as applied to the Christian church rests not in the connotation of an idea analogous to that of nationality but as expressing, through its Old Testament associations, close connection with God. The Christian church belongs to God. That is what is meant when it is said that Christians have been deemed worthy to be called " a people."

The holiness of the church, consequent upon its relation to God, finds acknowledgment in the qualifications laid down as a condition of entry into it. Only those are admitted who have accepted the Christian faith, and who undertake to regulate their lives by its rule. " As many as are persuaded and believe that what we teach and say is true and undertake to be able to live accordingly, are instructed to pray and to entreat God, with fasting, for the remission of their sins that are past, we praying and fasting with them " (*Apol.* I. 61). Repentance is therefore required as a precedent condition. The candidate must be cleansed from sin before he is fit to enter the church. The ceremony of entrance is therefore a " washing," as being symbolical of the cleansing required. " They are brought by us where there is water," says Justin (*ibid.*), and the meaning of the ceremony is emphasised by the application to it of a quotation from Isaiah, " Wash you, make you clean ; put away the evil of your doings from your souls " (Is. i. 16). The candidate for entrance into the church is baptized, in order that he " may obtain in the water the remission of sins formerly committed " (*Apol.* I. 61).

Entrance into the church is by a new birth ; it is the bestowal of a new life. Those who are brought to the water of Baptism " are regenerated," says Justin, " in the same manner, in which we were ourselves regenerated. For, in the name of God, the Father and Lord of the universe, and of our Saviour Jesus Christ and of the Holy Spirit, they then receive the washing with water. For Christ also said, Except ye be born again, ye shall not enter into the kingdom of Heaven" (*ibid.*). These words, in which Christ speaks of the new birth, are clearly interpreted by Justin as referring to the gift of Baptism, the rite through which the candidate becomes a member of the church. This is further emphasised by pointing its contrast with natural birth. "Since at our birth we were born without our own knowledge or choice, by the union of our parents, and were brought up in bad habits and wicked training ; in order that we may not remain the children of necessity and of ignorance, but may become the children of choice and knowledge and may obtain in the water the remission of sins formerly committed, there is pronounced over him, who chooses to be born again and has repented of his sins, the name of God the Father and Lord of the universe ; he who leads to the laver the person that is to be washed addressing God by this name alone " (*ibid.*). Here, it will be noticed, a triple contrast is pointed. The new spiritual birth is set over against the natural birth ; the spiritual birth is voluntarily entered into while the natural birth is by necessity ; the natural birth is from human parents, the spiritual from God, the Father of all. So the church, the Christian society, is the company of those who, through Baptism, have been endowed with the gift of spiritual life, received from God.

In accordance with this, there is a bestowal of spiritual gifts in the church. Baptism itself affords an enlightenment. " This washing is called illumination, because they who learn these things are illuminated in their mind " (*Apol.* I. 61). And this illumination carries with it spiritual gifts, which the disciples of Christ receive. " Every day some are becoming disciples in the name of Christ and leaving the way of error. These also receive gifts, each according as he is worthy, being illuminated through this name of Christ. For one receives the spirit of understanding, another of counsel, another of strength, another of healing, another of foreknowledge, another of teaching and another of the fear of God " (*Tryph.* 39). These are closely analogous to the χαρίσματα of the New Testament, with which according to St Paul the church is endowed. Indeed the actual word is used by Justin to express these spiritual endowments. " You may see among us both men and women who possess gifts of the Spirit of God (χαρίσματα ἀπὸ τοῦ πνεύματος τοῦ θεοῦ) " (*Tryph.* 88). The church is the sphere within which these spiritual gifts are bestowed.

Prominent among these χαρίσματα is the gift of prophecy. This distinctive gift was therefore still manifesting itself in the Christian church. And we notice that, just as in the days of the *Didaché* and of Hermas, so now in the time of Justin the claim to the possession of this gift had to be very carefully scrutinised. " The prophetical gifts remain with us, even to the present time. And hence you ought to understand," says Justin to Trypho, " that the gifts formerly among your nation have been transferred to us. And just as there were false prophets contemporaneous with your holy prophets, so are there now many false teachers amongst us, of whom

our Lord forewarned us to beware " (*Tryph.* 82). The
pretensions of men, who falsely claimed to possess the gift
of prophecy, were still therefore a danger in the Christian
church.

The church, thus endowed with spiritual χαρίσματα,
possesses an authority over its members. This authority
is like that of a mother over her children. Christians
are described as " children of the church " (Frag. *De
Resurrect.* 5). The church teaches authoritatively, as
a mother teaches her children. Recognised " teachers "
in the church perform this office (*Tryph.* 82). But the
teaching so given is referred back to the Apostles. Justin
says, for instance, that the account he gives of the
meaning of Baptism is that which has been derived
from the Apostles (*Apol.* I. 61). The teaching of the
church must be in accordance with apostolic tradition.

Justin claims the fulfilment in the Christian church
of those prerogatives and qualities which belonged
formerly to the Jewish church. Among these is the
quality of organic unity. " Such a thing also you may
witness in the body : although the members are enumerated as many, all are called one and constitute a body.
For, indeed, a people and a church, though consisting of
many individuals in number, form a single entity and are
spoken of and addressed by a single title " (*Tryph.* 42).
In this way the organic unity of the Jewish church is
described. It is like the harmonious unity of a body.
Such then also is the unity of the Christian church. For
the ordinances of the Jewish dispensation were "types and
symbols and declarations of those things, which would
happen to Christ, and of the people who it was foreknown
would believe in Him, and of those things likewise which
should be done by Christ Himself" (*ibid.*). The Christian

church therefore is thought of as essentially one, but organised as a body, in due harmony of internal relationships.

The royal marriage psalm (Ps. xlv.) is applied by Justin to the Christian church. The king's daughter, who is bidden to leave her father's home, is the church. In such a way the church is to separate itself from Judaism. "That to those, who believe in Him as being one soul and one synagogue and one church, the word of God speaks as to a daughter; that it thus addresses the church, which has sprung from His name and partakes of His name (for we are all called Christians), is distinctly proclaimed in like manner in the following words, which teach us to forget even our old ancestral customs, when they speak thus : Hearken, O daughter, and behold, and incline thine ear; forget thy people and the house of thy father, and the King shall desire thy beauty ; because He is thy Lord, and thou shalt worship Him" (*Tryph.* 63). Here then the old titles expressing inward and outward unity, unity of life and of organisation, are transferred from the old dispensation to the new. Christians are " one soul and one synagogue and one church." The inner unity of life, " one soul," is to find expression in unity of outward organisation, " one synagogue and one church."

This same idea of unity is also implied in the figure of a household, which Justin uses to express the church. The Christian community is "a household of prayer and worship" (*Tryph.* 86)[1]. This phrase, which marks the twofold attitude of the church towards God, implies that to the church there properly belongs the unity which should mark family life. The church is a family, which

---

[1] οἶκος εὐχῆς καὶ προσκυνήσεως. The context makes it clear that οἶκος must have the sense of " household."

exists as such in virtue of its relation to God. The natural expression of this relationship is public worship and public prayer.

Since then the church is " a household of prayer and worship," we are not surprised to find what an important place, according to Justin, is occupied by public worship in the life of the church. The newly baptized are, immediately after baptism, brought at once to share in the public worship of the church. " We, after we have thus washed him, who has been convinced and has assented to our teaching, bring him to the place where those who aré called brethren are assembled[1], in order that we may offer hearty prayers in common, both for ourselves and for the baptized person and for all others in every place " (*Apol.* I. 65). Thus at the very beginning of the Christian life, the keynote of church membership is struck by the recognition of its corporate character, as illustrated by public worship. Public worship thenceforward is to be a constant feature in the new life. " On the day called Sunday, all who live in the cities or in the country gather together to one place, and the memoirs of the Apostles or the writings of the prophets are read, as long as time permits " (*Apol.* I. 67). Stress is laid here upon the fact that the whole local church assembles for worship in " one place." The local church is one; it worships as one.

But the question arises how far the local church would be held to extend. Justin speaks, in the words quoted above, of all who live " in the cities or in the country "

---

[1] ἔνθα συνηγμένοι εἰσί. We may note that συνάγειν is twice used in the N. T. of the assembling of the church, on each occasion in reference to the church in Antioch (Acts xi. 26, xiv. 27). Cf. συναγωγή (*Tryph.* 63).

as gathering together "to one place." Does this mean that Christians of town and country all met together and that those living in the villages came into the town for their Sunday worship ? This seems improbable. The meaning probably is that each city and each country district or village had its own church. The arrangement of the country districts would no doubt be determined by the distribution of Christians dispersed through them. But this at least is clear, that in one locality, however its bounds might be determined, there was only one place of meeting for public worship. There was not a plurality of such centres, to which Christians, who lived side by side, might severally go. The local church united for public worship.

But further the character of the worship itself expressed the sense of unity. It was corporate, not individualistic. Its prayers were " common " prayers. " We all rise together (κοινῇ) and pray," says Justin (*Apol.* I. 67). There is unity of action.

And there is a feeling that this unity extends even to those who are absent. The deacons are charged to carry the Eucharist to the absent. So these also are made to feel that their place in the community is recognised. The community is one.

But the idea of unity is not exhausted by the unity of the local church. The whole church universal is one. And this greater bond of union is recognised in the united worship of the local church by the prayers which are offered for all. Prayers are offered not only for the immediate community but also " for all others in every place " (*Apol.* I. 65). A tie binds all together, however far apart they may be.

In direct opposition to this unity of teaching and of

10—2

life is " heresy and schism " (*Tryph.* 35). " Heresy " contradicts the teaching of the church ; " schism " separates from its fellowship. That there would be heresies and schisms was prophesied, says Justin, by Christ Himself (*ibid.*). And this had come about. " For some in one way, others in another, teach to blaspheme the Maker of all things and Christ, who was foretold by Him as coming, and the God of Abraham and of Isaac and of Jacob. But with these men we have nothing in common (οὐδενὶ κοινωνοῦμεν), since we know them to be atheists, impious, unrighteous and sinful, and confessors of Jesus in name only instead of worshippers of Him " (*ibid.*). The men so described are therefore outside the κοινωνία, the common life or fellowship of the church.

It will be noticed, however, that these men are not only heretics but also schismatics. " Some are called Marcians, and some Valentinians, and some Basilidians, and some Saturnilians, and others by other names " (*ibid.*). The men who are thus said to be cut off from the fellowship of the church (ὧν οὐδενὶ κοινωνοῦμεν) are therefore those who have joined some one of the sects and call themselves by its name. To these Justin will not even allow the name of Christian. With the heresy is associated the sect ; and it is the formation of the sect, with its separate worship, that destroys the κοινωνία, which is the bond of church life. The sect therefore is regarded by Justin as outside the church, not as a mutilation of Christianity within the church.

On the other hand, there may be variation of opinion within the church itself. An example of this is Millennarianism. Justin himself holds the millennarian belief but admits that " many, who belong to the pure and pious faith and are true Christians, think otherwise "

(*Tryph.* 80). This is a subject then upon which a man· was at liberty to believe as he chose without injury to his Christianity. There are, however, doctrines which admit of no compromise. Such a doctrine, according to Justin, is belief in the resurrection. Those who deny this doctrine have no title to the name of Christian (*ibid.*).

We may note that Justin would seem to allow the name of Christian to those who denied the doctrine of the Virgin Birth of our Lord. "There are some," he says, " of our race, who confess that He is Christ, while holding that He is man of men ; with whom I do not agree, nor would the majority of those, who hold the same opinions as myself, say so ; since we have been bidden by Christ Himself to put no faith in human doctrines, but in those proclaimed by the blessed prophets and taught by Himself" (*Tryph.* 48). It is to be noted that Justin does not regard the Virgin Birth of our Lord as in any sense an open question. It is a doctrine of revelation, as opposed to the merely human doctrine of the Ebionites. It rests upon the authority of our Lord Himself, and upon the prophetic Scriptures. It was the accepted doctrine, held by the generality of Christians. At the same time those few, who, like the Ebionites, admitted the Messianic authority of Jesus, while denying His miraculous conception, are allowed a place in the Christian family : they are still "of our race." The false teaching is not condoned, but neither, in the opinion of Justin, does it necessitate exclusion from Christian fellowship.

The unity of the church, then, is consistent with a certain variety of opinion. It is not however consistent with the formation of sects, based upon doctrines fundamentally antagonistic to " the pure and pious faith" (*Tryph.* 80). Those who join such sects forfeit the fellowship of the church and have no title to the name of Christian.

In close connection with the thought of the unity of the church is its character as a brotherhood. The church's worship is designed throughout to give expression to this brotherhood. The newly baptized is at once made to feel that he has come among " brethren." Thus the candidate for Baptism must fast; but he is not isolated. The whole church fasts and prays with him (*Apol.* I. 61). The new convert does not go alone to the laver of Baptism. He is led there by another, as illustrating the care of brother for brother. Then by this brother he is baptized in the name of God, the Father and Lord of the universe, " he who leads to the laver the person, that is to be washed, invoking upon him this name alone " (*ibid.*). But this act of admission, though performed by a single person, is really the act of the community, who thus admit the new brother to fellowship with themselves. " We, after we have thus washed him...bring him to the place where those who are called brethren are assembled " (*Apol.* I. 65). The same thought of brotherhood dominates the service ; and consequently a prominent place in it is given to intercessory prayer. Prayer is offered for the present assembly, including him who has been baptized, and " for all others in every place " (*Apol.* I. 65). That these " others " are Christians appears from the further description of them as those who " have learned the truth " (*ibid.*). The brotherhood of the church universal is thus secured by mutual bonds of intercession. Then follows the kiss, also a symbol of brotherhood. " Having ended the prayers, we salute one another with a kiss " (*ibid.*). Then the Eucharist is celebrated. This is emphatically a social sacrament, being the sacred meal

of those who form one family in Christ. The thanksgiving is offered by "the president of the brethren,"
himself a brother. "There is brought to the president
of the brethren bread and a cup of wine mixed with
water; and he, taking them, gives praise and glory to the
Father of the universe, through the name of the Son and
of the Holy Ghost, and offers thanks at considerable length
for our being counted worthy to receive these things at
His hands" (*ibid.*). Though one of the brethren must of
necessity lead the worship, an essential feature in it is
the co-operation of the people. The president acts, not
instead of the people, but as their mouthpiece. This is
shown by the united "Amen," at the end of the prayers
and thanksgivings, by which the people ratify his words.
"When he has concluded the prayers and thanksgivings,
all the people present express their assent by saying
Amen" (*ibid.*). Further, those who are absent are
recognised as belonging to the brotherhood. The sacred
social meal is to be shared by them as well. A portion is
therefore carried to them by the deacons (*ibid.*). This
sacred meal, the Eucharist, is only to be partaken of by
those who have been admitted by regeneration into the
Christian society. "This food is called among us the
Eucharist, of which no one is allowed to partake but the
man who believes that the things which we teach are
true, and who has been washed with the washing that is
for the remission of sins and unto regeneration, and who
is so living as Christ has enjoined" (*Apol.* I. 66). The
Eucharist is therefore the crowning privilege of brotherhood. "For not as common bread and common drink do
we receive these; but in like manner as Jesus Christ our
Saviour, having been made flesh by the word of God, hath
taken both flesh and blood for our salvation, so likewise

have we been taught that the food, which is blessed by the prayer of His word (τοῦ παρ' αὐτοῦ), and from which our blood and flesh by conversion are nourished, is the flesh and blood of that Jesus who was made flesh " (*ibid.*).

The acknowledgment of brotherhood must also issue in almsgiving. And so Justin says, "Those of us who are wealthy help all who are in want, and we always remain together" (*Apol.* I. 67). This almsgiving forms an integral part of the public service. " They who are well-to-do and willing give what each thinks fit; and what is collected is deposited with the president, who succours the orphans and widows and those who are in bonds, and the strangers sojourning among us, and, in a word, takes care of all who are in need " (*ibid.*).

The brotherhood of Christians transcends differences of custom. Thus Trypho instances to Justin the case of those Christians who continue to observe the Jewish law. This, says Justin, ought not in his opinion to be any barrier to the exercise of brotherliness, so long as they do not attempt to compel others to adopt their opinions. "I hold that we ought to join ourselves to such and associate with them in all things as kinsmen and brethren " (*Tryph.* 47).

Although so much stress is laid upon the fact of the Christian brotherhood, it should also be noticed that Justin, at the same time, maintains a brotherhood of mankind. Thus, writing to the people of Rome, he speaks of them as brethren. They are "brethren, even though they know it not" (*Apol.* II. 1). Indeed even those who persecute the Christians are with touching generosity appealed to as "brethren." " You curse in your synagogues all those who are called Christians after Him; and the other nations carry the curse into effect, by

putting to death those who merely confess themselves
to be Christians. But to all these we say, 'You are our
brethren ; recognise rather the truth of God'" (*Tryph.* 96).
Justin therefore confesses a universal brotherhood of all
mankind. But within this, and with deeper meaning, is
the sacred brotherhood of the church, a brotherhood
which colours all the relations which belong to the
Christian life.

The church has a sacrificial character, its central act,
the Eucharist, being of a sacrificial nature. Thus Justin
regards Malachi's prophecy of the "pure offering" as
being fulfilled in the Eucharist. He says that God, in
these words of the prophet, "speaks of those Gentiles,
namely us, who in every place offer sacrifice to Him, that
is the bread of the Eucharist and also the cup of the
Eucharist" (*Tryph.* 41).

Since then the central act of the church has a sacrificial character there must be a power of priesthood in
the church. Justin deduces this from his application of
Malachi's prophecy, "We are the true high-priestly race
of God, even as God Himself bears witness, saying that
in every place among the Gentiles sacrifices are presented
to Him, well-pleasing and pure. Now God receives
sacrifices from no one except through His priests"
(*Tryph.* 116). Christians, as such, possess a power of
priesthood, which they exercise in the Eucharist.

At the same time Justin admits (*Tryph.* 117) that
"prayers and giving of thanks, when offered by worthy
men, are the only perfect and well-pleasing sacrifices to
God." But these, he says, are in fact what Christians offer
in the Eucharistic memorial of the Passion of Christ (*ibid.*).

The same sacrificial view of the Eucharist occurs in the
interpretation of a prophecy of Isaiah (Is. xxxiii. 13—19).

"Now it is evident," says Justin, "that in this prophecy also there is a reference to the bread, which our Christ gave us to offer (ποιεῖν) in remembrance of His being made flesh for the sake of those who believe in Him, for whom also He became subject to suffering; and a reference to the cup, which He gave us to offer (ποιεῖν) in remembrance of His blood, with thanksgiving" (*Tryph.* 70). This passage is interesting in connection with the controversy as to the meaning of τοῦτο ποιεῖτε in 1 Cor. xi. 24 f. [? St Luke xxii. 19]. For, whatever be the meaning of the word in the New Testament account of the institution of the Eucharist, it is clear that in the above passage of Justin it must have the meaning "to offer." To render it "to do" would give no sense.

The Eucharist then, in the view of Justin, is an act of a sacrificial character. In it is offered a sacrifice of prayer and thanksgiving, in connection with the offering of the elements, whereby is made a memorial of the Incarnation and Passion of the Son of God.

It will be noticed that the Eucharist is, with Justin, the central act of the church. Every Sunday, when the church assembles for public worship, it is for the celebration of the Eucharist (*Apol.* I. 67).

We have now to examine the indications which Justin gives of the organisation of the Christian ministry in his time.

He does not speak of πρεσβύτεροι or ἐπίσκοποι, but uses instead the somewhat vague term "the president of the brethren" (ὁ προεστὼς τῶν ἀδελφῶν, *Apol.* I. 65). This is a term describing a function rather than the title of an office.

The vagueness of his description is probably to be accounted for by the fact that he is addressing himself to heathen readers, and would therefore naturally avoid technical terms as far as possible. It was no part of his plan to give a description of the Christian ministry, so that any allusions to it, which are necessitated by the purpose of his writing, will naturally be of as non-technical a character as possible. The term "president" explains itself. But when an allusion to a different function necessitated the mention of an order in the ministry by name, it is accompanied by the explanation "those who by us are called deacons" (*ibid.*).

It is however worth noting that the verb which describes the function of presidency (προΐσταμαι) is, in the New Testament, frequently used in connection with the rulers of the church. Thus "we beseech you, brethren, to know them...that are over you in the Lord (τοὺς προϊσταμένους ὑμῶν) and admonish you" (1 Thess. v. 12). In this passage the function of admonition shows that it is the rulers of the church who are referred to. In 1 Tim. the word is definitely connected with the position of the ἐπίσκοπος. The ἐπίσκοπος must be "one that ruleth well (προϊστάμενος) his own house," for how else "shall he take care of the church of God?" (1 Tim. iii. 4). Also the deacons must be able to rule their children well (καλῶς προϊστάμενοι, 1 Tim. iii. 12). The elders, who deserve honour, are those who have discharged well the office of ruler (οἱ καλῶς προεστῶτες πρεσβύτεροι, 1 Tim. v. 17).

We have already remarked that we are not to regard the scattered allusions in Justin as giving a complete account of the Christian ministry as he understood it. Certainly no negative conclusions can be drawn from his silence upon a subject which had no bearing upon his purpose in addressing a Defence of the Christian Faith to the heathen or in arguing about Christianity with a Jew.

But what can we infer as to the position of the president whom Justin describes ? Was he simply one of the brethren appointed for the occasion ? Or was he a presbyter ? Or a monarchical bishop ? Or did he occupy such a position as that which Clement held at the close of the first century in Rome ?

We may note his duties. He takes the lead in the celebration of the Eucharist. The offerings of bread and wine are brought to him, and he offers a thanksgiving in his own words over the gifts (*Apol.* I. 65). After the reading, which is taken from " the memoirs of the Apostles or the writings of the prophets," he instructs and exhorts the people (*Apol.* I. 67). He has charge of the alms for the sick and poor. Those who are in need are under his care (*ibid.*).

Now the duty, which " the president of the brethren " discharges as almoner, shows at once that it is no mere temporary presidency on the occasion of public worship which is here described. It is a permanent office. The phrase ὁ προεστὼς τῶν ἀδελφῶν does not mean merely " that one of the brethren who was presiding." It means a permanent president. It describes one who held a permanent office. For the duties of almoner, as here shown, imply a continuous work. " They who are well-to-do and willing give what each thinks fit; and what is collected is deposited with the president, who succours the orphans and widows, and those who through sickness or any other cause are in want, and those who are in bonds, and the strangers sojourning among us, and, in a word, takes care of all who are in need " (*ibid.*). Here then is the description of an officer who occupies a unique position in the community. Indeed we seem here to be reading a description of a monarchical bishop. True, the

technical title is not used, for it would convey no meaning
to the heathen, to whom the treatise is addressed. But
instead of the technical title, Justin describes by his
function of presidency one, who, as we see by his duties,
must have been a permanent official and who occupied a
unique position in the community to which he belonged.
He was in fact its bishop.

The only class of Christian ministers, whom Justin
mentions by the title of their office, are the deacons. It
is their duty to assist in the celebration of the Eucharist.
They administer the consecrated food to those who are
present, and, as we have seen, they carry it also to the
absent members of the church. "Those who by us are
called deacons give to each of those present to partake
of the bread and of the wine mixed with water, over which
the thanksgiving was pronounced, and to those who are
absent they carry away a portion" (*Apol.* I. 65; cf. also
Apol. I. 67).

Among the functions of the ministry is that of reading
in public worship. "The reader" (ὁ ἀναγινώσκων) has
his place in the service. It is doubtful, however, whether
we have here merely the description of a function or the
title of an office. We shall find that when in the Canons
of Hippolytus at the close of the century an order of
readers is referred to, the title given is ὁ ἀναγνώστης.
The participial form used by Justin suggests therefore
that "the reader" is simply the minister, upon whom
devolves the duty of reading on any particular occasion.
"The memoirs of the Apostles or the writings of the
prophets are read, as long as time permits; and when
the reader has ceased, the president verbally instructs
and exhorts to the imitation of these good things"
(*Apol.* I. 67).

The people (ὁ λαός) have their distinctive function in
the church. "The president," indeed, is their mouthpiece.
It is necessary that he should offer the thanksgiving. But
on the other hand it is equally necessary that the people
should add their assent to his words. "When he has
concluded the prayers and thanksgivings, all the people
present express their assent by saying Amen " (*Apol.* I. 65).
And again : " We all rise together and pray and, as we
before said, when our prayer is ended, bread and wine and
water are brought and the president in like manner offers
prayers and thanksgivings, according to his ability, and
the people assent, saying Amen " (*Apol.* I. 67).   We have
already seen how Clement (Clem. 41) in the same way
exhorts the people to take their proper part in the service
(ἐν τῷ ἰδίῳ τάγματι).

Justin uses the expression " the people " (ὁ παρὼν λαός,
Apol. I. 65) exactly in the sense of " the laity."   This use
had already occurred in the LXX. in regard to the Jewish
church.   In 1 Esdr. v. 46 (LXX. v. 45) we find ὁ λαός
used of the lay-folk, as distinguished from the rulers or
the priests (οἱ ἱερεῖς καὶ οἱ Λευῖται καὶ οἱ ἐκ τοῦ λαοῦ) [1].
But now we have the same title of privilege, which of old
was claimed by the Jews, transferred to the Christians.
They are " the people."   And, further, in Justin we find
the title used technically to denote those who are not of
the ministry.   The laity stand as distinguished from their
president.

But it should be noticed that there is nothing to
suggest a caste distinction between minister and laity.
The distinguishing phrase " the laity " occurs in the very
connection which unites them with their minister, the
president.   His ministry is not exercised as a thing apart.

---

[1] Cf. Lightfoot, *Christian Ministry* in *Phil.* p. 245.

It is necessary that the laity should co-operate with him, by giving their consent to his thanksgiving, and expressing this consent by their "Amen." The president is the representative or mouthpiece of the lay-folk. He leads their worship.

SECTION V.

THE MARTYRDOM OF POLYCARP.

The local church.—One church in one place.—The universal church.— Holiness of the church.—The teaching of the church.—Episcopacy.

The Asiatic tradition is carried a step further by the letter written from the church in Smyrna, shortly after the martyrdom of Polycarp in A.D. 155 or 156.

We still find the Ignatian description of the local church. "The church of God which sojourneth at Smyrna" writes to "the church of God which sojourneth in Philomelium" (*Mart. Polyc.* inscr.). Still therefore a form of expression is used which implies that there can be only one local church in one place. The local church is still in the position of an alien minority in a great heathen city. It makes as yet no claim of possession. In itself it still preserves its original character. It is a brotherhood. Its members are united in love (*Mart. Polyc.* 1).

Now in this document the epithet καθολικός is three times applied to the church. In what sense is it used? Salutation is sent from the church of God, which sojourneth at Smyrna, "to all the communities of the holy and catholic church (καθολικῆς ἐκκλησίας) sojourning in every place" (*Mart. Polyc.* inscr.). Polycarp's prayer on his way to martyrdom is offered for "all who at any

time had come in his way, small and great, high and low,
and all the catholic church throughout the world " (*Mart.
Polyc.* 8). Jesus Christ is " the Saviour of our souls and
Helmsman of our bodies and Shepherd of the catholic
church throughout the world " (*Mart. Polyc.* 19). Now
the context in each of these cases is fully satisfied by
the simple non-technical use of the word in its common
meaning of " universal." The catholic church (ἡ καθολικὴ
ἐκκλησία) is simply the one universal church, the body
which preserves its organic unity, notwithstanding its
extension throughout the world. Thus the phrase stands
in contradistinction to that which expresses a merely
local church, the Christian community in a particular
place. In this sense the epithet had already occurred in
Ignatius, as an epithet of the church (Smyrn. 8), and it
is perhaps worth noting that it is in a letter from Smyrna
that the same epithet reappears.

In none of the passages above quoted is it necessary
to suppose that the word was intended to convey any
other idea than that which belonged to it in common
speech, the idea, namely, of entirety or totality. In fact
it is not too much to say that in each context the
introduction of the idea contained in the technical sense
of " catholic " would be quite incongruous. The Muratorian Fragment however shows that, at least in Rome,
this new technical sense came shortly afterwards into use,
according to which the " Catholic Church " stands in
contradistinction to heretical sects. In other words, the
term " catholic " came to possess a doctrinal significance,
implying adherence to the entire and unperverted
Christian faith, instead of to such selections from it as
heretical bodies might happen to make, and such
perversions of it as fell short of the apostolic standard.

In this new and technical sense of the word it is possible to speak of the " Catholic Church " in a particular place, where the expression would imply its distinction from heretical or schismatic bodies of Christians in the same place.

Now according to some MS. authorities, this use is found in the Letter of the Smyrnæans. According to one reading, Polycarp is spoken of as " bishop of the Catholic Church which is in Smyrna " (*Mart. Polyc.* 16)[1]. In this case, if the word καθολικῆς is to stand, the local limitation, " in Smyrna," makes it necessary to give the word the technical sense above described. But the reading varies, and there is strong MS. support for ἁγίας in place of καθολικῆς. Now it is much easier to account for the alteration of " holy " into " catholic," when once the latter term had come into common use in its technical sense, than it would be to account for the reverse process. It is best therefore to read here " the holy church in Smyrna."

There is then no clear evidence that the technical meaning of the term καθολική had as yet come into use. It is not till the close of the century that the Muratorian Fragment supplies us with the first clear example of this technical use and shows that by that time the term was current in its technical meaning in Rome.

The epithet " holy " given to the local church, according to the best reading (*Mart. Polyc.* 16), is of interest. We have already found it in Ignatius and in Hermas. In the old Roman Creed it is predicated of the church, where the church universal is meant[2]. The local church is holy, as belonging to God.

---

[1] For the textual authorities see Lightfoot, *ad loc.*, *Apostolic Fathers*, Part II. vol. II. sect. 2, p. 976.

[2] πιστεύω εἰς......ἁγίαν ἐκκλησίαν.   Old Roman Creed.

Polycarp is "an apostolic and prophetic teacher" (*Mart. Polyc.* 16). The two epithets express well the two aspects of the teaching of the church. On the one hand that teaching is "apostolic": it is based on the apostolic tradition, from which it may not depart. On the other hand it is "prophetic": that is, the old teaching is subject to a living interpretation, according to the new needs, which arise with growth. There will, in fact, be a progressive and ever-deepening interpretation of the apostolic message. The church has its "prophets," whose function it is to interpret the message in the light of new conditions.

The Letter of the Smyrnæans corroborates what we have already learnt as to episcopacy in Asia. Polycarp is spoken of by them as "bishop of the holy church which is in Smyrna" (*Mart. Polyc.* 16). So Ignatius had described him. So too he had described himself.

SECTION VI.

THE ANTI-MONTANISTS.

The one universal church : (1) Its importance. (2) Its unity.—The church as implying (1) citizenship; (2) brotherhood.—Continuous life of the church.—Its holiness.—Its spiritual endowments, including prophecy.—Authority of the church : (1) In the exercise of discipline. (2) In teaching.—The local church in Rome.—Usages of the term " the church."—Ministry of the church.—Functions of the bishops.—The presbyterate.

The wild frenzy of Montanism in Phrygia and the neighbouring countries in Asia Minor called out in the second half of the second century a group of writers in defence of traditional Christianity in opposition to Montanist excesses. Among these were Serapion, bishop of

Antioch, Apollonius and an unnamed writer, mentioned by Eusebius in conjunction with Apollinaris of Hierapolis. All these flourished in the last quarter of the second century. To them must now be added Avircius of Hierapolis (not however the well-known city of the Lycus valley), whose inscription dating from the last decade of the second century has been so brilliantly reconstructed by the help of recent archæological research in Asia Minor. It will be convenient to group these writers together for the purposes of our present enquiry.

The Montanist schism naturally brought into prominence the doctrine of the one universal church. The anonymous writer in Eusebius contrasts the teaching of the church with "the recent schismatic heresy" (Euseb. *H. E.* v. 16). Montanus is spoken of, by the same writer, as "prophesying (save the mark!) contrary to the usage of the church, which follows the tradition and the succession from the beginning" (*ibid.*). His followers teach men "to revile the entire universal church under heaven" (*ibid.*). "Those who are called martyrs by the church" are contrasted with those whom the Montanists claim as martyrs (*ibid.*). In each case "the church" is the one universal church, which can admit no rival.

The importance attached to the church in the Christian scheme appears from the fact that blasphemy against "the holy church" is coupled by Apollonius with blasphemy against the Lord and the Apostles. His charge against the Montanists is that "they blaspheme against the Lord and the Apostles and the holy church" (Euseb. *H. E.* v. 18). The meaning seems to be that the false ideas of the Montanists in regard to spiritual manifestation are in conflict with the system of regular organisation, which marks the church. They condemned this organisation as unspiritual. So in making their claim to freedom of prophecy and in their impatience of restraint, they were guilty of impiety towards a system, which was no mere human invention, but a sacred institution, " the holy church."

The church universal is one. It is welded together as a single brotherhood. Nor did this unity exist only in name. It entered very deeply into Christian life. Wherever the Christian went he found himself among friends; he was received as a brother. Everywhere he found the religious practices observed to which he was accustomed at home. Everywhere the same teaching was given, the same spiritual privileges were cherished. The whole of Christendom throbbed with life. And the life was one.

The reality of this unity of life and faith and custom, pervading the entire church, is very vividly illustrated by the epitaph of Avircius[1]. This epitaph is incorporated in an apocryphal life of the saint, but had been thought by scholars to have a ring of genuineness about it. That it is genuine has now been proved by the remarkable discovery in central Phrygia of some fragments of the actual inscription. It was composed by Avircius himself in his seventy-second year. His purpose was that it should be erected in a public place, so that all might read his witness to the faith of the church. The pagan reader indeed would not recognise the character of the inscription, for its language is symbolic. But to the Christian the esoteric meaning would be plain. He would see in it a vindication of the faith and practice of the church, as against the Montanist heresies.

Avircius then, with a view to impressing upon his

[1] See the Frontispiece and Additional Note on pp. 199—201.

readers the unity both in faith and practice of the one
great church, tells us of his pilgrimages from west to
east. In the west he travels as far as Rome; in the
east he crosses the Euphrates. Wherever he goes he
finds fellow-worshippers, whose customs are the same as
his own (l. 11); he receives a welcome in each local
church. Everywhere he takes his part in the church's
spiritual life. No difference of nationality is a barrier to
him. The life of the church is on a higher plane than
national distinctions, and no such distinctions can break
its harmony. The "flocks of sheep on mountains and
plains" are all alike fed by the one "pure Shepherd"
(l. 4). His "great eyes looking on all sides" (l. 5) are
over all alike, and they, who owe one and the same
allegiance, are themselves united as one.

Everywhere too the same faith is held by the church.
"Everywhere," writes Avircius, "faith led the way and
everywhere set before me fish from the fountain, mighty
and stainless, whom a pure virgin grasped" (ll. 12 f.). In
symbolical language the full doctrine of the Incarnation is
here distinctly taught. There is thus shown to be a universal belief throughout the church in "Jesus Christ the
Son of God the Saviour" (ΙΧΘΥΣ), who is born of "a
pure virgin[1]" and who gives Himself to His worshippers
as their spiritual food. Everywhere the Eucharist is
received as the means whereby the Incarnate Life is
bestowed in response to faith. "At all times faith gave
this (i.e. the heavenly $ἰχθύς$) to friends to eat, having
good wine, giving the mixed cup with bread" (ll. 15 f.).
Here then is impressive evidence of the unity of the

---

[1] Lightfoot however suggests that the "pure virgin" may perhaps
symbolise the church. He cites 2 Cor. xi. 2 and Eph. v. 27. *Apostolic
Fathers*, Part ii. vol. i. p. 481.

church and of its teaching at the close of the second century.

This life of the united church is thought of, from one point of view, as a citizenship. Avircius describes himself as "the citizen of a notable city." The figure expresses the corporate character of Christian life[1]. The Christian, as the citizen of a spiritual city, has a duty to his fellow-citizens. The life in the church is not simply individual, but organic.

But, further, the Christian society is a brotherhood. Serapion for instance regards the whole church as a brotherhood. In speaking of the Montanists he says, "The influence of this lying party of a new prophecy, as it is called, is abominated by all the brethren in the world" (Euseb. *H. E.* v. 19). In the church, then, the ties of brotherhood extend through the world.

The church preserves a continuous life. It holds its tradition and succession unbroken from the beginning. The anonymous writer in Eusebius speaks of "the usage of the church, that accords with the tradition and the succession from the beginning" (Euseb. *H. E.* v. 16). There is not necessarily any distinct idea here of episcopal succession. The thought is probably of the successive generations in the church, each of which has handed on to its successor the doctrine and practice which it had itself received. This continuity of existence was a safeguard to the deposit of doctrine in the church.

The church is holy. Apollonius rebukes one of the Montanists for speaking blasphemously "against the Lord and his Apostles and the holy church" (Euseb. *H. E.* v. 18). The church is a sacred institution, not of worldly

---

[1] Cf. *Ep. to Diognetus*, § 5.

origin or of worldly character. In the world it is an alien body. Its true home is elsewhere. So Apollonius describes a local church as a παροικία, a sojourner in a foreign land[1].

In close connection with the holiness of the church is the richness of its spiritual endowment. The veiled language of the epitaph of Avircius clearly indicates this. His words are clothed in metaphor. To the heathen they would be unintelligible ; to the Christian the symbolism would be clear. The church is the source of spiritual sustenance. In it as we have seen " the pure Shepherd " feeds His " flocks of sheep." Everywhere Jesus Christ is present, symbolised by ἰχθύς, the fish. Everywhere is the cleansing " fountain " of Baptism. At all times the heavenly ἰχθύς is received as mystic food, in the bread and wine of the Eucharist. Such are the spiritual gifts enshrined in the church. Christ, everywhere present, is the source of its life.

Among the spiritual endowments of the church is the gift of· prophecy. Some of the characteristic features of the true Christian prophets may be inferred from the grounds upon which Apollonius denounces the Montanists. They made a claim to the possession of prophetical powers, but an examination of their methods and aims proves them to be false prophets. Great stress is laid, as in the *Didaché*, upon the fact that a true prophet does not prophesy for the sake of gain. " Is it not apparent to you that every Scripture forbids a prophet to receive gifts and money ? When therefore I see the prophetess receiving both gold and silver and precious garments, how can I fail to reject her ? " (Euseb. *H. E.* v. 18). This

---

[1] Euseb. *H. E.* v. 18, ἡ ἰδία παροικία αὐτόν, ὅθεν ἦν, οὐκ ἐδέξατο.

has been the general characteristic of the Montanist prophets. For Apollonius goes on to say, " We shall show that those, who among them are called' prophets and martyrs, derive gain not only from the rich but also from the poor and from orphans and widows " (*ibid.*).

Moreover, the life of the prophet must be consistent. " The fruits of a prophet must be examined; for by its fruit the tree is known " (*ibid.*). One whose life is evil cannot be inspired by the Holy Spirit. Tried by this test the Montanist leaders are proved to be no true prophets.

Further, worldly vanities are inconsistent with the life of a true prophet. " It is necessary," Apollonius says again, " that all the fruits of a prophet should be examined. Tell me, does a prophet dye his hair ? Does a prophet paint his eyebrows ? Does a prophet delight in ornament ? Does a prophet play with tablets and dice ? Does a prophet take usury ? " (*ibid.*).

Apollonius, it will be noted, assumes throughout that the characteristics of a true prophet would be well known and unquestioned. From this it would appear that prophecy was still recognised as having its place in the Christian church. No doubt the exercise of the gift had fallen into abeyance, but it can hardly have died out altogether, when Montanus and his followers revived it. The gift was regarded as especially sacred and as one which therefore in a peculiar degree demanded holiness of life from its possessor. There must be no worldly motive in exercising it.

The church exercises a disciplinary authority. Its decisions on matters of doctrine and discipline are arrived at by means of councils, or assemblies of the faithful. Thus local councils of the church were held, in which the doctrines of Montanus were examined and condemned. "The faithful in Asia," says the anonymous writer in Eusebius, "assembled frequently in many places in Asia on this account and examined these novel doctrines and pronounced them vain and rejected the heresy. So these men were expelled from the church and were excluded from the fellowship" (Euseb. *H. E.* v. 16). The deliberative body seems to have been the whole church, the entire company of the faithful, not simply the presbyters and the bishops.

But, on the other hand, the bishops took a leading part in these deliberations, as appears from a letter of Serapion, quoted by Eusebius (Euseb. *H. E.* v. 19). This letter, says Eusebius, contained the signatures of many other bishops in their own hand. It follows from this that many bishops had assembled together to deliberate on the Montanist heresy, to which this letter refers. So then, while the deliberative authority reposes in the whole church, the bishops as leaders take a prominent place in the assembly and give expression to the decision arrived at.

The local church again may exercise its disciplinary authority in the excommunication of unworthy members. Apollonius gives an instance of the exercise of this power in the case of one Alexander, a Montanist. "The church of the place, whence he sprang, would not receive him, because he was a robber" (Euseb. *H. E.* v. 18). Alexander was cut off from church-fellowship, or, in other words, he was excommunicated.

This exclusion from fellowship is conspicuously seen on an occasion of martyrdom. It may happen that Montanists and members of the church are to suffer martyrdom together. But even then those who hold the

true faith may have no communion with those who are
in heresy. " Whenever those of the church, who are
summoned to martyrdom for the faith that is in accord
with truth, meet with any of the so-called martyrs of the
heresy of the Phrygians, they stand apart from them and
suffer death without holding fellowship with them, for
they do not wish to give their assent to the spirit that
speaks through Montanus and the women " (Euseb.
H. E. 16).

The question now arises whether those who were condemned as heretics were regarded as being outside the
church, or as still within the church universal though
excluded from fellowship with the local church. We have
already seen that our anonymous writer states that the
Montanists were expelled from the church. Does this
mean that they were put outside the church universal ?
The words would be satisfied by the interpretation of
ἐκκλησία as meaning here " the local Christian community." It might then be held that all that is meant
is exclusion from the local church ; that being no longer
members of the local church, they were excluded from
the gatherings of that church ; but that they still
remained members of the church universal. But the
words equally bear the meaning that the heretics thus
condemned were regarded as cut off, not only from the
local church, but from the church universal as well.

The view taken by our writer is, however, determined
by another passage. He speaks of Montanism as " the
recent schismatic heresy in reference to the church "
(Euseb. *H. E.* 16, ἡ πρόσφατος τοῦ ἀποσχίσματος αἵρεσις
πρὸς τὴν ἐκκλησίαν). Here there is no ambiguity as to
the meaning of ἐκκλησία. It can only mean the church
universal. The Montanists therefore are regarded as

making a schism from the church. They are outside
the church universal.

The church, again, exercises authority as a teacher.
But its teaching does not permit innovation. It follows
the tradition which has been handed down from the first.
Our anonymous writer condemns the teaching of the
Montanists on the ground that it is contrary to the
ancient faith. It does not accord with " the tradition
and the succession of the church from the beginning "
(Euseb. *H. E.* v. 16). He had himself long been urged,
he says, to write a treatise in refutation of the Montanist
heresy, but had refrained from doing so, not from want
of argument, but for fear of himself unwittingly adding
something to the doctrine of the New Testament. " For
one, who has determined to order his life in accordance
with the Gospel, may," he says, " neither add to nor sub-
tract from this doctrine " (*ibid.*). So then the New
Testament supplies the permanent standard of doctrine.
To this standard the teaching of the church conforms.

From this it follows that the teaching of the church
is everywhere the same. The entire church throughout
the world presents a united front in this matter, as is
illustrated by the unanimity with which the tenets of
Montanus were everywhere condemned. Montanus taught
his followers " to revile the entire universal church under
heaven, because this spirit of pretended prophecy neither
received honour, nor was admitted into it " (Anon. in
Euseb. *H. E.* v. 16). The entire church was agreed.
Its teaching was everywhere the same. Here then we
find the limits of the authority of the church as a
teacher. The church indeed is authorised to teach, but
not to introduce new teaching. The substance of its
teaching must be the New Testament tradition, to which

nothing may be added and from which nothing may be taken away.

The epitaph of Avircius has a bearing upon the question as to what position was assigned to the local church in Rome in the second century. Avircius tells us that he was sent by "the pure Shepherd" to Rome "to behold the king, and to see the golden-robed, golden-slippered queen, and there he saw a people bearing the splendid seal." Now a pagan reader of the inscription would of course understand this as meaning the Emperor, the Empress and the people of Rome. But the question for us is, what meaning the Christian reader was intended to find in the words. Clearly they suggest a spiritual sovereignty, the sovereignty of Jesus Christ. And what place could more vividly suggest the spiritual empire of Christ than the imperial city of Rome? Outwardly the church in Rome had little to suggest thoughts of empire, but the eye of faith would recognise in the devoted company, mostly drawn from the lower orders though they were, a nobler seat of sovereignty than that which so dazzled the outward eye in the rule of the Cæsars. Cæsar held outward sway. The eye of faith could see even in Imperial Rome the truer sovereignty of Christ. "Thine eyes shall see the king in his beauty" (Is. xxxiii. 17). May it not be that the Messianic fulfilment of such prophecies as this was in the mind of Avircius? But if Christ, visible to the eye of faith, is suggested by the king, then the queen, golden-robed, golden-slippered, must be the church, thought of ideally as the bride of Christ. The "people bearing the splendid seal" are those who in Rome have received the seal of Baptism, and who therefore compose the local church. But the question arises, why Avircius should go to Rome in order to see Christ

present in His church. The key to the meaning is
probably to be found in the fact that the idea here dwelt
on is that of sovereignty. Christ is sovereign, His
church is sovereign; and no less sovereign in that very
place, where the only sovereignty seems to be of an utterly
different kind. The true sovereignty in Rome, as the
eye of faith clearly recognises, is that of Christ and the
church.

Clearly a special pre-eminence attaches to the local
church in Rome. Its seat is the imperial city. It shares
the imperial city's prestige. "The splendid seal" may
well include an allusion to the seal of martyrdom. And
the church in Rome was rich in its company of martyrs.
It held a glorious record. What wonder that the prestige
of its imperial situation and its own honourable record
should have given to this local church a unique place in
Christendom. In Rome under the very shadow of the
palaces of the Cæsars, the true and abiding sovereignty
found local representation in an obscure company of
persecuted slaves. The sovereignty is that of Christ.
The special honour of the local church in Rome was that
its position and its circumstances enabled it to exhibit
Christ's sovereignty more conspicuously than it could
be seen elsewhere.

We may note that the anonymous writer in Eusebius
employs the term ἐκκλησία in a sense which is not found
in the New Testament. The New Testament does not
speak of the church in a district or country. We read
here, however, of "the church in Pontus" (Euseb.
H. E. v. 16)[1]. We have already noted a similar use in
Ignatius (Rom. ix., "the church in Syria"). Now
it is possible that the phrase means no more than "the

---

[1] There is however a various reading τὴν κατὰ τόπον ἐκκλησίαν.

universal church, as represented in the country of Pontus by the sum of the local churches there." But the context seems to suggest that it does in fact mean more than this, and that it implies the union of the local churches within the country of Pontus in an organic relationship. We need not suppose that this relationship was very clearly or precisely defined, but we seem to see here in an incipient form the shaping of the idea of a national church, an organic unity rather than a federation of independent units.

We gather little from the Anti-Montanists as to the ministry of the church. A function of the bishop, which not unnaturally is prominent in their writings, is that of teaching. Bishops are regarded as the natural guardians of the faith. So our anonymous writer relates how two bishops, Zoticus of Comana and Julian of Apamea, attempted to refute the teaching of the Montanist prophetess, Maximilla (Euseb. *H. E.* v. 16). The case of Serapion, bishop of Antioch, also illustrates the fact that to the bishops pre-eminently belonged the responsibility of teaching. It was their duty to guard the church against heresy. We hear of them writing admonitory letters. Eusebius says of Serapion: " In a private letter which he wrote to Caricus and Ponticus, he mentions [Montanus] and also refutes his heresy " (Euseb. *H. E.* v. 19). In this letter Serapion enclosed a letter of Claudius Apollinaris, bishop of Hierapolis, on the subject of the Montanist heresy. Eusebius further states that the signatures of many other bishops were appended to Serapion's letter, among them that of Ælius Publius Julius, bishop of Debeltum. The bishops therefore took the lead in the campaign against Montanism. That they were accustomed to meet together for counsel is shown by the fact of many bishops' signatures being appended to Serapion's letter " in their own hand " (*ibid.*).

To this pre-eminence of the bishops the city of Ancyra seems to have been an exception. We may quote our anonymous writer's account of his visit to the church there. " Having lately been at Ancyra, a city of Galatia, and having understood that the church in Pontus was very much agitated by this new prophecy, as they call it, but which, as shall be shown, with divine assistance, deserves rather the name of false prophecy, I discoursed many days in the church, both respecting these matters and others that were proposed ; so that the church indeed rejoiced and was strengthened in the truth ; but the adversaries were put to flight and the opponents were cast down. But as the presbyters of the place requested that we should leave some account of those things that we said, in opposition to the enemies of the truth, Zoticus Otrenus also being present, who was our fellow-presbyter ; this, indeed, I did not perform, but I promised to write thither if the Lord permitted, and to send the letter to them as soon as possible " (Euseb. *H. E.* v. 16). Here then we seem to find the presbyters taking the lead in the church of Ancyra. There is no mention of a bishop. It would of course be highly precarious to assume that the church was without a bishop. The argument from silence is almost worthless. Was our writer himself a bishop or simply a presbyter ? The fact that he calls Zoticus his " fellow-presbyter " is not conclusive. He was certainly a presbyter. But the greater includes the less. Was he also a bishop ? The authoritative way in which he teaches and the respect which he inspired among the presbyters of Ancyra, who asked him for a written summary of teaching, prove him to have been at all events a man of weight. More than this we cannot say.

SECTION VII.

DIONYSIUS OF CORINTH.

Relations between the local churches.—Unity in the local church.—The
bishop as representing the local church.—Disciplinary authority
(1) of the bishop, (2) of the church.—Public worship in the church.

Dionysius, bishop of Corinth in the third quarter of
the second century, vividly illustrates the spirit of unity
and brotherhood as essentially characteristic of the church
(Euseb. *H. E.* iv. 23).

It is felt that strong ties bind together the various
local churches. Dionysius is in the constant habit of
writing, from his church in Corinth, letters to other local
churches. Eusebius gives a long list of such letters. There
is one to the Lacedæmonians, one to the Athenians, one
to the Nicomedians, one to the church in Gortyna, one to
the church in Amastris, one to the Gnossians, one to the
Romans. These letters show a wide range of interest on
the part of Dionysius. Each one indicates his recognition
of the tie binding local churches together, a tie which
made the welfare of each the concern of all.

This intimate relationship between the local churches
is illustrated further by the hospitality shown by one
church to another. This had been from the beginning a
noble characteristic of the church in Rome. So Dionysius
writes to Soter : " This practice has prevailed with you
from the beginning, to do good to all the brethren in
every way, and to send contributions to many churches in
every city, thus refreshing the needy in their want and
succouring the brethren condemned to the mines. So
by these contributions, which you have been accustomed

to send from the beginning, you preserve, as Romans, the practice of your ancestors. And this practice your good bishop Soter has not only observed, but has also added to, in that he furnished plentiful supplies to the saints, and also encouraged the brethren that came from abroad, as a loving father his children, with consolatory words " (*ibid.*). Here we have a fine example of the spirit of love and brotherhood that animated the church, and made the welfare of the brethren an object of solicitude to all.

Further, in each local church the spirit of unity must prevail. Clement of Rome in his letter to Corinth, which, as Dionysius shows, was still read and cherished there, had conspicuously taught this. Dionysius in writing to the Lacedæmonians hands on to them from Corinth the same exhortation. His letter " inculcates peace and unity " (*ibid.*).

We may gather from Dionysius the position occupied by the bishop in the local church. He is thought of as gathering up in himself the life of the church, and so he becomes the representative, the *persona* of the church. The correspondence between Soter, bishop of Rome, and Dionysius, bishop of Corinth, is really a message from one church to another. The church speaks through its bishop, who gives it articulate voice. The letter of Dionysius is, indeed, according to Eusebius, addressed to Soter, bishop of Rome. But the letter itself, so far as it is preserved, shows quite clearly that it is written to the church. The church is addressed in the person of the bishop. Dionysius mentions in the same way the letter which he has received from Soter. He speaks of it not as Soter's letter but as " your letter." It is the letter of the church in Rome. The bishop in each case is the mouthpiece of the collective voice of the local church.

A disciplinary authority resides in the bishop. He has, for instance, power to lay down regulations in regard to marriage. Thus the bishop of the church of the Gnossians is admonished by Dionysius to be careful in the exercise of this power. "He admonishes Pinytus, the bishop of the church, not to impose upon the brethren without necessity a burden in regard to purity too great to be borne, but to pay regard to the infirmity of the many" (*ibid.*).

But a disciplinary authority is also represented as residing in the church. The local church has a power of excommunication from its society and a power to grant readmission. This is illustrated by a letter of Dionysius to the church at Amastris. In this letter, according to Eusebius, "he enjoins upon the church to receive kindly all that return again from their backslidings, whether of delinquency or of heresy" (*ibid.*).

Public worship is the necessary expression of the life of the local church on the Lord's day. Dionysius gives some indication as to its character. It was the custom to read certain edifying writings. Thus at Corinth the letter of Clement was still read in the time of Dionysius. He tells Soter that his letter will take its place by the side of Clement's, to be used in the same way. "To-day," he writes, "we have passed the Lord's holy-day, in which we have read your letter; in reading which we shall always have our minds stored with admonition, as we shall also from that written to us before by Clement" (*ibid.*).

SECTION VIII.

MELITO.

Witness to the church.

Melito, bishop of Sardis (circ. 160—180), wrote an essay " On the Church " and another " On the Lord's Day." Neither of these has come down to us, but it is perhaps fair to infer from the fact of his writing them that he had a high sense of the place of the church in the scheme of salvation and of the church's disciplinary authority.

SECTION IX.

THE LETTER FROM LYONS AND VIENNE.

Unity of the churches.—Brotherhood in the church.—The church as mother.—Living membership in the church.—The Christian ministry : (1) The episcopate. (2) The presbyterate.

The seventeenth year of the Emperor Marcus Aurelius, A.D. 177, was signalised by terrible persecutions. These fell with special violence upon the churches of southern Gaul, of which those in Lyons and Vienne were conspicuous. After the persecution, the brethren of these two churches wrote a letter telling of the tortures which had been heroically endured. Of this letter a large portion is preserved by Eusebius.

The bond of a common faith and hope binds together into one the various local churches. The practice of writing letters from one church to another is an outcome of a sense of this bond of union. The fortunes of each local church are of deep interest to all. The churches of Gaul show a recognition of this by their letter to the churches of Asia. Note the salutation with which their letter opens. " The servants of Christ, dwelling at Lyons and Vienne in Gaul, to the brethren in Asia and Phrygia, who have the same faith and hope of redemption with us; peace and grace and glory from God the Father and Christ Jesus our Lord " (Euseb. *H. E.* v. 1).

These distant Christians then are addressed as brethren. The whole universal church is thought of as a vast brotherhood.

A victim of the persecution, Vettius Epagathus, is described as " one of the brethren " (*ibid.*). When the persecution began, he "asked to be permitted to testify in behalf of his brethren, that there is among us nothing ungodly or impious " (*ibid.*). And, finally, he rejoiced " to lay down his life in defence of the brethren " (*ibid.*). This repeated reference to brotherhood shows the close tie which was recognised as existing in the church. Irenæus again, to whom the bearing of the letter was entrusted, is spoken of by the writers as " our brother " (Euseb. *H. E.* v. 4).

But as the members of the church are brethren, so the church itself is described as " mother." " The virgin mother had much joy in receiving alive those whom she had brought forth as dead. For through their influence (*i.e.* the influence of the steadfast witnesses) many, who had denied, were restored and re-begotten and rekindled with life and learnt to confess " (*ibid.*). The phrase, " the virgin mother," is a striking one. We may compare the words of Hegesippus, " They called the church as yet a virgin, for it was not yet corrupted by vain cries " (Euseb. *H. E.* iv. 22). The virginity of the church then expresses the purity of its doctrine. Its motherhood expresses the fact that the new birth is given through the church and that so through the church comes the gift of spiritual life.

The gift of spiritual life is bound up with the church. But there may be a church membership which is spiritually dead. Thus the Christians who failed under trial are children of the church, but were still-born. The church "brought them forth as dead." They have had no spiritual life; or their spiritual life, if they once possessed it, has been destroyed. But if they return to steadfastness, their spiritual life revives. They are "re-begotten." This corresponds with the teaching which is given, for instance, by Hermas, in whose visions the tower represents, not the institutional church, but the spiritual nucleus of the church; it is the company of those who possess, not merely a formal external membership, but true spiritual life.

That the church in Gaul possessed the threefold ministry is shown by this letter. The episcopate is represented by "the blessed Pothinus, who had been entrusted with the bishopric of Lyons" (Euseb. *H. E.* v. 1). The presbyterate is represented by Irenæus, who is described as holding the office (τόπος) of church presbyter (πρεσβύτερος ἐκκλησίας, Euseb. *H. E.* v. 4). The diaconate finds a representative in Sanctus "the deacon from Vienne" (Euseb. *H. E.* v. 4).

The high esteem in which the bishop's office was held is illustrated by the terms in which Pothinus is referred to. His office is a trust. It is, indeed, a service (διακονία). But it is a service of authority, an office of oversight. Eleutherus, bishop of Rome, is in the same way addressed in terms of honour and respect by the writers of the letter. He is given the title of "father." "We pray, that thou mayest rejoice in God in all things and always, father Eleutherus" (Euseb. *H. E.* v. 4).

Pothinus is an important link with an earlier genera-

tion. He was at the time of his martyrdom "more than
ninety years of age."   His birth must therefore have been
previous to A.D. 87.   A later tradition states that he came
from Asia Minor, so that he would bring with him the
Johannine traditions and the ideas of church government,
which the Ignatian letters show to have prevailed in Asia
when he was a young man.

We have seen that Irenæus is described as a "church
presbyter." This implies that he bore office in a particular
local church, that namely in Lyons. But does the expression imply that a presbyter was not a presbyter everywhere and indelibly, but that he was only such in virtue
of holding office in a particular local church? According to
this view, a man might give up his office in a particular
church and would then cease to be a presbyter.   He
might be reappointed there or elsewhere, and would then
again become a presbyter in virtue of holding office.

The form of expression seems however to point more
reasonably to an opposite conclusion. The fact that the
title $\pi\rho\epsilon\sigma\beta\acute{\upsilon}\tau\epsilon\rho\sigma\varsigma$ requires further definition as $\pi\rho\epsilon\sigma\beta\acute{\upsilon}$-
$\tau\epsilon\rho\sigma\varsigma$ $\dot{\epsilon}\kappa\kappa\lambda\eta\sigma\acute{\iota}\alpha\varsigma$, when the bearing of office in a local
church is referred to, implies that a presbyter did not
necessarily bear such office. It is implied that his position
as presbyter was independent of his appointment to office
in a local church.   There is, therefore, in this expression
nothing inconsistent with the belief that the presbyterate
was an order indelibly conferred and that it was not
merely held temporarily during the occupancy of a local
office.   We shall find that the view which regards the
presbyterate as indelible is upheld by the Canons of
Hippolytus.

SECTION X.

THE PASCHAL CONTROVERSY.

Deliberative councils of the church: the exercise of authority.—Sacred character of the church.—Unity of the church.—Apostolic tradition.—Monarchical episcopacy.—Sacerdotal character of the church.

In the last quarter of the second century the Paschal controversy reached an acute form. This controversy had reference to the proper time for the observance of Easter. The Asiatic tradition fixed the 14th day of the lunar month as the date for commemorating the Resurrection. In the west it was held that the festival of Easter should always be observed on a Sunday. This controversy became the occasion of the calling together of councils, composed of bishops, to deliberate on the points at issue. "Synods and convocations of bishops were held upon this question," says Eusebius (Euseb. *H. E.* v. 23). Here then we have the record of an important feature in the life of the church. In order to ascertain the mind of the church, synods or councils are summoned, and these synods are composed of bishops. Each bishop would doubtless sit as the delegate or representative of his own local church.

The question then arises as to the precise authority of these councils. The councils or synods of bishops, which were held in order to deliberate on the Paschal controversy, gave their decision, according to Eusebius, in an "ecclesiastical decree (ἐκκλησιαστικὸν δόγμα)" (*ibid.*). We cannot indeed be sure whether this description is due merely to Eusebius or whether it preserves the original description of the resolutions passed. Dr Hort has shown that the word δόγμα expresses varying degrees

of imperativeness, according to the circumstances of
each particular case[1]. The context suggests that in this
case, as in that of the Jerusalem decrees, the word that
best expresses its meaning is "resolution." For it will
be noted that there is no word expressive of necessity
or obligation (such as δεῖ or χρή) but rather a tone of
persuasive recommendation. It is "a resolution......that
the mystery of the Lord's Resurrection from the dead
be celebrated (ὡς ἂν......ἐπιτελοῖτο) on no other than
the Lord's day." The resolution of the synod would no
doubt be treated with great respect, but its function would
seem to be to recommend rather than to command.

We gather the same impression from a further account
of a synod or conference of bishops summoned by Polycrates.   Polycrates was bishop of the church in Ephesus
at the close of the second century. Eusebius has preserved
a fragment of his letter to Victor of Rome on the subject
of the Paschal controversy.

In accordance with Victor's request, he invited the
bishops of Asia to meet him in conference to consider the
question under dispute. As the outcome of the conference
he wrote his letter. "I could mention," he says, "the
bishops who were present, whom you requested that I
should summon, and whom I summoned. Their names,
if I were to write them, would be many in number. And
they, though seeing the insignificance of my person, con-
sented to the letter, since they knew that I did not bear
my grey hairs for naught, but that I have at all times
ruled my life in the Lord Jesus" (Euseb. *H. E.* v. 24).
Here then is a further example of a provincial council or
synod, consisting of bishops, called to deliberate upon the
Paschal question. The letter embodying the decision

[1] Hort, *Christian Ecclesia*, pp. 81—83.

arrived at was drafted by Polycrates, but it derived its
authority from the fact that the bishops assembled gave
their consent to it. The effect of the decision was that
the churches represented committed themselves to a continuance of the practice approved by the council. This
is shown by the fact that Victor, in reply, " attempted
to cut off the churches of all Asia, together with the
neighbouring churches, from the common unity " (*ibid.*).
The decision of the council was therefore regarded as
having great weight in the local churches concerned.

The character of each local church as an alien community in the world receives early expression in the
association with ἐκκλησία of the ideas of παροικία, παροι-
κεῖν. Thus Clement of Rome has spoken of ἡ ἐκκλησία
τοῦ Θεοῦ ἡ παροικοῦσα ῾Ρώμην (Clem. inscr.). The
Letter of the Smyrnæans on the Martyrdom of Polycarp
speaks of αἱ κατὰ πάντα τόπον τῆς ἁγίας καὶ καθολικῆς
ἐκκλησίας παροικίαι. But in the joint letter of the
eastern bishops, written as the outcome of their council,
the word παροικία is used absolutely as meaning " the
local church." " Endeavour," they say, " to send copies of
the letter to every church" (κατὰ πᾶσαν παροικίαν, Euseb.
H. E. v. 25). The same absolute use of παροικία, as
meaning a local church, is found also in the letter of
Irenæus to Victor on the subject of this same controversy
(Euseb. *H. E.* v. 24)[1]. The usage vividly illustrates the
fact that the church was thought of as being a sacred
institution. It is in the world, but not of it. It is
necessarily an alien community.

The Paschal controversy raises the important question
as to what the unity of the church involves. Does it
involve uniformity of custom, or are differences of local

[1] See also Apollonius in Euseb. *H. E.* v. 18.

practice consistent with fundamental unity ?   Consider
first the view taken in the east. The Palestinian bishops,
who met in council to deliberate upon the observance of
Easter, commend their decision upon the ground that
their custom is that which is uniformly adopted within
the range of their experience. " Endeavour," they say,
" to send copies of the letter to every church, so that we
may not be held accountable to those whose minds are
easily led astray.   But we inform you that at Alexandria
also they observe the same day as we ourselves do.   For
letters are carried from us to them and from them to us,
so that we celebrate the holy season with one mind and
at one time " (Euseb. *H. E.* v. 25). The aim of the eastern
bishops is to secure a clear realisation of the bond of
union between the local churches under their care.   It
would be too much to say that uniformity of practice is
insisted on, but at least a high value is attached to it.
Uniformity of custom makes easier the unity of spirit, which
is a fundamental necessity of the church.   There is, however, no indication of a desire to interfere with the churches
of the west, where a different custom had prevailed.
The bishops state their own practice, uniformly pursued
among themselves : they give reasons why they themselves
adhere to it : they state its value as promoting harmony,
in that they all celebrate Easter " with one mind and at
one time ": but they utter no word respecting other
churches, in which a different custom may have prevailed.

We come next to the position taken up by Victor.
He will allow no departure at all from strict uniformity of
practice.   As soon as he received the letter of Polycrates,
" he forthwith endeavoured," says Eusebius, " to cut off
the churches of all Asia, together with the neighbouring
churches, as heterodox, from the common unity ; and he

published abroad'by letters and proclaimed that all the
brethren there were wholly excommunicated " (Euseb.
H. E. v. 24). Here then the view is clearly expressed
that no divergence of custom could be permitted : that
the unity of the church requires uniformity of practice.

But we do not find that Victor obtained any great
support for his view that those churches, which refused to
fall in with western practice, should be regarded as heterodox and ought therefore to be excommunicated. " This,"
adds Eusebius, "was not pleasing to the bishops as a whole.
In fact they exhorted him on the contrary to be disposed
towards a course favouring peace and unity and love one
towards another " (*ibid.*). This opinion of the western
bishops, who were led, as subsequently appears, by Irenæus,
is based upon the fundamental truth of the unity of the
church. It is just because they hold the doctrine of unity
so strongly that they give the advice they do. Victor had
held that unity required uniformity ; and he was in fact
prepared to embark on a course which would destroy
unity in a vain attempt to secure uniformity. Irenæus
and those who followed his lead take the truer line
that the unity of the church is a bond of love, and
that the course adopted should be one dictated by love.
Individuals or churches might indeed forfeit their fellowship for grave cause, but the gravity of excommunication
was strongly felt. Hence the vigorous remonstrance
addressed to Victor for attempting a course so contrary to
the spirit of the church. There must indeed be a true
inward unity, a real sense of inter-communion, but this
might perfectly well subsist together with variety of local
use. There is no hint that such variety is a good thing in
itself ; only that the differences arising from it are a far
less evil than would have been the breach of unity, which
would have resulted from the high-handed attempt of

Victor to secure uniformity, if that attempt had been allowed to take effect.

Polycrates expresses his own sense of the unity of the church by his thoughts of brotherhood. He addresses the Christians at Rome as " brethren." His own long life has brought him into contact with " the brethren throughout the world " (*ibid.*). So the whole church universal is united in a brotherhood.

The church, both in deciding its practice and in formulating its teaching, has respect to tradition. So Polycrates gives as his reason for maintaining the Quartodeciman method of determining Easter the ancient tradition of Asia, handed down, as he implies, from the Apostles through St John. Thus, after quoting the great names in the spiritual ancestry of the churches of Asia, including John and Philip among Apostles, and Polycarp, Thraseas, Sagaris and his own relatives among bishops, he says, " These all observed the fourteenth day of the Passover, according to the Gospel, deviating in no respect, but following the rule of faith " (*ibid.*). Here then is the appeal to apostolic tradition. It is the same appeal as that which was made in the west (Euseb. *H.E.* v. 23). So then, although Polycrates and the churches of the east differed from the west in their custom, all were agreed upon the principle upon which their practice should be based. The appeal to apostolic tradition was universal.

Polycrates, himself bishop in Ephesus in the last decade of the second century, is a witness to the long establishment of monarchical episcopacy. " Polycarp too, who was a bishop and martyr, [fell asleep] in Smyrna ; and there is Thraseas, bishop and martyr from Eumenia, who fell asleep in Smyrna. Why should I mention Sagaris, bishop and martyr, who fell asleep at Laodicea ?...

And I also, Polycrates, the least of you all, act according to the tradition of my relatives, some of whom I have closely followed. For seven of my relatives were bishops, and I am the eighth" (Euseb. *H. E.* v. 24). Now Polycrates, at the time of writing, in the last decade of the second century, was,.as he tells us himself, " sixty-five years in the Lord." He had already been preceded by seven relatives, who had been bishops. Now on any reasonable calculation, these must be supposed to extend back at least two generations, to the generation namely of the grand-parents of Polycrates. So having regard to the age of Polycrates, the episcopal tradition in his family must be carried back well towards the early part of the second century. Polycrates therefore supplies an important corroboration of the evidence of Ignatius as to the early establishment of episcopacy in Asia.

Further, the Quartodeciman controversy illustrates the important position occupied by bishops in the government of the church at large. In addition to the rule of the bishop over his own local church, we find councils of bishops assembled to deliberate on questions affecting the church in general, with a view to determining upon a common course of action.

Polycrates uses sacerdotal language in connection with St John. " He became a priest ($\iota\epsilon\rho\epsilon\upsilon\varsigma$), wearing the sacerdotal plate ($\tau\dot{o}\ \pi\acute{e}\tau\alpha\lambda o\nu$) " (Euseb. *H. E.* v. 24). The sentence would seem to imply that, in the view of Polycrates, the $\pi\acute{e}\tau\alpha\lambda o\nu$ was the Christian counterpart of the breastplate worn by the Jewish high-priest, as his distinguishing badge of office, the token of his intercessory function. St John then was thought of as having duties of priesthood, closely connected with the work of intercession. He was invested with a sacerdotal character.

SECTION XI.

THEOPHILUS OF ANTIOCH.

Sacred character of the local churches.—Their continuity.—The church
as the means of salvation.—And as the depository of the truth.

Theophilus, bishop of Antioch, flourished during the
third quarter of the second century and somewhat later.
His Apology, addressed to one Autolycus, may perhaps be
dated about the year A.D. 180. His only evidence bearing
upon our present subject is contained in a single passage.

" As in the sea there are islands, some of them
habitable and well-watered and fruitful, with havens and
harbours, in which the storm-tossed may find refuge, so
God has given to the world, which is driven and tempest-
tossed by sins, assemblies, that is holy churches, in which
survive the doctrines of the truth, as in the island-harbours
of good anchorage; and into these run those who desire to
be saved, being lovers of the truth and wishing to escape
the wrath and judgment of God. And as, again, there are
other islands, rocky and without water, and barren, and
infested by wild beasts, and uninhabitable and serving
only to injure navigators and the storm-tossed, on which
ships are wrecked and those driven among them perish,
so there are doctrines of error, that is heresies, which
destroy those who approach them. For they are not
guided by the word of truth; but as pirates, when they
have filled their vessels, drive them on the afore-mentioned
places, so that they may spoil them, so also it happens in
the case of those who err from the truth, that they are all
totally ruined by their error" (Theoph. *ad Autol.* ii. 14).

Here then we have a clear view of the position and
function of the local churches. They are described as

" holy," for they derive their being from God.   It is God who has given them to the world.

The local churches are regarded as possessing a continuity of life. This is implied by the fact that in them the doctrines of the truth are said to " survive."   The church, originally the depository of the truth, has retained the truth committed to it.

We may note that Theophilus applies the term συναγωγαί to the local churches.   " God has given to the world assemblies (συναγωγάς), that is holy churches." There is doubtless a thought here of the Jewish ecclesiastical use of the word.   But if there is an idea of comparison, there is also, and more prominently, an expression of contrast.   The " holy churches " of Christianity are something essentially different from the συναγωγαί of the Jews.

The local churches are havens of safety in the storm-tossed world.   It is their possession of the truth which gives them the saving power which they possess.   In the church, then, is the way of salvation, divinely appointed. Theophilus illustrates his contention by comparison with the fruitful islands, in whose harbours the mariner may find refuge.   But safety is only for those " who desire to be saved."   The sailor must use his own exertions : he must run his ship into the haven.   The blessings of the church must, in the same way, be actively sought.   There must be moral co-operation with the purpose of God.

The church is the depository of sacred truth.   In contradistinction to the truth, which rests in the church, there are the destructive errors of heresy.   Like dangerous rocky islands, upon which ships are wrecked, are these " doctrines of error," whereas in the " holy churches " there survive " the doctrines of the truth."

SECTION XII.

HEGESIPPUS.

Little is known of the life of Hegesippus. Fragments
of his writings are preserved for us by Eusebius. He was
a considerable traveller, being of Jewish origin and visiting
Corinth and Rome. He wrote during the episcopate of
Eleutherus at Rome, and his work may therefore be dated
about A.D. 180.

Hegesippus has a clear conception of the unity of the
universal church. His complaint against the heretics is that
by their varying doctrines they have destroyed this unity.
He enumerates various sects, of which he says, " They
each introduced their own opinions, peculiar to themselves
and differing from one another. From these sprung the
false Christs and false prophets and false apostles, who
divided the unity of the church by the introduction of
corrupt doctrines against God and against His Christ "
(Euseb. *H. E.* iv. 22).

In contrast to this varied teaching of the heretical
sects, the teaching of the church is everywhere the same.
In all parts of the church the same doctrine is found.
Everywhere there is unanimity. Hegesippus, like Avircius,
was able to test this unanimity by his travels. " He
states," says Eusebius of him, " that he conversed with
most of the bishops, when he travelled to Rome, and that
he received the same doctrine from all " (*ibid.*). This is

impressively illustrated by the words of Hegesippus himself. "The church of the Corinthians continued in the true faith, until Primus was bishop there ; with whom I had familiar conversation, as I stayed many days with the Corinthians when on my voyage to Rome, during which we were mutually refreshed with the true doctrine. And when I was in Rome, I made a stay with Anicetus, whose deacon was Eleutherus. And after Anicetus, Soter succeeded, and after him Eleutherus. But in every succession and in every city the prevailing conditions are such as are preached by the law and the prophets and the Lord " (*ibid.*). Everywhere Hegesippus finds " the true doctrine " and " the true faith."

And this doctrine, which he describes as " the true faith," and which he finds everywhere current, is the same that has been handed down in the church from the beginning. It is the doctrine of the Scriptures, the Old Testament and the New, " the law and the prophets and the Lord." Hegesippus is therefore able to say that the church in his time was still uncorrupt, in that it had kept its teaching pure. " For this reason they called the church a virgin, for it was not yet corrupted by vain cries " (*ibid.*). Its teaching was still that of the original tradition. But even then corruption was beginning. The heretical sects were starting their new teaching, the effect of which was to divide the unity of the church " by the introduction of corrupt doctrines against God and against His Christ " (*ibid.*). But in the universal church there is one standard of doctrine, that of the Scriptures.

What position are the heretics thought of as occupying in respect to the church ? It would appear that Hegesippus does not regard them as cut off from the church. Rather they are regarded as being within the

D. 13

church and as exercising there a corrupting influence.
For, after stating that the church had till then preserved
its virgin purity, Hegesippus adds : " Thebuthis is making
a beginning to corrupt it (ὑποφθείρειν), because he was
not made a bishop" (*ibid.*). Now the word used describes a
gradual process of corruption and implies that Thebuthis
was in a position to exercise an insidious influence, such
as he could hardly have exerted if he had been definitely
excluded from the church. The word describes a process
of corruption from within rather than an attack from
without. And yet Thebuthis is described as belonging to
one of the seven Jewish sects (αἱρέσεις). We should gather
then that though the false teaching of Thebuthis draws
down upon him the condemnation of Hegesippus, it had
not resulted in his exclusion from the church.

Moreover the same conclusion is suggested by the
result, which is said to follow from the teaching of the
Valentinians and others. "They divided the unity of the
church " (*ibid.*). This could hardly be said if by their
action they were thought of as having cut themselves off
from the church. For in that case the unity of the
church would still be preserved, they themselves being
outside it. It would seem then that the heretical sects
are thought of by Hegesippus as being still within the
church, whose harmonious unity of life and doctrine they
have, by their teaching and action, impaired.

Hegesippus throws a curious light upon the custom
of the early Palestinian church in regard to the ministry.
Eusebius, on the authority of Hegesippus, whose name he
mentions in the context, describes the appointment of the
successor of St James at Jerusalem. " After the martyrdom of James and the capture of Jerusalem, which
immediately followed, it is reported that those of the

Apostles and disciples of the Lord, that were yet surviving, came together from all parts, with those that were related to the Lord according to the flesh. For the greater part of them were yet living. These consulted together, to determine whom it was proper to pronounce worthy of being the successor of James. They all unanimously declared Simeon, the son of Cleophas, of whom mention is made in the sacred volume, as worthy of the position to rule there " (Euseb. *H. E.* iii. 11). Thus Simeon was appointed to the headship of the church at Jerusalem by the surviving Apostles, disciples and relatives of the Lord. Such a method of appointment must indeed be regarded as unique. Appointments by representatives of the first generation of Christians could, of course, only take place in the first age. And moreover the circumstances of the church in Jerusalem were peculiar, and this no doubt must be held to account for the appointment there not being made by the local church itself.

In this connection, however, it is necessary to refer to another passage. Eusebius recurs to the subject of the appointment of Simeon, quoting words from Hegesippus, which, had they stood by themselves, might have been held to imply that the appointment was made by the whole local church instead of by the earthly associates and kinsmen of the Lord. " After James the Just had suffered martyrdom, as our Lord had for the same reason, Simeon, the son of Cleophas, the Lord's uncle, was appointed bishop. For all proposed him as the second [bishop] as being the Lord's kinsman " (Euseb. *H. E.* iv. 22). But a reference to the earlier passage in Eusebius (*H. E.* iii. 11) shows that he is there referring to the same passage in Hegesippus of which he here quotes a part. Hence we must understand that those

13—2

who unanimously appointed Simeon as the second bishop were not " all " the church at Jerusalem, but " all " the surviving Apostles and kinsmen of the Lord. This narrative is of great interest, but has no bearing on the general question of appointment of bishops, since the circumstances of the local church in Jerusalem, especially in the first age, were unique.

Another narrative illustrates the position of the Lord's kinsmen in the Palestinian church. After their dismissal by Domitian, the grandsons of Jude, says Hegesippus, " ruled the churches, both as witnesses and relatives of the Lord " (Euseb. *H. E.* iii. 20). Both from this passage and from those relating to the appointment of Simeon, it appears that the Lord's kin occupied a special position in the churches of Palestine. Evidently a high degree of authority was conceded to them. Their presence introduced a unique local factor into the conception of church order in Palestine. The language used of them would seem to imply that in the churches of Palestine they were recognised as possessing an authority not different from that which in the earlier generation had belonged to the Apostles. Doubtless their influence would be confined to Palestine. The description of the work of Jude's grandsons, as tillers of the soil, shows that in point of fact they cannot have travelled much or far. But within a limited local range their authority over the churches was great. " They ruled the churches," not in virtue of a special appointment, but as being the Lord's kin.

But, going back to a time previous to the appointment of Simeon, we have to ask what was the position of James in the church in Jerusalem. He may perhaps be best described as *primus inter pares*, his peers being the Apostles. " James, the brother of the Lord, who, as there

were many of this name, was surnamed the Just by all,
from the days of the Lord until now, received the government of the church with the Apostles" (Euseb. *H. E.* ii. 23).
In these words Hegesippus describes James' position at
Jerusalem. The meaning of the phrase seems to be that
a position of primacy was conceded to James (διαδέχεται
τὴν ἐκκλησίαν), but that this primacy was exercised in the
presence of equals (μετὰ τῶν ἀποστόλων). There is, however, a various reading ἐπὶ τῶν ἀποστόλων found in an
ancient codex in the Bodleian[1]. This would mean " in
the time of the Apostles." The position of headship would
then be ascribed to James without qualification[2]. It
seems best however to read μετὰ. We shall then understand Hegesippus to say that James exercised a headship
over the church in Jerusalem in conjunction with the
Apostles. It would then naturally follow that after the
death of the Apostles, or their departure from Jerusalem,
James would be left in the position of simple headship
which is freely ascribed to him by the later tradition.
Thus Eusebius speaks of him as " James, the brother
of the Lord, to whom the episcopal seat at Jerusalem
was committed by the Apostles" (Euseb. *H. E.* ii. 23).
That he occupied at the time of his death a defined
and unique position of headship, is shown by the fact
of a successor to him being appointed with the careful
deliberation described by Eusebius on the authority of
Hegesippus (Euseb. *H. E.* iii. 11). Indeed we may go
further than this and may infer that Hegesippus would
himself give to James the title of bishop. For in relating
the appointment of Simeon as bishop, he states that he was

---

[1] Routh, *Rel. Sacr.* vol. I. p. 229 ; Codex Bodl. no. 142.

[2] Gruter conjectures παρὰ τῶν ἀποστόλων, " from the Apostles," but
no MS. authority is quoted for this reading.

second in reference to James. "All put him forward as the second, because he was the cousin of the Lord" (Euseb. *H. E.* iv. 22). Second what? Surely, second bishop; taking up the word in the earlier part of the sentence, "Simeon was appointed bishop." We may therefore take it that the position of James at Jerusalem in his later years was not distinguishable from that of a monarchical bishop, and that Hegesippus regarded him as such.

The idea of episcopal succession is normal and universal in the time of Hegesippus. The church in every city has its succession (διαδοχή), and this succession cannot plausibly be explained as meaning anything else than the succession of bishops. "In every succession and in every city," says Hegesippus, "the doctrine is that of the law and the prophets and the Lord" (Euseb. *H. E.* iv. 22). Of this, Hegesippus gives examples. A succession of bishops is implied at Corinth. "The church of the Corinthians continued in the true faith, until Primus was bishop there" (*ibid.*). Again, at Rome, where the names of three successive bishops are mentioned. "After coming to Rome, I made my stay with Anicetus, whose deacon was Eleutherus. After Anicetus, Soter succeeded, and after him Eleutherus" (*ibid.*). And again at Jerusalem. "After James the Just had suffered martyrdom, as the Lord had for the same reason, Simeon, the son of Cleophas, the Lord's uncle, was appointed bishop" (*ibid.*). In each church, then, bishop succeeded bishop, as its ruler: and this continuity of organisation provided a security that the true doctrine of the apostolic tradition would be handed on unimpaired.

We may notice a point respecting the diaconate. It would seem that a deacon was especially delegated to attend upon a bishop. Such at least appears to have been the case at Rome. Hegesippus speaks of " Anicetus, whose deacon was Eleutherus " (Euseb. *H. E.* iv. 22). For this position of singularity we may compare the words of Ignatius in regard to Burrhus. " Burrhus, your deacon " he calls him, writing to the Ephesians. Ignatius asks that he may remain with him as his attendant " to the honour of yourselves and of your bishop " (Ign. Eph. 2).

ADDITIONAL NOTE.

THE EPITAPH OF AVIRCIUS.

Three sources are available, from which the text of the epitaph may be reconstructed. These are (1) the MSS. of *Acta Abercii*, in which the complete epitaph is given; (2) the fragments of the actual inscription, discovered by Prof. Ramsay, in the bath house at the hot springs three miles south of Hierapolis, and now in the Lateran Museum at Rome; (3) the epitaph of one Alexander the son of Antonius (date A.D. 216), in which the epitaph of Avircius is imitated.

The text as given by the MSS. is faulty. This is due partly to mistakes originally made in transcription, partly to errors arising in transmission. These may be to some extent corrected by comparison with the inscriptions. The following is the Greek text given by Prof. Ramsay. In it those letters or words which do not occur either in any published MS. of *Acta Abercii* or on the recovered fragments of the original stone or in the epitaph of Alexander, are enclosed in square brackets[1].

ἐκλεκτῆς πόλεως ὁ πολείτης τοῦτ᾽ ἐποίησα
  ζῶν, ἵν᾽ ἔχω φανερῶ[ς]² σώματος ἔνθα θέσιν,

---

[1] Ramsay, *Cities and Bishoprics of Phrygia*, vol. I. pt. II. p. 722.

[2] The MSS. read καιρῷ. The stone of Alexander shows that we should read φανερῶς. The word indeed is emphatic. It was the determination of Avircius that this witness to the faith should be placed where all might see it.

οὔνομ' Ἀουίρκιος [ὦν, ὁ] μαθητὴς Ποιμένος ἁγνοῦ,
4 ὃς βόσκει προβάτων ἀγέλας ὄρεσι[ν] πεδίοις τε,
ὀφθαλμοὺς ὃς ἔχει μεγάλους [καὶ πάνθ'] ὁρόωντας·
οὗτος γάρ μ' ἐδίδαξε [.........]¹ γράμματα πιστά,
εἰς Ῥώμην ὃς ἔπεμψεν ἐμὲν βασιλῆαν² ἀθρῆσαι
8 καὶ βασίλισσαν ἰδεῖν χρυσόστολον χρυσοπέδιλον·
λαὸν δ' εἶδον ἐκεῖ λαμπρὰν σφραγεῖδαν ἔχοντα·
καὶ Συρίης πέδον εἶδα καὶ ἄστεα πάντα Νίσιβιν,
Εὐφράτην διαβάς· πάντη δ' ἔσχον συνομή[θεις].
12 Παῦλον ἔχων ἐπό[μην], Πίστις πάντη δὲ προῆγε
καὶ παρέθηκε τροφὴν πάντη, Ἰχθὺν ἀπὸ πηγῆς,
πανμεγέθη, καθαρόν, ὃν ἐδράξατο Παρθένος ἁγνή,
καὶ τοῦτον ἐπέδωκε φίλοις ἔσθειν διὰ παντός,
16 οἶνον χρηστὸν ἔχουσα, κέρασμα διδοῦσα μετ' ἄρτου.
ταῦτα παρεστὼς εἶπον Ἀουίρκιος ὧδε γραφῆναι·
ἐβδομηκοστὸν ἔτος καὶ δεύτερον ἦγον ἀληθῶς.
ταῦθ' ὁ νοῶν εὔξαιθ' ὑπὲρ [αὐτοῦ]³ πᾶς ὁ συνῳδός.
20 οὐ μέντοι τύμβῳ τις ἐμῷ ἕτερόν τινα θήσει.
εἰ δ' οὖν, Ῥωμαίων ταμείῳ θήσει δισχείλια χρυσᾶ,
καὶ χρηστῇ πατρίδι Ἱεράπολ[ι] χείλια χρυσᾶ.

¹ The metre shows that some words must have dropped out at this
point. De Rossi conjectures that we should insert τὰ ζωῆς. I venture
to suggest that we should rather supply a participle, such as πορίζων or
δεδωκώς.

² The MSS. read βασιλείαν. The stone as originally read by Ramsay
had ΒΑΣ ΛΗ. In the course of transport to Rome, the stone unfor-
tunately suffered injury and the Η was obliterated. Ramsay, however,
tells us that he had verified every letter with the most scrupulous care.
There can be no doubt therefore that the reading βασιλῆαν ἀθρῆσαι must
be accepted.

³ The MSS. have ὑπὲρ Ἀβερκίου, which cannot have been the original
text. For not only is this a late form of the name, but the metre will
not allow it. Ramsay conjectures ὑπὲρ αὐτοῦ. He points out that the
transition from the pronoun of the first person to αὐτὸς is a well-marked
characteristic of Phrygian Greek. And on the other hand the writer of
the *Life* might well think that his readers would find some difficulty in
determining who was meant. He would therefore substitute the name
for the pronoun, and would write the name in the form Abercius, with
which he was familiar.

The epitaph may be thus translated:

" I, the citizen of a notable city, made this [tomb] in my lifetime, that I may have openly a resting-place for my body. Avircius by name, I am a disciple of the pure shepherd, who feedeth flocks of sheep on mountains and plains, who hath great eyes looking on all sides. For he taught me faithful writings, and he sent me to Rome to behold the king and to see the golden-robed, golden-slippered queen ; and there I saw a people bearing the splendid seal. And I saw the plain of Syria and all its cities, even Nisibis, having crossed the Euphrates. And everywhere I had associates. With Paul as my companion I followed, and everywhere faith led the way and everywhere set food before me, even fish from the fountain, mighty and stainless, which a pure virgin grasped, and this at all times faith gave to friends to eat, having good wine, giving the mingled cup with bread. These words I, Avircius, standing by, ordered to be here inscribed ; in truth I was in my seventy-second year. Let everyone of like mind, who sees this, pray for me. No one shall place another in my tomb. If he should do so, he shall pay two thousand gold pieces to the treasury of the Romans and to my good fatherland, Hierapolis, one thousand gold pieces."

CHAPTER IV.

IRENÆUS.

SECTION I.

IRENÆUS.

The Gnostic Æon "Ecclesia."—The church as the goal of Judaism.—
Its continuity.—Its destiny.—Relation of the church : (1) to Christ ;
(2) to the Father ; (3) to the Holy Spirit.—The "charismata" in
the church.—Their exercise dependent on prayer. —The church the
sole channel of the spiritual gifts.—The heretics are outside the
church.—The church compared to (1) a tower ; (2) a mother ;
(3) an Eden ; (4) the people of the Exodus.

The writings of Irenæus belong to the last quarter of
the second century. He was of Asiatic origin and, as a
young man, had been a pupil of Polycarp. His later life
was spent in Gaul. He succeeded Pothinus as bishop of
the church in Lyons.

The chief aim of Irenæus is to set forth the true faith,
in opposition to the fantastic systems of the Gnostics. In
these systems the church had a place as an æon or emana-
tion from the Eternal Being. According to Valentinus,
Anthropos and Ecclesia were brought forth by the conjunction of Logos and Zoë (I. 1. 2)[1]. Anthropos and
Ecclesia in turn produce twelve other æons, Paracletus
and Pistis, Patricus and Elpis, Metricus and Agapé, Ainos

[1] The references throughout this chapter are to the great work of
Irenæus *Against Heresies*.

and Synesis, Ecclesiasticus and Macariotes, Theletus and Sophia (I. 1. 3). This curious system at least recognises the fact that the church is of high spiritual origin and that, through the church [Ecclesia], man [Anthropos] may produce noble spiritual qualities and virtues, faith, hope, love, understanding, wisdom and the like. Valentinus then agrees so far with the traditional faith in assigning to the church an important place in the scheme of salvation, but as a system his teaching is of course utterly foreign to that faith.

Another Gnostic system represents Ecclesia as the off-spring of Achamoth, the divine Wisdom (I. 5. 6). The Demiurge, the creator of the material world (I. 5. 5), makes Ecclesia, or the church, the special object of his care. It is said "that he will administer the affairs of the world so long as is necessary and especially that he will at the same time exercise a care over the church" (I. 7. 4). This, of course, has no significance for us, except as illustrating the important place which the idea of the church occupied in the thought of the second century. The Gnostics were obliged to take account of the church and to incorporate it into their systems.

The church, according to Irenæus, is the goal for which the old dispensation had prepared the way. The old dispensation prefigured the new. The saints of the Old Testament have their reward in the progress made by the church, for it was their preparatory labour which made that progress possible. "For as in the first dispensation we were prefigured and foretold; so, on the other hand, are they represented in us, that is, in the church, and receive their reward for their labours" (IV. 22. 2). So again : " The patriarchs and prophets sowed the word concerning Christ, but the church has reaped the fruit"

(IV. 25. 3). The church is the true " seed of Abraham "
and, as such, is the heir to the promises of God. " His
seed is the church, which receives through the Lord the
adoption which is toward God " (v. 32. 2). " The church is
the seed of Abraham " (v. 34. 1). God "brings into the kingdom of heaven through Jesus Christ Abraham and his
seed, which is the church, upon which also is conferred
the adoption and the inheritance promised to Abraham "
(IV. 8. 1). So then it is not the Jewish nation, but the
Christian church, which inherits the promises. Irenæus
finds a further figure of this in the history of Jacob and
Esau. " The entire blessing is in Christ : and for this
reason, the later people [*i.e.* the church] has taken at the
Father's hands the blessing of the elder people [*i.e.* the
Jews], just as Jacob took away the blessing of Esau. And
for this reason, a brother endured the plots and persecutions of his brother, just as the church suffers this
self same thing from the Jews " (IV. 21. 3). The church,
having inherited the Old Testament promises, is persecuted by the Jews, as was Jacob by Esau.

The parable of the Labourers in the Vineyard is likewise cited by Irenæus in support of the truth. " God
planted the vineyard of the human race, in the first
instance through the creation of Adam and the election
of the fathers ; then He handed it over to husbandmen
through the Mosaic legislation ; then He hedged it round
about, that is, He set a local limit to their worship ; also
He built a tower, that is, He chose Jerusalem ; also He
digged a winepress, that is, He prepared a receptacle for
the prophetic Spirit " (IV. 36. 2). Then follows the
account of the Jewish apostasy, with its consequence :
the vineyard is given to others. " The Lord God has
handed it over to other husbandmen, who will render the

fruits in their season. It is no longer hedged about, but opened out into all the world. The tower, which signifies election, has everywhere been raised on high in its beauty. For the illustrious church is everywhere; and everywhere the winepress is digged, for everywhere are they who receive the Spirit" (*ibid.*). Not only then has the church inherited the prerogative of the Jews, but its privilege is of a nobler degree. It is not national, but universal. The Christian church is everywhere, and everywhere claims its spiritual endowment.

Irenæus interprets a passage of Jeremiah as a prophecy of this expansion. " That the promises were not announced to the prophets and the fathers only, but also to churches from among the nations, united with these, which also the Spirit describes as 'the isles'......Jeremiah thus declares : Hear the word of the Lord, ye nations, and declare it to the isles afar off" (v. 34. 3).

Again, the Lord's residence in Egypt in infancy, "whence also He made for Himself a church" (IV. 20. 12), is taken as a prophecy of the inclusion of the Gentiles. And the same thing is also prefigured by Moses' Ethiopian wife, through whom "the Gentile church (ἡ ἐξ ἐθνῶν ἐκκλησία) was portrayed" (*ibid.*).

All this is, of course, very fanciful. But it at least leaves no doubt as to the view held by Irenæus regarding the position of the Christian church. In the Christian church are fulfilled the promises of God, given indeed in the first instance to the Jews, but always intended to have a wider than national fulfilment. Owing to their apostasy, the Jews as a nation have forfeited their claim to privilege and the church takes their place. No limit may be set to the expansion of the church. No spirit of exclusiveness hedges it in. Everywhere it holds its ground ; everywhere the Holy Spirit inspires it. Such are the points which the contrast with Judaism leads Irenæus to emphasise.

The continuous life of the church is illustrated by a curious tradition in respect to Lot's wife. It was related that the pillar of salt, into which Lot's wife was transformed, retained the vital forces of womanhood and ever renewed its form when portions of it were from time to time broken away. This is said to show that " the church, which is the salt of the earth, has been left behind within the confines of the earth, subject to human sufferings; and while often entire limbs are broken away from it, it still endures as a statue of salt, which represents the firm foundation of the faith, that holds men firm and sends them forth as sons to their Father " (IV. 31. 3). The church, then, passing through many crises preserves its continuous life, holding the ancient faith and in the strength of that faith leading men to God. This is " the true and life-giving faith, which the church has received from the Apostles and has imparted to her sons " (III. pref.). " Having received this message and this faith, the church, though dispersed throughout the whole world, carefully guards it, as if occupying but a single house " (I. 10. 2, cf. I. 10. 1). This implies that the church has a continuity of existence. It is not merely the body of the faithful at any particular time, but it preserves a continuous organic life from age to age. So Irenæus speaks of the time of Marcion's heresy as " the intermediate period of the church " (III. 4. 3), a particular epoch in the church's continuous life. So also the Apostles by means of the succession of bishops are said to have " handed down the church, which is in every place " (IV. 33. 8).

In the same way, each local church, as a part of the whole, has a continuous existence. Irenæus speaks of

Peter and Paul as "preaching at Rome and laying the foundations of the church" (III. 1. 1). The local church in Rome in the time of Irenæus is that identical church which had been founded upwards of a century before by the Apostles. But further, to the idea of identity is added that of organic growth. The local church is as a building, of which the foundation is first laid and which then grows upon that foundation, but, growing, preserves its identity.

The church in this world is not yet in its true home. It is as an alien in a foreign land. "In a foreign land were born the twelve tribes, the people of Israel : and so Christ also in a foreign land called into being his twelve-pillared foundation of the church" (IV. 21. 3). Christ, by means of Old Testament types and prophecies, "accustoms His inheritance to be obedient to God and to live as foreigners in the world" (*ibid.*). The church, then, must look beyond this world for the realisation of its destiny. For this glorious future the church must be continually fitting itself, by taking the Son of God as the pattern which it is to follow. So the purpose of God's work is said to be "that goodness may be manifested and righteousness made perfect and the church conformed to the image of His Son" (IV. 37. 7). Finally, when the process is complete, "the church shall suddenly be caught up from hence" (v. 29. 1) in the midst of the last apocalyptic woes, and so shall reach its true home, no longer "an alien" in a strange land, but having entered into its inheritance in "the kingdom of God."

Irenæus follows St Paul in his metaphor expressive of the relation of the church to Christ. Christ is "the Head, from whom the whole body of the church, being knit together, increaseth" (v. 14. 4, see Col. ii. 19). The relation of the Holy Trinity is thus expressed: "The Father is above all and is the Head of Christ: the Word is through all things and is the Head of the church: the Spirit is in us all and is the Living Water" (v. 18. 2). It was for the sake of the church therefore that Christ patiently laboured, as Jacob had done for Rachel (iv. 21. 3).

From this relation of the church to Christ, there results its progressive sanctification. The church is gathered out of the wicked world in order that it may be sanctified by fellowship with Christ. This process of sanctification is prefigured by the command given to Hosea to take as his wife a woman of evil repute. So "it will be God's good pleasure to take to Himself, from among men of that kind, a church, to be sanctified by fellowship with His Son, just as that woman was sanctified by fellowship with the prophet" (iv. 20. 12). What therefore the prophet did by way of figure, "the Apostle shows[1] to have been done in reality in the church by Christ" (*ibid.*).

Closely connected with the relation of the church to Christ is the bond which unites it with the Father. In that it is Christ, Himself God, who has gathered the church out of the world, the church is therefore the special possession of God. "It is the synagogue of God, which God, that is the Son, hath Himself of His own act gathered together" (iii. 6. 1). And, further, it stands to God in a relation of adoption. Irenæus says respecting "those who have received adoption," that "these are the church" (*ibid.*). The church therefore is united to God by the strong tie of love. This love, a divine χάρισμα (iv. 33. 8), has borne rich fruit in a long roll of martyrs. "The church in every place, on account of that love

[1] *i.e.* St Paul in Rom. ix. 25 f.

which it hath toward God, doth send forth a multitude of martyrs in every age to the Father" (IV. 33. 9).

Further, the relation of the church to Christ is rendered effective by means of the operation of the Holy Spirit. In the church " has been planted the means of fellowship with Christ, that is the Holy Spirit, the earnest of incorruption and the confirmation of our faith and the ladder of ascent to God. For in the church, God hath set apostles, prophets, teachers and all other channels through which the Spirit works" (III. 24. 1). The Holy Spirit has been bestowed upon the church, in all the fulness of His manifold operations, and everywhere in the church the gracious influence of the Spirit's presence is felt. "Where the church is, there also is the Spirit of God ; and where the Spirit of God is, there is the church and every grace " (*ibid.*). This endowment is the gift of God, who " conferred upon the church the Spirit Himself, in that He sends into all the world the Paraclete from heaven " (III. 17. 3).

That these gifts of grace, the outcome of the indwelling Spirit, were strikingly apparent in the church in the days of Irenæus, is evident from the way in which he appeals to them in support of his argument. " Those who are in truth the disciples of the Son of God receive grace from Him, and work for the benefit of other men, according as each one of them has received the gift from Him. For some certainly and truly drive out devils, so that oftentimes those who have been cleansed from the evil spirits become believers and are now in the church. Others again have foreknowledge of things to come, and visions, and prophetic utterance. Others also heal the sick by the laying on of hands, and they are made whole. Yea moreover, as I have said, even the dead have been raised, and abode with us many years. And what shall I say more ? It is not possible to tell the number of the gifts (χαρίσματα), which through all the world the church has received from God in the name of Jesus Christ, who was crucified under Pontius Pilate, and which it now employs every day for the benefit of the nations" (II. 32. 4). The church therefore in the time of Irenæus was richly endowed with the divine *charismata* or spiritual gifts. There is, first, the power of exorcism ; then that of prophetic knowledge, which is associated with the seeing of visions; then the healing of the sick; and then the raising of the dead. But these are given as examples, not as an exhaustive list. So rich is the variety of gifts, with which the church is endowed, that it is impossible fully to describe them.

But among the *charismata*, Irenæus lays greatest stress upon the gift of prophecy. This emphasis was necessitated by the denial by certain opponents that the church possessed the gift of prophecy at all. " Wretched men, indeed, they are, who wish to be false prophets—for this is what it amounts to—and who set aside the gift of prophecy from the church" (III. 11. 9). The question arises as to who these opponents were. Irenæus does not name them ; but it is clear, from the way in which he speaks of them, that they were men of a materialising tendency. They rejected the work of the Holy Spirit, and this had led them to a repudiation of the Gospel of St John. Now Epiphanius (who wrote after A.D. 350) describes, in language closely resembling that which Irenæus uses in this passage, a heretical sect, to whom he gives the nickname of Alogi or Irrationalists. " I put upon them," he says, " this nickname ; from henceforth they shall be so called, and therefore, my beloved, let us

give them this name" (Epiph. *Hær.* 51. 3). The re-
semblance between the two descriptions raises a considerable presumption that Irenæus, in the passage under
discussion, is speaking of the sect afterwards nicknamed
the Alogi. They were strong opponents of Montanism ;
for their rejection of the work of the Holy Spirit required
them to deny the reality of prophecy. But this denial
brought them into conflict with the church as well as
with the Montanists ; and so Irenæus joins issue with
them. He says that their attitude is tantamount to
claiming for themselves the power of prophecy, while all
the time they are denying that prophecy has any reality.
So they condemn themselves by their inconsistency. With
all their self-assertion, they are no better than false
prophets[1].

Irenæus in reply to them claims for the church of his
day the same gift of prophecy as was attributed to the
church by St Paul, who "in his Epistle to the Corinthians
speaks expressly of prophetical gifts and recognises men
and women as prophesying in the church" (III. 11. 9).
"We hear," he says again, "many brethren in the church,
who possess prophetic gifts ($\chi\alpha\rho\acute{\iota}\sigma\mu\alpha\tau\alpha$) and who through
the Spirit speak many different tongues and bring to light
the things hidden from men and declare the mysteries of
God. These are they whom the Apostle terms spiritual,
they being spiritual because they partake of the Spirit"
(V. 6. 1).

It is probable indeed that in the time of Irenæus
prophecy in the church had lost, at least in some degree,

[1] It seems best to give this interpretation to the words *qui pseudo-
prophetæ esse volunt*, rather than to adopt Lightfoot's emendation *pseudo-
prophetas* (*Biblical Essays*, p. 115) or Zahn's suggestion *nolunt* (*Canon,*
II. p. 971). Cf. Stanton, *The Gospels as Historical Documents*, p. 199.

14—2

those striking outward manifestations, which seem to have accompanied it in the days of the Apostles, and which in an exaggerated form marked the frenzies of the Montanist claimants of the gift. Prophecy in the church was a quiet spiritual insight into the meaning of things that were hidden from the common run of men, and into the divine mysteries. It was a gift, which would be of great value in the edifying of believers, but which could hardly be used by way of evidence to convince opponents. On the other hand, however, we have to note that the gift of tongues is still associated with it by Irenæus.

The spiritual character of the *charismata* is emphasised by the fact that their exercise is dependent upon prayer. "The church does not perform anything by means of angelic invocations or by incantations or by any other wicked curious art; but, directing its prayers in a pure, sincere and straightforward spirit to the Lord, who made all things, and calling upon the name of our Lord Jesus Christ, has exercised its powers for the advantage of mankind and not to lead men into error" (II. 32. 5). This intimate connection of prayer with the exercise of the *charismata* is illustrated by the case of the raising of the dead. "When the entire church in a particular place has prayed with much fasting and supplication, the spirit of the dead has returned and the man has been granted to the prayers of the saints" (II. 31. 2). So then in response to the united prayer of a local church, the dead, says Irenæus, have been restored to life. Such was the spiritual power of the church.

This spiritual character of the church is further shown by the motives which prompted the exercise of the *charismata*. The heretical bodies, it is said, used their pretended powers for the sake of gain: the church worked for the benefit of men, asking nothing in return. " Whereas among them error and misleading influences are found and magical illusions are impiously wrought in the sight of men, in the church on the other hand not only are sympathy and compassion and steadfastness and truth displayed in aid of mankind without fee or reward, but also we ourselves lay out for the benefit of mankind our own possessions " (II. 31. 3). All this emphasises the spiritual character of the church. By these graces of character the church evinces the stamp of genuineness upon its spiritual life. An unselfish care for the welfare of mankind is its distinctive aim.

The church then is the means through which the gifts of the spiritual life are brought to men. But, further, it is the sole means. Separation from the church involves the loss of these gifts. " They are not partakers of the Spirit who do not join themselves to the church, but they defraud themselves of life through their perverse opinions and shameful behaviour " (III. 24. 1). Separation from the church, then, involves loss of the Holy Spirit, and loss of the Holy Spirit carries with it deprivation of the gifts He bestows. " Those who do not partake of Him are neither nourished into life from the mother's breasts nor do they enjoy that most limpid fountain which issues from the body of Christ ; but they dig for themselves broken cisterns out of earthly trenches and drink putrid water from the mire, in that they flee from the faith of the church, lest they should be exposed, and in a word reject the Spirit, that they may not be instructed " (ibid.). The heretics, then, are regarded as being outside the church. They are not thought of as being erring members, but as being completely separate from it. And this separation from the church means separation from the channels of spiritual life, which the church, as a mother, imparts to its members.

This conception of the church, which regards the heretics as standing outside its pale, is consistently maintained by Irenæus. Of Tatian, on his lapsing into heresy after Justin's martyrdom, it is said that "he severed himself from the church" (I. 28. 1). Irenæus, writing to Florinus, speaks of "the heretics outside the church" (*Frag.* 2). Speaking of the Gnostic teaching he says, "As many as separate from the church and give heed to such old wives' fables as these are truly self-condemned" (I. 16. 3). On the other hand those who abjure their heresy are said to return to the church. Women who have been led astray by the Gnostics are spoken of as confessing their sins and "returning to the church of God" (I. 6. 3). Women, again, who had become followers of the magician Marcus, had repented and "returned to the church" (I. 13. 5). Polycarp, meeting in Rome many who had attached themselves to Valentinus, Marcion and other heretics, induced them "to turn away from these heretics to the church of God" (III. 3. 4). "The actual church" (I. 10. 3, ἡ οὖσα ἐκκλησία, Lat. ecclesia universa) is contrasted with the Gnostic bodies. Their assemblies are merely meetings (IV. 18. 4, hæreticorum synagogæ). The church alone, it is said, offers the pure oblation; the Jews do not offer it; nor do the meetings of heretics. The heretics therefore are consistently regarded as being completely separate from the church. Their meetings have no title to the name of a church.

It should be noted that this view of separation from the church was accepted by the heretics themselves. They made no claim to church membership. Indeed they despised the church, holding that it was on an altogether lower spiritual level than themselves. They looked down in a contemptuous way upon the church, as being tied by a soulless ecclesiasticism. "These men"—Irenæus is speaking of the Valentinians—"discourse to the multitude about those who belong to the church, whom they refer to as 'mere churchpeople'" (III. 15. 2). They mean, no doubt, that the organised society, with its appeal to tradition, is fettered by unspiritual conditions, and is therefore on a lower plane than those who have capacity for such exalted speculations as the Gnostic teachers. "The early heretics," says Dr Swete, "gloried in being the minority and not of the vulgar herd of churchmen [1]." They contended that their special doctrine gave them a distinction. They had therefore no desire to claim communion with the church.

But none the less Irenæus claims that the church, as the channel of spiritual gifts, provides the true way of salvation. In the church "one and the same way of salvation is set forth in all the world. For to it is entrusted the light of God, and therefore 'the wisdom of God,' through which it saves all men, 'uttereth her voice in the way [2]'" (v. 20. 1). The church, then, is said to save men by means of "the wisdom of God." The bestowal of the Divine Wisdom is here thought of in direct connection with the Incarnation. So when, in the Magnificat, Mary gives thanks for the Incarnation, whereby the blessings of the new dispensation of grace are brought to man, she is said to do so "on behalf of the church" (III. 10. 2).

---

[1] Swete, *The Apostles' Creed*, p. 80 n.
[2] Prov. i. 20, LXX.

Under various figures this truth is illustrated from different points of view.

Thus the tower in the parable of the Labourers in the Vineyard is compared to the church. It is "a tower of election" (IV. 36. 2). That is, those who are privileged to enter the tower do so in virtue of divine election. Thus membership of the church is a divine privilege. We may compare this with the imagery of the tower worked out elaborately in the *Shepherd* of Hermas.

The church, again, is thought of as a mother. Those who belong to the church "receive the nourishment of life from the mother's breasts " (III. 24. 1). "It behoves us therefore to fly for refuge to the church, and to be brought up in her bosom, and to be nourished with the Scriptures of the Lord" (V. 20. 2). The Scriptures are a source whence the church, as mother, feeds those who are hers. These, in continuation of the metaphor, are spoken of as her sons. The church, receiving her doctrines from Christ, "has transmitted them to her sons" (V. pref.). It is their duty, as sons, to defend the faith of the church, as against the heretics. "Faithfully and strenuously shalt thou resist them in defence of the only true and lifegiving faith, which the church has received from the Apostles and has imparted to her sons" (III. pref.). This doctrine of the motherhood of the church is contrasted with the teaching of the Gnostics. The last of the Gnostic æons, Achamoth or Sophia, is spoken of as the mother (I. 4. 1 ; cf. II. 5. 2). Irenæus prays that the Gnostics "may separate themselves from a mother of this nature... and that they may be converted to the church of God and lawfully begotten, and that Christ may be formed in them" (III. 25. 7). Here the true mother, the church, is set over against the false mother, of the Gnostic system. The church is a mother; for it is through the church that the new birth is given, and in the church the new life is lived. Further this new birth, "the power of regeneration unto God," is bestowed through Baptism, in accordance with our Lord's commission to His disciples (III. 17. 1).

The church has been planted in the world as an Eden, a "Paradisus" (V. 20. 2). The Scriptures are the fruit of the trees of this garden, which is a figure of the church. Of this fruit all may freely eat. But there is also the tree of knowledge, whose fruit is that false Gnosis which results from the wrong exercise of the reason upon subjects that are above reason. For the Gnostics "profess that they have themselves the knowledge of good and evil; and they set their own impious minds above the God who made them. They therefore exercise their reason upon that which is beyond the sphere of reason" (ibid.). The fruit of this tree of knowledge is heresy, and to eat of it is "to be cast forth from the Paradise of life" (ibid.). Into this Paradise, which is the church, all those are brought who obey the call of God (ibid.).

The people of Israel, coming out of Egypt, was a type of the church. Egypt represents the nations of the world, from whom the church is drawn. "The entire exodus of the people from Egypt, which was effected by God, was a type and figure of the exodus of the church, which was to take place from out of the nations. For this cause He is leading it out hence in these latter days into His own inheritance, which Moses the servant of God did not bestow, but which Jesus the Son of God will give for an inheritance" (IV. 30. 4). The church, drawn from out of all the nations of the world, is brought by the guidance of Jesus the Son of God into a position of spiritual privilege. This spiritual privilege of the church is contrasted with the position of the people under the old dispensation, when " the inheritance " had not yet been bestowed.

But on the other hand the new dispensation, thus contrasted with the old, is regarded as its fulfilment. " Christ Himself fulfilled all things by His coming and still in the church He is fulfilling, even to its consummation, the new covenant predicted by the Law " (IV. 34. 2). The coming of Christ was a fulfilment of the Law and the Prophets. But this fulfilment was not completed by His earthly life. It goes on continuously and will go on until the final consummation. And, further, the sphere within which this progressive fulfilment is taking place is the church.

In connection with this idea of the continuity of the old and new, it may be noted that the term " member of Christ " is not confined to the new dispensation. The prophets also are called " members of Christ " (IV. 33. 10). For by their united work they manifested Christ beforehand, as a person is manifested by the action of the members of his body.

SECTION II.

IRENÆUS (*continued*).

Unity of the church an organic unity.—Founded on the common faith.—
Marked by the apostolic ministry.—Marred by schism.—Expressed
by true fellowship.—Authority of the church, in relation to (1) The
synods, (2) Excommunication, (3) Penance, (4) Doctrine.—The
church the sole guardian of the faith.—Apostolic tradition.—The
creed of Irenæus.—The creed in the church.—The church as teacher,
in relation to the Scriptures.

The church everywhere is one and the same. It is "the
church throughout all the world" (II. 9. 1). It has no local
boundary, for the "hedge," which formerly fenced in the area
of God's special dealings with men, has been taken away ;
and now " the illustrious church is everywhere, and everywhere the winepress is digged : for everywhere are those
who receive the Spirit " (IV. 36. 2). One church then
covers the whole ground of God's dealings with men
throughout all the world. There is an ideal completeness
in the church, scattered as it is through all countries. It
stands, as it were, four-square, upon the pillars of the four
Gospels. " It is not possible for the Gospels to be more in
number than they are, nor again for them to be fewer.
For since there are four quarters of the world in which
we live, and four principal winds, while the church has
been scattered throughout all the world, and the pillar
and ground of the church is the Gospel and the spirit of
life, it is fitting that it should have four pillars, breathing
out immortality on every side and vivifying men afresh "
(III. 11. 8). Such is the ideal completeness of the church,
standing upon the fourfold support, which symbolises a
foundation ideally perfect. Herein too is expressed its
mission. The Gospels in the church are to be a source of
new and endless life. But the power, which effects this

through the church, is that of the Holy Spirit. And this also finds symbolic expression. For of the four living creatures of the Revelation, which like the fourfold Gospel express ideal completeness, "the fourth was like a flying eagle, symbolising the gift of the Spirit hovering in flight over the church" (*ibid.*). So then the church, brooded over by the one Spirit, preaching everywhere the one faith of the fourfold Gospel, possesses an ideal unity throughout the world.

But, further, the unity of the church is organic. The church is described as "a cohort of faith" composed of men "from various and divers nations" (IV. 21. 3). The metaphor implies a visible unity, a unity of organisation. The point is that though its members are of very varied nationalities, yet they form, as it were, a single regiment, united under a discipline, which transcends national distinctions. The bond of unity in this regiment is the common faith. It is a "cohort of faith." All alike hold the same faith, the apostolic tradition.

The outward organic unity of the church is secured by adherence to the apostolic succession of bishops. The presbyters derive their authority from association with this succession. Obedience therefore is due to them. "It is incumbent to obey those presbyters who are in the church, those who, as I have shown, possess the succession from the Apostles; those who, together with the succession of the episcopate, have received the sure gift of truth according to the good pleasure of the Father" (IV. 26. 2). Indeed so jealous is Irenæus for this organic unity of the church, so emphatic is he as to the necessity of keeping it unimpaired, that he not only condemns heresy and schism, but even says that all bodies of Christians are to be held in suspicion who gather together, no matter where, apart

from the apostolic ministry. They are to be viewed with
suspicion as being possibly either heretics or schismatics
or hypocrites. These are all included in those who have
lapsed from the truth. "All those who keep aloof from
the primitive succession, and assemble together in any
place whatsoever, we must suspect of being either heretics
of perverse opinions, or schismatics, puffed up and self-
pleasing, or again hypocrites, acting thus for the sake of
profit and vainglory. For all these have fallen from the
truth" (*ibid.*).

So then it is not only the heretics, who have fallen
from the truth, but the schismatics also. Thus schism,
the setting up of separate and independent organisation,
is in itself, apart from the question of whether a different
doctrine is taught, a violation of fundamental truth, a
departure from the apostolic tradition. The unity of the
church is not merely a moral unity, a unity of affection
and the like. It is a unity which should find external
expression. And such a unity is violated by schism, the
formation of separate communities. The essence of schism
is not the holding of erroneous doctrine, but the setting
up of separate organisation and holding aloof from the
fellowship of the primitive succession.

Schism is thought of as division within the church
rather than as separation from it. The schismatics are
spoken of as "those who cut and cleave asunder the unity
of the church" (IV. 26. 2). Or again, they "cut in
pieces and divide the great and glorious body of Christ"
(IV. 33. 7). A schism is not said to make the church
smaller by removing men from its pale: it is said to
destroy the church's unity. The schismatics still belong
to the church.

Their action however is to be strongly condemned.

The spiritually-minded man " will condemn those who give rise to schisms, who are destitute of the love of God, and who look to their own private advantage rather than to the unity of the church, and who for trifling or indeed any reasons cut in pieces and divide the great and glorious body of Christ and, so far as in them lies, destroy it. They talk of peace while they are giving rise to war, and do in truth strain out the gnat, while they swallow the camel.   For no reformation of so great importance can be effected by them, as will compensate for the mischief arising from their schism " (IV. 33. 7).   The attitude of " the spiritually-minded disciple " (IV. 33. 1) is contrasted with that of the schismatics.   For schism is the outcome of a self-assertive and self-seeking spirit, which is incompatible with true churchmanship.   For the unity of the church requires the subordination of self-interest to consideration of the common good.

An excuse, often advanced in justification of schism, is mentioned by Irenæus.   It is pleaded that there is something imperfect in the church, something that needs reformation.   Forthwith those who are discontented, instead of trying to correct the evil, make a schism.   They set up a community of their own, which is to be free from the particular error in question.   But, says Irenæus, the remedy is far worse than the disease.   It is a veritable case of straining out the gnat, by which he means the flaw complained of in the church, and swallowing the camel, which expresses the miserable disunion that follows.   No amount of reformation, which they may be able to effect, can make up for the grievous harm done by the divisions caused.

It may be noted that this passage in condemnation of schismatics is followed by a reference to heretics.   This same spiritually-minded disciple " will also condemn those who are outside the truth, that is those who are outside the church " (IV. 33. 7). Here, then, we have a further emphasis of the view of Irenæus that, while schism does not of itself result in exclusion from the church, heresy does so. No doubt the statement must be qualified by bearing in mind the type of heretics with whom Irenæus is concerned, those, namely, who are mentioned in the preceding sections, Ebionites, Marcionites and Valentinians. Their errors were so fundamental that there could be no place in the church for those holding such beliefs.

In direct contrast with the self-assertive spirit of schism is the spirit of Christian fellowship, which marks the true life of the church. Irenæus notes this fellowship in the apostolic church in Jerusalem. Peter and John, when dismissed from the chief priests, are said to have " returned to the rest of their fellow-Apostles and to the disciples of the Lord, that is, to the church....The whole church then lifted up their voice to God with one accord " (III. 12. 5). The local church, which Irenæus here defines as the company of believers, speaks with one voice. Its life is an expression of brotherhood (II. 31. 2).

Nor does this fellowship exist only within the limits of the local church. It is a bond uniting the various local churches with one another. And this spiritual fellowship was more strikingly manifested by the fact that it was unaffected by certain differences of custom, which subsisted in various parts of the church. Of this divergence of custom the time of observance of Easter was a conspicuous example. When the Quartodeciman controversy arose, Victor, Bishop of Rome, as we have already seen, broke this long-continued harmony by attempting to enforce a uniformity of custom and claiming to cut off from the

common unity those local churches in which his own custom
was not followed. This drew down upon him the dignified
rebuke of Irenæus, who pointed out that the variety was
of long standing and had never been allowed to interrupt
the fellowship of the churches. "In spite of it," he says,
"all lived in peace one with another and we also are
in peace. So our difference as regards the fast confirms
our agreement in respect of the faith" (*Ep. ad Vict.*).

This conscious fellowship between the local churches
was beautifully symbolised by the practice of sending the
Eucharist from one church to another. Irenæus points
out that the predecessors of Victor at Rome had been
accustomed to send the Eucharist to those churches in
which the Quartodeciman practice prevailed, making no
distinction in this respect (*ibid.*).

He then cites the case of Polycarp, whose relations
with Anicetus of Rome so beautifully illustrated the true
spirit of fellowship, which united the churches and which
rose superior to differences of local custom. Each might
think it his duty to observe his own traditional custom :
each was sure that the supreme duty of fellow-Christians
was that of Christian love. Each indeed tried to persuade
the other to change his usage, when Polycarp was visiting
Anicetus at Rome. But each was inflexible. "And
under these conditions they held fellowship with one
another; and Anicetus conceded to Polycarp the celebration of the Eucharist, by way of showing him respect"
(*ibid.*).

This Quartodeciman controversy is, further, of value
as throwing light upon the question of the authority of
the church. Eusebius (*H. E.* v. 23, 24) gives us the
history of the controversy. In each district the bishops
of the churches met together in synod or convocation.

There was, for instance, a synod of the bishops of Pontus, under the presidency of Palmas. There was a synod of the bishops of Gaul under the presidency of Irenæus. Theophilus presided at Cæsarea, Narcissus at Jerusalem. Polycrates guided the deliberations of the bishops of Asia. In each synod the question of the observance of Easter was considered and all the synods, with the exception of that of Asia, arrived at the same conclusion, that the Lord's Resurrection should be celebrated on the Lord's day. This decision was embodied by each synod in an ἐκκλησιαστικὸν δόγμα and was sent to all the churches.

We cannot indeed be sure whether this term is due simply to Eusebius or whether it represents the language in which the synods themselves described the embodiment of their conclusion. The expression is therefore of little value for our present purpose. We may however note that δόγμα has not the force of a " decree " or " command," but is rather an " opinion." The opinion is expressed that the churches should act in the way therein defined : they are not commanded to do so[1].

On the other hand, the claim of Victor to command is at once repudiated. When the decision of the synod of Asia was received at Rome, and the attempt was made to enforce uniformity, the answer of Polycrates is, "We ought to obey God rather than men." When Victor still tried to enforce his will and attempted to excommunicate the churches of Asia, he met with the rebuke from Irenæus of which we have already spoken.

Although it so happened that all but one of the synods arrived at the same conclusion (οἱ μίαν καὶ τὴν αὐτὴν δόξαν τε καὶ κρίσιν ἐξενηνεγμένοι), this comparative unanimity

---

[1] ὡς ἂν μὴ...ἐπιτελοῖτο. The optative does not express a command. Cf. the use of δόγματα in Acts xvi. 4.

was not a matter of necessity. Each synod sat inde-
pendently, and each wrote letters expressing its own δόξα,
its own opinion. There is no attempt to enforce uniformity
throughout the church, except the attempt of Victor,
which at once met with strong rebuke. But on the other
hand we must suppose that within the locality represented
by each separate synod the opinion put forth by the synod
would have great moral authority. The wish implied
would not be lightly disregarded.

Victor's action was the illegitimate use of an authority
which had a true existence within rightful limits. He
had indeed no authority to excommunicate the churches
of Asia, " to cut them off from the common unity," but on
the other hand there was a real authority of excommunication resident in each local church. Thus the
church in Rome exercised its power of excommunication
in the case of Cerdon, the predecessor of Marcion.
" Having been denounced for his false teaching, he was
excluded from the assembly of the faithful" (III. 4. 3).

In the case of penitence after excommunication,
restoration to the church was accompanied by an act of
public penance. It is said of a woman who had been led
away and corrupted by a pretended magician, that " when
with no small difficulty the brethren had converted her,
she spent her whole time in the exercise of public confession, weeping over and lamenting the defilement which
she had received " (I. 13. 5). Here then we have an
example of the penitential discipline of the church.

The commission of the church includes the guardian-
ship of the faith. This faith the church has received from
the Apostles and " she alone guards it in its integrity
throughout the world and has transmitted it to her sons "
(v. pref.). This faith it is the function of the church not

only to hold but to preach (*ibid.*). It follows then that
" the preaching of the church is alone true " (v. 18. 1).
The particular doctrine, which Irenæus here has in his
mind, is that of the Incarnation, as opposed to the wild
theories of the Gnostics. But the same claim is made for
the church in respect of the entire scheme of salvation.
" The preaching of the church is true and constant, in
which one and the same way of salvation is shown throughout the whole world....For the church preaches the truth
everywhere and is the seven-branched candlestick, which
carries the light of Christ [1] " (v. 20. 1). The faith of Christ
shines forth from the church in all parts of the world. It
is therefore from the church that the faith is received.
Those in danger of falling under the influence of false
teachers are warned to " hold firm the faith, which from
the beginning they received through the church " (I. 13. 4).
This faith, as taught by the church, constituted a standard
by which all doctrines might be tested. When Florinus
lapsed into Valentinianism, Irenæus wrote in reference to
his new opinions that " they are not in agreement with
the church " (*Ep. ad Flor.*). This was a sufficient condemnation of them.

This prerogative of the church has its origin in the
Apostles, who first committed the truth to its care. All
therefore that is necessary is to examine the proofs of the
continuity of the church from the apostolic days. This
Irenæus does (III. 3). " Since therefore," he continues, " we
have such proofs, we must not seek among others that
truth which it is easy to obtain from the church; since
the Apostles, like a rich man making a deposit in a bank,
bestowed upon the church in fullest measure all things
which pertain to the truth; so that everyone who wishes

---

[1] Cf. Rev. i. 12 f.

may take from it the water of life.   For the church is the
entrance into life : all others are thieves and robbers.   For
this reason we ought to avoid them, but to value most
highly all that pertains to the church and to lay hold of
the tradition of the truth " (III. 4. 1).   Here is stated the
exclusive prerogative of the church as the entrance to
eternal life.   The covenanted way of salvation is found in
the church, and in the church alone.   It will be noted
that the teaching of Irenæus in no way falls short of the
later Cyprianic phrase " Extra ecclesiam nulla salus."

Our Lord's illustration of the household, over which
the faithful steward is placed to give to all their meat in
due season (Matt. xxiv. 45 f.), is interpreted by Irenæus as
meaning the church.   " Where therefore the gifts of the
Lord have been placed, there we ought to learn the truth,
namely from those who possess that succession of the
church which comes from the Apostles " (IV. 26. 5).   The
divine χαρίσματα are deposited in the church, and therefore to the church men must resort in order to learn the
truth.   That the truth remains in the church is guaranteed
by its possession of the apostolic succession (cf. IV. 26. 2).

That the church possesses the truth is further
evidenced by the uniformity of its teaching.   " The
preaching of the church is everywhere consistent, and
continues ever the same and receives testimony from prophets and Apostles and from all the disciples" (III. 24. 1).
This account of the teaching of the church amounts to
nothing less than the Vincentian Canon "Quod semper,
quod ubique, quod ab omnibus."   It is a body of truth,
which Irenæus describes as " a gift of God entrusted to
the church " (ibid.) and as " conducive to salvation " (ibid.).
" We keep guard over our faith, which we have received
from the church " (ibid.).   The heretics on the other hand

have no fixed body of truth. They think one thing at one time, another at another. They are not founded upon the "one rock," by which it would seem that Irenæus means the apostolic tradition of faith (III. 24. 2). The heretics "who bring to the altar of God strange fire, that is strange doctrines," are compared to Nadab and Abihu, and shall be punished in like manner (IV. 26. 2).

We have now to examine in closer detail the appeal of Irenæus to the apostolic tradition. The ground of the appeal lies in the action of Christ Himself. For it was He who shaped "the twelve-pillared foundation of the church" (IV. 21. 3), which of course is a reference to the twelve Apostles. The church, therefore, by Christ's ordinance is built upon the foundation of the Apostles and their teaching.

The teaching of the church has not varied. "The Apostles and their disciples used to teach just the same as the church now teaches" (III. 12. 13). Nothing has been added to the original deposit. "The preaching of the church is without interpolation" (III. 21. 3). It is one and the same everywhere and always, since it is the faith which has come down from the Apostles. "The church throughout all the world, having its origin firm from the Apostles, perseveres in one and the same belief with regard to God and His Son" (III. 12. 7). This is noted as standing in contrast with the new and ever-changing teaching of the heretics. "These are of much later date than the bishops to whom the Apostles committed the churches....These heretics then, since they are blind to the truth, must needs walk in various paths outside the true course; and for this reason the footprints of their doctrine are scattered about, without either agreement or consecutive purpose" (V. 20. 1). On the other hand, " the fenced path of those who are of the church traverses the whole world, as possessing the sure tradition from the Apostles " (*ibid.*).

Irenæus appeals to the teaching of the elders, on the ground that they had themselves been instructed by Apostles. Thus he remarks that " the elders, the disciples of the Apostles," give a certain interpretation of the parable of the Wedding Feast. He gives as a reason for condemning the new teaching of Florinus that "the elders, who preceded us and who were pupils of the Apostles, did not hand down these opinions " (*Ep. ad Flor.*).

Irenæus examines the history of the church in order to establish his contention that the apostolic tradition, and that alone, has been handed down in the church's teaching. Looking to the beginning he finds that the Apostles instituted bishops in the churches, and to the bishops severally the charge of the churches was committed. In each church bishop was succeeded by bishop. A record of these successions was kept, and Irenæus was in a position to give them, if required to do so. Thus in each place the church preserved a continuous existence, witnessed to by the continuity of the succession of bishops. And this, again, guaranteed the preservation of apostolic tradition in the several churches. Upstart leaders might have introduced other teaching ; but not so those who had derived their instruction from the Apostles. " It is possible for all those who wish to see the truth to trace clearly in every church the tradition of the Apostles, manifested in all the world, and we are in a position to enumerate those who were appointed by the Apostles as bishops in the churches, and their successors even to our own time ; men who neither taught nor even had knowledge of any such things as these, about which they [*i.e.* the

Gnostics] rave. For if the Apostles had known hidden mysteries, which they were in the habit of imparting to the perfect by themselves, keeping them secret from the rest, they would have delivered them first of all to those to whom they were committing the churches themselves. For they earnestly desired that these men, whom they were leaving behind as their successors and to whom they were handing over their own seat of authority, should be perfect and blameless in all things. For if they discharged their functions well, great benefit would ensue ; but if they should fail, then deepest misfortune" (III. 3. 1). The argument of Irenæus is that the Gnostic teaching could never have had a place in the apostolic tradition. It was claimed for this teaching that it had formed part of an esoteric body of doctrine, which the Apostles had taught only to the inner circle of the " perfect " and which the uninitiated had not the capacity to understand. The answer of Irenæus to this is that, in that case, the bishops, appointed by the Apostles themselves, would of all people have been recipients of this teaching. But an examination of the actual teaching of the bishops shows they possessed no such esoteric knowledge. It would be wearisome, says Irenæus, to show this by examining the succession of bishops in all the churches. He therefore selects the church at Rome as an example and gives a detailed account of its line of bishops. Of these Clement is an important witness for the purpose of Irenæus. " He had seen the Apostles and had associated with them and had the preaching of the Apostles still ringing in his ears and their traditions before his eyes " (III. 3. 3). We may look therefore to his writings to ascertain the apostolic tradition. His letter to the Corinthians gives no countenance to the Gnostic theory of esoteric teaching. It is fundamentally opposed to their tenets. "From this writing all who will may learn that He, the Father of our Lord Jesus Christ, was preached by the churches, and may also understand the apostolic tradition of the church" (*ibid.*). At the close of his enumeration of the bishops at Rome, Irenæus draws his conclusion. "In this order and by this succession the church's tradition, which is from the Apostles, and the preaching of the truth have come down to our times. And this is most abundant proof, that there is one and the same lifegiving faith, which has been preserved in the church from the Apostles until now, and has been handed down in truth" (*ibid.*).

But just as the church in Rome affords striking collective witness, so Polycarp is cited as an important individual witness. For on the one hand he was the pupil of Apostles, and by Apostles had been appointed bishop, and on the other hand he had survived to the lifetime of Irenæus himself, who had actually seen him as a boy. Polycarp suffered martyrdom as a very old man, "having always taught that which he had learnt from the Apostles, and which the church hands down, and which alone is true" (III. 3. 4).

The witness also of the church in Ephesus is specially important owing to the long-continued stay there of the Apostle St John. "The church in Ephesus, founded by Paul but having John dwelling with it up to the time of Trajan, is a true witness of the tradition of the Apostles" (*ibid.*).

Irenæus has proved then that the teaching, which has been handed down in the church, is the teaching of the Apostles. There exists therefore in the Scriptures a means of testing the teaching, a corroborative proof of its truth. For the Scriptures of the New Testament are

the work of apostolic writers and therefore contain the
apostolic teaching. "Since therefore the tradition from
the Apostles is thus held in the church and endures
among us, let us turn to that scriptural proof provided by
those Apostles who also wrote the gospel" (III. 5. 1). The
Scriptures are regarded as furnishing a permanent
standard, by which the teaching of the church can be
checked. Its agreement with the Scriptures proves its
title to be the apostolic tradition.

We may note the terms in which Irenæus sums up
this teaching. It requires "a full faith in one God
Almighty, from whom are all things; and a firm belief in
the Son of God, Jesus Christ, our Lord, through whom are
all things; and in His dispensation, whereby the Son of
God became man; and in the Spirit of God, who bestows
upon us a knowledge of the truth, and has revealed the
dispensation of the Father and of the Son, in virtue of
which He dwells in every generation of men, even as the
Father wills" (IV. 33. 7). And again: "the church, though
dispersed through all the world unto the ends of the earth,
has received from the Apostles and their disciples belief
in one God the Father Almighty, maker of heaven and
earth and the seas and all that is in them; and in one
Christ Jesus, the Son of God, who became man for our
salvation; and in the Holy Ghost, who proclaimed through
the prophets the dispensations of God and the Advents and
the Birth from a Virgin and the Passion, and the Resurrection from the dead and the Ascension in the flesh into
heaven of the beloved Christ Jesus our Lord and His
return from the heavens in the glory of the Father, to
sum up all things, and to raise all flesh of the whole
human race" (I. 10. 1).

This then is the creed which the church everywhere

proclaims. " Having received this preaching and this
faith, the church, though scattered abroad in the whole
world, carefully guards it, as though dwelling in a single
house. And she believes these doctrines, just as though
she had one soul and one single heart; and with one voice
she proclaims them and teaches them and hands them
down, as though she had one mouth. For though the
languages of the world are various, yet the vital force of
the tradition is ever the same. The churches planted in
Germany have neither believed nor handed down other
doctrine; nor have those planted in Spain or in Gaul or in
the East or in Egypt or in Libya or in the central parts of
the world. But just as the sun, the creature of God, is
one and the same in all the world, so the preaching of the
truth appears everywhere, and lightens all men who wish
to come to the knowledge of the truth. And neither does
he who is mightiest in speech among the rulers in the
churches pronounce other doctrines than these (for no one
is above the Master); nor does he who is feeble in speech
belittle the tradition. For since the faith is one and the
same, neither does he magnify it who is able to discourse
much concerning it, nor does he who can say but little
make it any the less" (I. 10. 2).

Such then is the faith in the church. The universal
church has, as it were, a single soul, a single organic life, and
so speaks everywhere with a single voice. Everywhere its
teaching is that one faith, which it has to guard and to
hand on unimpaired. The local churches may be inter-
rogated, and it will be found that this general statement,
in whatever part of the world it be tested, is universally
true. Languages may vary, but though the medium
changes the faith itself is constant. Spain and Gaul in
the west, Germany in the north, Africa in the south, Asia

in the east and Italy in the centre will be found, each in their several languages, to teach the one unchanging faith.

We have seen that the teaching of the church everywhere conforms to a certain standard, the "regula veritatis" (ὁ κανὼν τῆς ἀληθείας, I. 9. 4; I. 22. 1). We have now to examine more closely the relation of the Scriptures to this rule of faith.

In the church the Scriptures and the apostolic tradition stand side by side. The apostolic tradition supplies a standard for the interpretation of the Scriptures. Irenæus says of the Gnostics that both alike are rejected by them. "It has come about that they agree neither to the Scriptures nor yet to the tradition" (III. 2. 2). The Gnostics did indeed claim to be possessors of a tradition of esoteric truth. They held that a knowledge of this esoteric tradition was necessary for the true understanding of the Scriptures (III. 2. 1). Thus they interpret Scripture in a mystical and allegorical sense, rejecting the plain meaning of the words. To the parables in particular they delighted to give their own private interpretations. The result of such methods must necessarily be chaotic. "In consequence of this no one will possess the rule of truth; but the number of those who interpret the parables will be equalled by the number of systems of truth which will appear, in mutual opposition to each other and setting forth antagonistic doctrines, like the questions current among the Gentile philosophers" (II. 27. 1). The Scriptures therefore are to be interpreted by the rule of the apostolic tradition. But this rule differs essentially from the canons of interpretation arbitrarily set up by the Gnostics. For it is in accordance with the plain meaning of the Scriptures. "The entire Scriptures, both the Prophets and the Gospels, can be understood by all openly and without ambiguity and with a single meaning" (II. 27. 2). Those portions of the Scriptures which, like the parables, " admit of many interpretations " (II. 27. 3) are to be interpreted by the same standard. Or, again, there is the difficulty occasioned by the Old Testament. Unless the true method of interpretation of the Old Testament be understood, it will seem to be contradictory to the New. Marcion was led to regard it as the work of a different God from the God of the New Testament. The Old Testament must be read in the light of the New and regarded as designed to lead up to the New. " Then shall every word seem consistent, if one diligently read the Scriptures in company with those who are presbyters in the church, among whom is the apostolic doctrine, as we have proved " (IV. 32. 1). The Scriptures must be read as interpreted by the church, in which is handed down the apostolic tradition. The presbyters are the recognised mouthpiece of the church in voicing this tradition.

SECTION III.

IRENÆUS (*continued*).

Sacerdotal character of the church, illustrated by (1) the Eucharist, (2) the oblations.—The glorified Lord as High-priest in the church.—The ministry of the church.—The apostolic succession.—Its historic character.—Its importance as guaranteeing purity of doctrine.—And as witnessing to the continuity of the church.—A matter of principle, not merely of utility.—The gifts of grace associated with it.—Hence the external organisation of the church is a matter of fundamental importance.—Orders in the ministry : (1) bishops, (2) presbyters, (3) deacons.—Ministerial authority.—The local churches in Rome and in Jerusalem.

Irenæus ascribes to the church a sacerdotal character, transferring to the Christian dispensation the sacerdotal terms which are used in the Old Testament of Judaism. The Lord Himself is compared to the Jewish high-priest, whose offices it is said that He performs (IV. 8. 2). So too a sacerdotal character is attached to the Apostles. "All the Apostles of the Lord are priests. They inherit neither fields nor houses, but ever serve the altar and God" (IV. 8. 3). Theirs is "a Levite's portion" (*ibid.*). They occupy in the Christian dispensation a position analogous to that held by the priests and Levites under the Mosaic law.

The church is a sacerdotal body, offering sacrifice to God and, through sacrifice, winning access to God's presence. There rests upon Christians the general obligation to offer sacrifice. They should offer many sacrifices to God out of gratitude for His many benefits. All gifts made to God with pure hearts are of the nature of sacrifice, as for instance the gift of the Philippians conveyed to St Paul by Epaphroditus. "Inasmuch as the

church makes its offering with singleness of heart, its gift
is justly reckoned a pure sacrifice with God. As also
Paul says to the Philippians, 'I am filled, having received
from Epaphroditus the things that came from you, an
odour of a sweet smell, a sacrifice acceptable, well-pleasing
to God[1].' For it is our duty to make oblation to God,
with pure mind and in faith unfeigned, in firm hope, in
fervent love, offering the firstfruits of those things which
are His creatures " (IV. 18. 4).

But foremost among all such offerings stands the
Eucharist, which derives its meaning and its power from
its institution by Christ Himself. " Giving directions to
His disciples to offer to God the firstfruits of His creatures,
not as though He needed anything, but that they themselves might be neither unfruitful nor ungrateful, He took
bread, which is a created substance, and gave thanks,
saying, 'This is My body.' And the cup likewise, which
belongs to that creation, which is of our nature, He
confessed was His blood, and taught that it was the new
oblation of the New Testament; and this the church,
having received it from the Apostles, offers in all the
world to God, to Him who affords to us as our sustenance
the firstfruits of His own gifts in the New Testament,
concerning which Malachi among the twelve prophets
thus spoke beforehand: 'I have no pleasure in you, saith
the Lord Almighty, neither will I accept a sacrifice at
your hands. For from the rising of the sun even unto
the going down of the same My name is glorified among
the Gentiles; and in every place incense is offered unto
My name and a pure offering: for My name is great among
the Gentiles, saith the Lord Almighty[2].' "

Thus the Eucharist is the central offering of the

¹ Phil. iv. 18.   ² Mal. i. 10 f.

church.   The sacrifice is not here thought of as consisting
of the offerers themselves, but of the gifts.   The gifts are
spoken of as the body and blood of Christ.   Irenæus therefore clearly contemplates, in some sense, an offering of the
body and blood of Christ in the Eucharist.

The thought of this oblation is further emphasised.
" The oblation of the church, which the Lord taught to be
offered in the whole world, is accounted with God a pure
sacrifice, and is accepted by Him : not because He needs
a sacrifice from us, but because he who offers is himself
honoured in that which he offers, if his gift be accepted.
For through his gift both honour and love are shown
towards the King : and the Lord, wishing us to offer it in
all simplicity and innocence, preached, saying, ' When therefore thou offerest thy gift at the altar and rememberest
that thy brother hath aught against thee, leave thy gift
before the altar, and first go thy way to be reconciled to
thy brother, and then come back and offer thy gift.'   We
ought therefore to offer to God the firstfruits of His
creation, as also Moses said : ' Thou shalt not appear before
the Lord thy God empty ' ;   so that in the things in
which a man proves his gratitude, in those he is accounted
to be grateful, and receives that honour which comes from
God " (IV. 18. 1).

The Eucharist then is a sacrifice, which is offered by
the church.   Irenæus does not make any mention, in this
connection, of the Christian ministry.   The church itself
is the sacerdotal body that offers the sacrifice and its
action is described in terms of our Lord's precept in the
Sermon on the Mount.   No doubt these words, of leaving
the gift at the altar, have reference, in their original
context, to the ceremonial of Jewish worship.   But
Irenæus transfers them to the worship of the Christian

church, to which he ascribes altar, priesthood and sacrifice. It does not however appear certain that Irenæus would give the name "altar" to the *mensa* upon which the Eucharist is celebrated on earth. It may be contended that he reserves the name to the spiritual altar in heaven. "He wishes us to offer our gift at the altar frequently and without intermission. The altar then is in heaven, for thither our prayers and our oblations are directed; and the temple is there, as John saith in the Apocalypse, 'And the temple of God was opened'; and the tabernacle is there, 'For behold,' he saith, 'the tabernacle of God, in which He will dwell with men'" (IV. 18. 6).

The church then offers to God its gifts of firstfruits, in return for innumerable benefits; it offers, as its central sacrifice, the Eucharist, where the oblation is the body and blood of the Lord. It may be noticed that in this connection the incense of the prophecy of Malachi is interpreted metaphorically. While the "pure offering" of the prophecy is declared to have its fulfilment in the Eucharist, the incense is said to symbolise prayer. "In every place incense is offered unto me and a pure sacrifice. But the incense, saith John in the Apocalypse, means 'the prayers of the saints'" (IV. 17. 6).

The pure oblation of the Eucharist is offered only by the church; not by the Jews, whose rejection of the Logos makes it impossible that they should offer it; nor by the heretics, whose misbelief precludes them from such a service. "The church alone offers this pure oblation to the Creator, offering to Him of His creation with giving of thanks. But the Jews do not offer it, for their hands are full of blood: for they have not received the Word, through whom it is offered to God. Nor again do any of the synagogues of heretics offer it. For some, who maintain that the creator is other than the Father, do, when they offer to Him what belongs to this creation of ours, set Him forth as covetous of what is not His own" (IV. 18. 4). We may note that the obstacle, in the way of heretical bodies offering the Eucharist, is not connected by Irenæus with the ministry, but arises from their heretical doctrine. The Marcionites, for instance, who ascribe the work of creation to another than the Father, cannot consistently with their belief offer the Eucharist to the Father. For the elements in the Eucharist must on such a supposition be alien from Him. In the same way Irenæus shows that Gnosticism is inconsistent with the offering of the Eucharist.

So far from oblations having ceased in the Christian church, there is a greater place for them even than there was in the Jewish church. For Christians owe a greater debt of gratitude to God, as having received the blessings of freedom. "The class of oblations in general has not been set aside; for there were oblations there [*i.e.* under the Jewish dispensation], and there are oblations here [*i.e.* under the Christian dispensation]: there were sacrifices among the people [*i.e.* the Jews], and there are sacrifices in the church : but the species certainly has been changed, inasmuch as the offering now is made, not by slaves, but by freemen. For the Lord is one and the same ; but there is a distinctive character in a slave's oblation, and a distinctive character in that of freemen, so that through the oblations an index of freedom is given" (IV. 18. 2). The Eucharistic oblations of the Christian church correspond in character to that liberty which marks the dispensation of the Gospel. In this they stand in contrast to the Jewish sacrifices, which were a badge of servitude.

The church then has a sacerdotal character, which

D.   16

however is to be viewed in close connection with the priesthood of the glorified Lord. In the opening vision of the Apocalypse, in which the glorified figure appears in the midst of the golden candlesticks, St John is said to " behold the sacerdotal and glorious coming of His kingdom " (IV. 20. 11). The coming of Christ's kingdom means the acknowledgment of His rule. Its sacerdotal and glorious character is expressed by the features of the vision. The majesty of the Lord's appearance indicates His glory : the long garment down to the feet is a symbol of His priesthood (*ibid.*). We have seen that elsewhere Irenæus regards the seven-branched candlestick as figuring the church, " which carries the light of Christ " (v. 20. 1). Doubtless the thought is the same in the passage under discussion. The glorified Lord is seen in the midst of the golden candlesticks : He stands in the midst of His church as its great High-priest.

Irenæus is a witness to the importance attached by the church to episcopal government. He is in a position to give, if required, the list of episcopal successions in many of the churches. In fact he implies that such successions could be enumerated in the case of all the churches. " It is possible for all who wish to see the truth to contemplate in every church the tradition of the Apostles, manifested in the whole world, and we are in a position to enumerate those who by the Apostles were appointed bishops in the churches, and their successors even to our own time " (III. 3. 1). Thus all the churches, according to the evidence of Irenæus, were episcopally governed and attached so much importance to the episcopate, that they had kept the lists of all who had held the office of bishop in succession.

The institution of monarchical episcopacy is ascribed

to the action of the Apostles. Polycarp is said to have been "appointed by Apostles as bishop of the church in Smyrna" (III. 3. 4). Or, again, we read of "the bishops to whom the Apostles committed the churches." We need however the caution that Irenæus is apt to read into the apostolic writings the ideas of his own day. Thus the company who came to meet St Paul on his last journey to Jerusalem are spoken of as "the bishops and presbyters who came from Ephesus and from the other adjoining cities" (III. 14. 2). Now both the terms ἐπίσκοποι and πρεσβύτεροι occur in the narrative of the Acts. "From Miletus he sent to Ephesus and called to him the πρεσβύ-τεροι of the church" (Acts xx. 17). "Take heed unto yourselves and to all the flock, in the which the Holy Ghost hath made you ἐπίσκοποι" (Acts xx. 28). Here clearly the two terms refer to the same set of men. They were the men set over the local church at Ephesus. But Irenæus takes the terms in the sense which they had come to bear in his own day, as titles of two orders in the ministry. Further, he takes it for granted that the episcopacy of St Paul's day must have been monarchical, and he therefore gets over the difficulty of the plural ἐπίσκοποι by supposing that the bishops had come in from the adjacent cities as well as from Ephesus. Irenæus therefore, though an excellent witness to the beliefs and practices of his own day, is not always to be relied on as an interpreter of the past.

The fact, to which he bears unimpeachable witness, is that great importance was attached in his day to the episcopal successions in all the local churches. One reason for attaching this importance was that an unbroken succession provided a guarantee of purity of doctrine. For by its means the apostolic tradition was handed down

16—2

from one bishop to another in the church. The continuous line of bishops was a witness to the continuity of the life of the church. This stands in contrast with the new departures made by the heretics. A heretic, coming with his novel doctrine, is set in contrast with the bishop, who is ruling the local church at the time. So the visit of the Gnostic heretic Marcellina to Rome is dated by the episcopate of Anicetus (I. 25. 6). The visit to Rome of Cerdo, the follower of Simon Magus, is said to have taken place while Hyginus was bishop, "who held the ninth place in the episcopal succession from the Apostles" (I. 27. 1). No doubt the episcopal succession provided a convenient mode of dating. But to say this, does not give sufficient reason for its employment for this purpose. It is doubtless intended to have the significance already indicated, namely to be a reminder of the continuity of the teaching of the church, as witnessed to by the succession of bishops. We can count up the succession of bishops in each local church ; we can satisfy ourselves that there has been no break in the line ; and hence that there has been no break in the transmission of the truth.

It is not however a sufficient account of the meaning of apostolic succession as taught by Irenæus to say that it is simply of value as guaranteeing the transmission of the apostolic tradition. Apostolic succession has a value of its own, apart from this secondary attendant circumstance. Those who depart from the primitive succession are to be treated with suspicion as being heretics, schismatics or hypocrites. They have fallen from the truth. This shows that in the apostolic succession of bishops is involved a question, not merely of convenience or advantage, but of principle. " We ought to obey those presbyters who are

in the church, those who have the succession from the
Apostles, as I have shown ; who together with the succession in the episcopate have received the sure gift of
truth according to the good pleasure of the Father : but
those who hold aloof from the primitive succession, and
assemble together in any place whatsoever, we ought to
hold in suspicion, either as being heretics and of evil mind,
or as schismatics, puffed up and self-pleasing, or again as
hypocrites, acting thus for the sake of lucre and of vainglory " (IV. 26. 2).

The divine *charismata* are definitely associated with the
apostolic succession.   " Where the gifts of the Lord have
been placed, there we ought to learn the truth, from those
I mean with whom is the succession from the Apostles "
(IV. 26. 5).   It is to be noticed that the particular *charismata* here spoken of are the ministerial gifts, the endowments of Apostles, prophets and teachers, whom " God has
placed in the church " (*ibid.*).

Irenæus makes the external organisation of the church
a matter of fundamental importance.   Let us notice a
paraphrase of the creed in the church.   " The path of
those who belong to the church goes round the whole
world, in that it has the sure tradition from the Apostles
and enables us to see that the faith of all is one and the
same, since all receive one and the same God the Father,
and believe the same dispensation of the Incarnation of
the Son of God, and know the same bestowal of the Spirit,
and think upon the same precepts and guard the same
external organisation as regards the church, and look for
the same coming of the Lord and await the same salvation
of the entire man, that is soul and body " (v. 20. 1).   Now
this seems quite clearly to be in part a summary, in part
a paraphrase of the old Roman Creed.   It will be noticed

that the clause of the old Roman Creed, "I believe in the
holy church," is paraphrased as referring to the external
organisation of the church[1]. Everywhere the church is
organised in the same way, and this organisation is
thought of as part of the faith. We can hardly be wrong
if we interpret this as referring to the apostolic succession
of bishops.

Another passage corroborates this interpretation.
" True knowledge consists in the teaching of the Apostles
and the ancient constitution of the church in all the world
(τὸ ἀρχαῖον τῆς ἐκκλησίας σύστημα κατὰ παντὸς τοῦ
κόσμου), and the external organisation (χαρακτήρ) of the
body of Christ according to the succession of bishops, to
whom they [i.e. the Apostles] committed the church, which
is in every place " (IV. 33. 8). The constitution then and
the external organisation of the church are of its essence.
For together with the apostolic teaching they form part of
the true Gnosis. This external organisation is characterised
by the fact of episcopal succession from the time of the
Apostles. The position of the words κατὰ παντὸς τοῦ
κόσμου, quoted above, shows that they are to be taken with
σύστημα rather than with τῆς ἐκκλησίας. The thought
is not of the universal spread of the church, but of the
universal existence of episcopal organisation wherever the
church is found. Nowhere is the church organised on any
other system. Nowhere does " the body of Christ " in the
world exhibit any other χαρακτήρ. But everywhere it
has its apostolic succession of bishops. And this moreover
is of necessity.

The question arises how far the doctrine of the church
in Irenæus reproduces that of the apostolic age. Irenæus
is not conscious of anything new in his doctrine. Indeed

[1] Figuram ejus, quæ est erga ecclesiam, ordinationis custodientibus.

it is a fundamental principle with him that there should be nothing new. He is not like a brilliant Alexandrian, forming theories and elaborating a philosophy. He is a simple-minded man, appealing continually to the past, to the teaching of the Apostles, to the words of the elders. True, he is not always to be relied on in his interpretation of the past. But none the less it is inconceivable that the doctrine of apostolic succession, as the necessary constitution of the church, can have been new in the time of Irenæus. The belief in it must go back well behind his own generation. His witness shows that it was very widely, not merely locally, held at the close of the second century, and this fact must set it back to very early times.

We have now to consider separately the several grades in the Christian ministry. We have seen how deeply imbued Irenæus is with the idea of episcopacy. By the side of this, we have the somewhat curious fact that he uses the term "presbyter" in speaking of bishops. In his letter to Victor, he writes, " The presbyters before Soter, who presided over the church which you now govern, I mean Anicetus and Pius and Hyginus and Telesphorus and Sixtus, neither observed these customs themselves nor permitted those who were with them to do so " (*ad Vict.*, Euseb. *H.E.* v. 24). Now having regard to the uncompromising language used by Irenæus on the subject of episcopal succession, it seems impossible to suppose that he regards the terms " bishop " and " presbyter " as interchangeable [1]. We cannot imagine that he would call a mere " presbyter " a " bishop." But on the other hand he might speak of a bishop as a presbyter, inasmuch as the greater includes the less. And there is a reason here for

[1] Such however is the view of Bp Wordsworth. *Ministry of Grace*, p. 127, 2nd ed.

the use of this title. For it is doubtless used in reference
to the priority in time of the early bishops. They were
" elders " or seniors, as belonging to an earlier generation.
The point is that neither in recent times nor in earlier
times had the Quartodeciman custom been observed in
Rome.

This same passage from the letter to Victor illustrates
the kind of authority which the bishops exercised. They
had a disciplinary authority over the church which they
are said to " govern " and over which they " preside[1]."
They control its practices. They do not allow " those who
are with them," that is the members of their church, to
follow traditions of which they disapprove. Thus the
bishop claims obedience within the limits of his local
church.

There is little else in the writings of Irenæus that
throws light upon the distinctive work of the bishop. He
says indeed that he has himself " been given a place in
the administration of the word " (v. pref.), in virtue of
which he does his best to guard the faith against the
attacks of heretics. But this charge is not distinctive of
his episcopal office.

Of the position and work of the presbyters somewhat
more may be gathered. The presbyters constitute an
order (IV. 26. 4, presbyterii ordo), which must mean that
they form a definite body, authoritatively recognised.
They occupy the " chief seat " (IV. 26. 3, principalis con-
sessio) in the church, which shows that they are associated
with the bishop as his assessors in the government of the
church. They are therefore in a position of authority.
" We ought to obey those presbyters who are in the

---

[1] οἱ προστάντες τῆς ἐκκλησίας ἧς σὺ νῦν ἀφηγῇ.

church, those who, as I have shown, have the succession from the Apostles " (IV. 26. 2).

It is the office of the presbyters to teach. Believers are to " read the Scriptures in company with those who are presbyters in the church, among whom is the apostolic doctrine, as I have pointed out " (IV. 32. 1). To the church belongs the truth, the ancient tradition. This body of truth is committed to the presbyters, whose duty it is to teach. They require, not deep power of reasoning, but sound knowledge (*agnitio*). For it is not their function to invent or discover something new, but to hand on the tradition. " They, therefore, who forsake the preaching of the church call in question the knowledge of the holy presbyters, not considering of how much greater value is a religious person, even though he be unskilled, than is a blasphemous and shameless sophist. But such are all the heretics and those who think that they are discovering something beyond the truth " (v. 20. 2). Heresies arise from a misuse of the reason, an attempt to go beyond revelation. The church through its presbyters hands on the ancient faith. The necessary qualification of the presbyter then is that he should have the requisite knowledge to be able to teach the faith of the church. He does not need inventive genius. Nor is eloquence necessary for the presbyter, for the tradition, which forms the substance of his preaching, is independent of the personality of the preacher. " Neither will he who is mightiest in speech of the rulers in the churches preach other things than these (for no one is above the Master); nor will he who is weak in speech diminish aught of the tradition " (I. 10. 2).

Further, in addition to the ministry of teaching, the presbyters are charged with the administration of the

spiritual gifts of the church. "Such presbyters does the
church nourish......, of whom the Lord said, 'Who then will
be a faithful steward, good and wise, whom the Lord shall
set over His household, to give them their meat in due
season?'" (IV. 26. 5). It is impossible not to believe that
prominent in this stewardship lay the function of the
administration of the Eucharist.

Irenæus traces the origin of the diaconate to the
appointment of the Seven, as recorded in the Acts. He
speaks of "Nicolaus, one of the Seven who were the first
to be ordained to the diaconate by the Apostles" (I. 26. 3).
Stephen is described as "the first elected into the diaconate
by the Apostles" (IV. 15. 1) and again as "the first of the
deacons" (III. 12. 10). In this we no doubt have an
example of the tendency of Irenæus to read into the first
age the ideas of his own time. We do not find the term
διάκονος used as a title of office till we come to the
Pastoral Epistles.

It is not so used in the opening verse of the Epistle to
the Philippians, where it occurs as a generic description
of those whose office in the church is characterised by
service. But though the title is not given to the Seven
in the New Testament, their position in the economy of
the church at Jerusalem answered pretty much to that of
the order afterwards known as the diaconate. Their work
was διακονεῖν τραπέζαις. So Irenæus, by an anachronism
but with substantial accuracy, gives to Stephen the title
of deacon.

But his words contain a more important error. The
Seven were not, as he says, chosen by the Apostles. They
were chosen by "the whole multitude," that is the entire
local church. Now does this mistake on the part of
Irenæus reflect a departure from the primitive conception

of the authority of the church ?   Does it point to a growing hierarchical conception ?   In the New Testament it is
the entire church which is the authoritative body.   It is
the brethren, not the Eleven, who " put forward " the two
for the vacant Apostleship.   It is " the Apostles and the
elders with the whole church " who choose delegates to
carry the decrees from Jerusalem.   But here again
Irenæus speaks of the letter accompanying the decrees as
" the letter of the Apostles " (III. 12. 14), whereas the
narrative of the Acts represents it as the letter of the
Apostles and elder brethren, backed by the whole church
at Jerusalem.   It would be easy to draw too large an
inference from these expressions of Irenæus, which after
all are only incidental.   We have already seen how closely
he connects the authority of the presbyters with the
authority of the church.   They have no originating power :
they cannot go beyond the teaching committed to them.
And that teaching is the teaching of the church.

One word must be added as to the positions occupied
by the local churches in Rome and in Jerusalem.

In examining the witness of the local churches to the
continuity of the apostolic tradition, Irenæus notes that
there is one church whose witness, owing to its special
circumstances, is of peculiar value.   This is the local
church in Rome.   As the meaning of the words, which he
uses in regard to this church, is to some extent uncertain,
we shall do best to quote the passage, bearing in mind
however that the existing Latin is only a translation of the
lost Greek original.   " Ad hanc ecclesiam propter potentiorem principalitatem necesse est omnem convenire
ecclesiam, hoc est, eos qui sunt undique fideles, in qua
semper ab his, qui sunt undique, conservata est ea quæ
est ab apostolis traditio " (III. 3. 2).   Now the first question

in this passage is as to the meaning of "convenire ad." Does it mean " to resort to " or " to agree with " ? Of the second proposed interpretation no example is quoted by the lexicons, but it is perhaps a possible one. And having regard to the fact that we do not know the original Greek, it is necessary to take this interpretation into account as being possibly right. "With this church every church must needs agree." Note that the word used is not "oportet" ($\delta\epsilon\hat{\iota}$) but "necesse" ($\dot{a}\nu\acute{a}\gamma\kappa\eta$). It is an expression not of moral obligation, but of necessary and inevitable result. Why inevitable ? Now whatever may be doubtful in the interpretation of this passage, it seems at least clear that "eos qui sunt undique fideles" must refer to visitors to Rome, the faithful who come to Rome from every quarter. If Irenæus had meant merely the faithful who live in every quarter, we should have expected not "undique" but "ubique." These visitors, Irenæus implies, supply a corrective to local Roman tendencies. This continued intercourse between the local Roman and all other churches made inevitable the agreement between them.

But if we set aside this unauthorised interpretation of "convenire ad" and give the verb instead its ordinary meaning, we shall translate the passage as follows. " To this church, owing to special pre-eminence, every church must needs resort, the faithful, that is, who come from every quarter ; [a church] in which the apostolic tradition is ever preserved by those who come from every quarter." This continuous intercourse would prevent any departure from the apostolic tradition, for any such departure would be at once noted by some of the numerous visitors. There was therefore a special guarantee of the purity of the tradition as held by the church in Rome.

A further question of interpretation may be discussed. Does " propter potentiorem principalitatem " refer to the pre-eminence of the church or of the metropolis ? If we take " convenire ad " as meaning " to resort to," we must refer the pre-eminence to the metropolis. For the pre-eminence of the local church in Rome would not constitute an adequate reason for laying upon the faithful in all parts the necessity of a visit to it. But on the other hand Rome as the centre of empire drew visitors from all parts on business of every kind.

But undoubtedly the local church in Rome possessed in the time of Irenæus a special prestige. It had taken a leading part in the Quartodeciman controversy. It had made a request to Polycrates, bishop of the church in Ephesus, to summon the bishops of his district to a synod to consider the question (Polycrates, Euseb. *H.E.* v. 24). This request, it may be noted, came not from the bishop but from " Victor and the church of the Romans " (*ibid.*) acting conjointly. There is no indication that this request, coming from the Roman church, was deemed presumptuous. It was acknowledged that the church of the metropolis occupied a position of special importance, which entitled it to make a request on a matter affecting the welfare of the churches at large. It was only when Victor began to dictate to other churches that he was rebuked for assuming an authority that he did not possess. The earlier attitude of the Roman bishops is illustrated by the position of Anicetus with respect to Polycarp. He tried to persuade Polycarp to change his practice, but made no attempt to command his obedience. Though his persuasion proved ineffective, this was not allowed in any way to destroy the harmony of their intercourse.

But though a special prestige was attaching to the

church in the world's metropolis, yet it was not the local church in Rome, but the local church in Jerusalem, to which, according to Irenæus, the central and fundamental position in the church universal belonged. The words in which the Jerusalem church returned thanks to God for the delivery of Peter and John from the chief priests are quoted by Irenæus, with this comment: " This is the voice of that church from which every church had its origin ; this is the voice of the metropolis of the citizens of the new covenant ; this is the voice of the Apostles ; this is the voice of the disciples of the Lord " (III. 12. 5). In the utterance of the church in Jerusalem we are brought to the very fountain-head of apostolic tradition. The church in Jerusalem is the centre and focus of the church universal. True, the centre of secular authority was at Rome, and the church in Rome necessarily derived a special importance from the prestige attaching to the metropolis of the world. But the metropolis of spiritual primacy belonged not to Rome but to Jerusalem, to that church to which all other churches owed their being.

CHAPTER V.

THE CLOSE OF THE CENTURY.

SECTION I.

THE EPISTLE TO DIOGNETUS.

The life of the church a spiritual citizenship.

This singularly beautiful Apology for Christianity probably belongs to the close of the second century. It describes the life of the Christian church under the figure of citizenship. Christians discharge indeed the duties of citizenship towards the state in which they live, but an altogether higher citizenship is theirs. " They dwell in cities of Greeks and barbarians, as the lot of each is cast, and follow the native customs in dress and food and the other arrangements of life, yet the constitution of their own citizenship which they set forth is marvellous and confessedly contradicts expectation. They dwell in their own countries but only as sojourners; they bear their share in all things as citizens and they endure all hardships as strangers. Every foreign country is a fatherland to them, and every fatherland is foreign.......Their existence is on earth, but their citizenship is in heaven " (§ 5).

This metaphor of citizenship expresses the corporate character of the life of the church. Its members are not isolated individuals. Just as their membership of an earthly city lays upon them the duties of citizenship, so their membership of the church carries with it a spiritual citizenship, with its appropriate duties. The life of the church is a corporate life. The welfare of each is the concern of all.

SECTION II.

APPENDIX TO THE EPISTLE TO DIOGNETUS.

The one universal church.—All its endowments derived from Christ.—The church typified by Paradise.—The church and the apostolic tradition.—Public worship of the church.

The Epistle to Diognetus has attached to it, at its close, a fragment of an entirely independent work. This work is clearly Alexandrian in character, and should probably be dated at the close of the second century. Like the letter to which it is attached, it is anonymous, though the writer describes himself as "a disciple of Apostles" and "a teacher of the Gentiles."

His theme is the one church universal, that church which "is enriched" by the eternal Son and which exults with joy in that grace of God, "which confers understanding, which reveals mysteries, which announces seasons, which rejoices over the faithful, which is bestowed upon those who seek her, even those by whom the pledges of faith are not broken nor the boundaries of the fathers overstepped" (§ 11). Our writer has the full conception of the church as the glorious Christian society, founded on apostolic tradition, inspired by the indwelling Logos and so filled with grace and endowed with a spiritual life, which issues in triumphant joy.

All the spiritual power of the church comes, then, from Christ. It is He "through whom the church is enriched and grace is unfolded and multiplied among the saints" (§ 11). The effect of this divine connection of the church is broad and deep. "The fear of the law is sung and the grace of the prophets is recognised and the faith of the Gospels is established and the tradition of the Apostles is preserved and the joy of the church exults" (*ibid.*).

We find in this fragment an allegorical interpretation, which regards Paradise as representing the church. This interpretation was a favourite one. Among second century writers it is found in Papias, Justin Martyr and Pantænus[1], in addition to the present fragment. This allegorical interpretation implies a high conception of the spiritual character of the church and of the grace which it enshrines. "Ye shall know how much God bestoweth on those that love Him rightly, who become a Paradise of delight, a tree bearing all manner of fruits and flourishing, growing up in themselves and adorned with various fruits" (§ 12). So then he who belongs to the church is as a tree in the garden of God and is endowed with grace, which will enable him to bear the fruit of a holy life.

It is indeed the function of the church to teach. But its teaching must follow the old lines of apostolic tradition. It is noted as a characteristic of the church that "the tradition of the Apostles is preserved" (§ 11). The writer of the fragment insists that his own teaching is of this kind. "Mine are no strange discourses nor perverse questionings, but having been a disciple of Apostles I came

---

[1] *Vide* Routh, *Rel. Sacr.* vol. i. p. 15.

forward as a teacher of the Gentiles, ministering worthily
to them, as they present themselves disciples of the truth,
the lessons which have been handed down " (*ibid.*).   So
the teaching of the church consists of τὰ παραδοθέντα,
further defined as ἀποστόλων παράδοσις. It is because
the apostolic teaching has been handed down in the
church that the writer is able to call himself "a disciple
of Apostles." He does not claim to have himself heard
the living voice of Apostles. This would have been
impossible, for he belonged to a later generation. But
though he cannot have listened to the Apostles themselves,
yet, having been trained in the church, he had learnt the
apostolic tradition and so could call himself their disciple.
Then, further, being himself instructed in the apostolic
tradition, he claims to be qualified to act as teacher to
others.

Public worship has its place as a normal element in
the life of the church. " The passover of the Lord goes
forward and the congregations are gathered together "
(§ 12). The passover of the Lord can be nothing else than
the Eucharist, which therefore receives special mention as
the characteristic worship of the Christian church.

SECTION III.

THE MURATORIAN FRAGMENT.

The Catholic Church.—The local churches and the one universal church.—Unity of the church.—Unity in the local church.—Mode of designating the local church.—Discipline in the church.—Teaching of the church.—Monarchical episcopacy.—Public worship.

This archaic fragment on the Canon of the New Testament is of Roman origin, as may fairly be inferred from the way in which the episcopate of Pius at Rome is referred to. From the fact that this episcopate is spoken of as being quite recent, it used to be supposed that a date not later than A.D. 170 must be assigned to this document. But the allusion at the close to the Cataphrygians, or Montanists, shows that this early date is impossible. For the chronology of Montanism makes it improbable that the Montanists were regarded as heretics in the West much before the close of the second century. A work, therefore, which speaks of them in this way could hardly have been written at Rome earlier than this. On the other hand the episcopate of Pius could not have been spoken of as recent in the third century. The probable date of the Fragment is therefore in the last decade of the second century.

It supplies us with the earliest known use of the phrase " the Catholic Church " in the sense of " the true church," as opposed to heretical communities. In the first passage in which the phrase occurs (l. 61) it would not be necessary to understand it in this sense, if the passage stood alone. " To Philemon one [epistle], to Titus one and to Timothy two were put in writing from personal inclina-

tion and attachment, to be in honour however with the
Catholic Church for the ordering of the ecclesiastical mode
of life" (ll. 59—63). This sentence indeed requires no other
meaning to be given to the phrase than that of " the one
universal church," a sense in which the phrase ἡ καθολικὴ
ἐκκλησία has already occurred in Ignatius and in Polycarp.
The sentence would be sufficiently explained as meaning
that the letters addressed to certain individuals were not
intended for themselves alone, but for the edification of
the whole church.

But the phrase "catholica ecclesia" recurs in the
following sentence. And here the epithet must have the
technical sense of " true " or " orthodox," as distinguishing
the true church from the bodies of heretics. "There is
current also one [epistle] to the Laodicæans, another to the
Alexandrians,[both] forged in Paul's name to suit the heresy
of Marcion, and several others, which cannot be received
into the Catholic Church" (ll. 63—67). The Catholic
Church is the true church, as opposed, for instance, to the
Marcionites. Indeed the epithet is now so fixed in its
technical sense, as applied to the church, that the word
" ecclesia " can even be dispensed with, and " catholica,"
standing by itself, is written for " the Catholic Church."
" The Epistle of Jude no doubt, and the couple bearing
the name of John, are accepted in the Catholic [Church] "
(in catholica habentur, ll. 68 f.).

There is however not yet any such phrase occurring as
" the Catholic Church in Rome," or other city : as meaning
the true local church in a particular city, as opposed to the
heretical communities in the same place. We have already
seen that the phrase, " the Catholic Church which is in
Smyrna," in the *Martyrdom of Polycarp* (§ 16) is almost
certainly corrupt. "The Catholic Church " in the Mura-

torian Fragment is the one universal church, regarded in its aspect as the one true church. From this use it would be a single and easy step to use the phrase as meaning the local community, the local church, regarded as representing in its own locality the one true universal church. We should then get such a phrase as that which a scribe has introduced into the *Martyrdom of Polycarp*, " the Catholic Church which is in Smyrna."

The universal church is one. Each place indeed has its own local church, but these churches are not independent units. They go to form the one universal church. " The blessed Apostle Paul himself, following the order of his predecessor John, writes only by name to seven churches in the following order—to the Corinthians a first, to the Ephesians a second, to the Philippians a third, to the Colossians a fourth, to the Galatians a fifth, to the Thessalonians a sixth, to the Romans a seventh ; whereas, although for the sake of admonition there is a second to the Corinthians and to the Thessalonians, yet one church is recognised as being spread over the entire world" (ll. 47—57). Paul, that is, writes separately to different churches, but this fact of separate address is not to be taken as inconsistent with the unity of the church at large The church is one.

In each local church the principle of unity is to be observed. This principle is violated by heresies and schisms. So the Fragment says of St Paul's First Epistle to the Corinthians that " he wrote at some length first of all to the Corinthians, forbidding schisms and heresies " (ll. 42 f.). The healing of divisions in the local church of Corinth is regarded by the writer of the Fragment as the object with which St Paul wrote his letter.

We note a slight change of form in the description of

the local church, which is a subtle indication of a change in the way in which the local church was viewed in relation to the place in which it was situated. In the first days of Christianity the church was small and obscure, out of all relation to the great city in which it was planted. Numerically it was swamped by the vastly greater heathen population around it. So in the New Testament and in the Apostolic Fathers the local church is described by such phrases as " the church in Ephesus," " the church in Jerusalem." It was too small to have any possessory power over the city. It was simply placed in the city.

But in the Muratorian Fragment a mode of description is used for the first time which implies that the local church claims to stand in relation to the whole city. The Christian community at Rome is not simply " the church in Rome "; it is "the church of the city of Rome." It has grown in numbers and so has advanced its claim.

The church has a disciplinary authority. It lays down regulations for the ordering of the life of its members. This is described as " ordinatio ecclesiasticæ disciplinæ " (ll. 62 f.). It also exercises a discretionary power in the formation of the Canon. Certain books " cannot be received into the Catholic Church " (ll. 66 f.); others " are accepted in the Catholic Church " (l. 69). The question which determines the decision of the church is not whether a book is edifying, but whether it is apostolic. Thus " the *Shepherd*," says the Canonist, " was written quite lately in our times by Hermas, while his brother Pius, the bishop, was sitting in the chair of the church of the city of Rome ; and therefore it ought indeed to be read, but it cannot to the end of time be publicly read in church to the people, either among the prophets, who are complete in number, or among the Apostles " (ll. 73—80). The

Shepherd of Hermas, though regarded as edifying and therefore suited for private reading, cannot be received into the Canon, because it is not apostolic, being only of recent origin.

Here, then, we receive illustration of another fundamental fact. The teaching of the church is apostolic, based on the apostolic tradition. The church is therefore careful to sift the writings which claim apostolic sanction. There are current two letters " forged in Paul's name, to suit the heresy of Marcion, and several others, which cannot be received into the Catholic Church ; for it is not fitting that gall be mixed with honey " (ll. 64—67). The church can allow no corruption of the apostolic tradition.

The Fragment shows that monarchical episcopacy was certainly established at Rome by the middle of the second century. It speaks of "Pius, the bishop," as "sitting in the chair of the church of the city of Rome " (ll. 75 f.). The position so described is clearly that of monarchical bishop. So our writer uses the title " bishop " in its monarchical sense. But the word occurs again in the Fragment, for we are told that John was exhorted to write his Gospel by " his fellow-disciples and bishops " (l. 10). We must suppose that the Canonist uses the word "bishop" here in the same sense as that which it undoubtedly has below. It will follow, then, that he believed monarchical bishops to have existed in the time of St John. In other words, he regards the institution of episcopacy as apostolic.

Public worship is taken for granted. " In ecclesia " (ll. 73 and 78) means " in church," that is, in the assembly of the Christian community, gathered for the purpose of worship. An integral part of the service is the reading of the sacred writings.

SECTION IV.

THE CANONS OF HIPPOLYTUS.

The church : (1) its sacred character ; (2) its continuity.—Usages of the
term "the church " : the sacred building.—The church the normal
way of salvation.—But not exclusively so.—Baptism the entrance
into the church.—Its ritual : (1) Exorcism ; (2) Unction ; (3) Confirmation.—Unity of the church.—The charismata in the church.
—Authority of the church resident in the whole body.—Exercised
in respect of (1) teaching ; (2) discipline.

The so-called Canons of Hippolytus are the earliest
existing Church Order of the Roman church. They are
the result of working over an earlier book of Church
Order, now lost, which seems to have been of Palestinian
origin. They should probably be dated about the close of
the second century, as for the most part they show a very
archaic character, though certain passages must, if this
supposition be correct, be regarded as interpolations.

The church, in the view of the Canons of Hippolytus,
is a divine society, for it owes its being to God. It is
God who has "set up the borders of the church" (*C. H.*
III. 12). It is therefore " holy" (*C. H.* v. 41), as being a
sacred institution.

It is thought of as possessed of a continuity of
existence. The church known to the Canons is that
church which was founded by the Apostles and which
goes on from age to age. The Apostles "founded the
church to the honour and glory of the holy name " of
Jesus Christ (*C. H.* III. 13).

Not only is the term " the church " used of the sacred
society, as in the passages quoted above ; and as meaning
the assembly of the faithful, as, for instance, when it is

said that those who have lapsed into evil courses after
baptism are to be "expelled from the church" (*C. H.* xv.
79), or when a woman is bidden to "come to church"
soberly dressed (*C. H.* xvii. 81); but the term is also
used of the building dedicated to purposes of public
worship. And this use of the word has an important
place in the Canons. There must be no laughing or talk-
ing in the church "because it is the house of God. It is
not a place of conversation, but is a place of prayer with
fear. Let him who talks in the church be put out and
let him not be admitted to the mysteries" (*C. H.* xvii.
88—90). This shows that the building used for public
worship was regarded as possessing a special sanctity[1].

That the sacred society of the church is regarded as
the sphere within which men are to be brought to salvation appears from the ordination prayer spoken over a
deacon. The bishop prays that he may be endowed with
"a doctrine, whereby he may guide an abundant people in
the holy church to salvation" (*C. H.* v. 41). The holy
church, holy because of divine origin, is the way by which
salvation may be attained.

But though the church is thus thought of as the
normal way of salvation, cases are contemplated of salvation outside the church. Thus the Canons cite the case
of a slave who is converted to Christianity, but whose
heathen master does not wish him to be baptized. "Let
him be content, because he is a Christian. And if he
should die without having received the gift [*i.e.* of
Baptism], let him not be separated from the rest of the
flock" (*C. H.* x. 63). Although such a one has not been

---

[1] The same use of the word as applied to the building used for public
worship is found in the following passages : *C. H.* x. 60, 61 ; xxxii. 157,
159 ; xxxvi. 186 ; xxi. 217 ; xxvi. 226, 227, 230, 231 ; xxvii. 232, 245.

admitted into the church, he still belongs to "the flock," the people of Christ.

Baptism then is the rite of entrance into the church and, as such, is normally a necessity. The admitted exceptions to the general rule do but emphasise its importance. Another case is cited. "A catechumen, who is taken prisoner and led out to martyrdom and put to death before receiving Baptism, shall be buried with the rest of the martyrs; for he has been baptized with his own blood" (*C. H.* XIX. 101). This case, it will be noted, is not regarded as an exception to the rule requiring Baptism. The catechumen, dying as a martyr, is received into the fellowship of the faithful, not on the ground that though unbaptized his case is an exception, but on the ground that he has in fact been baptized. The shedding of his blood has been his Baptism.

The ritual of Baptism is carefully prescribed. "On the fifth day of the week let those who are to be baptized wash themselves with water and let them eat. But on the sixth day let them fast. A woman, however, who chances to be unclean, should not be baptized on that occasion, but should be put off to such time as she shall be clean. Then on the day of the sabbath let the bishop call together those who are to be baptized and let him admonish them to kneel with their faces turned towards the east and let him spread his hands over them in prayer, so that he may drive the evil spirits from all their members. But let them beware themselves lest these return to them by their own actions. Then after he has completed the exorcism, let him breathe in their faces and sign their breasts and foreheads, their ears and mouths. Then let them keep vigil all that night, occupied with sacred discourse and with prayers. Then about cockcrow let them stand near rippling water of the sea, pure and prepared and sanctified. Let those who reply for little infants divest them of their garments : but let those who are able to do so occupy themselves in private with this part of the preparation. Let all the women however have other females as companions to divest them of their clothes. Let the women put off their ornaments of gold and of other kinds, let them unloose the folds of their hair, lest there descend into the water of regeneration anything alien, coming from alien spirits. Then let the bishop pray over the oil of exorcism and let him hand it to a presbyter. Then let him pray over the oil of unction, that is the oil of thanksgiving, and let him hand that to another presbyter. Let the presbyter who holds in his hand the oil of exorcism stand on the left of the bishop ; and let him who holds the oil of unction stand on the bishop's right. He who is being baptized shall stand with his face towards the west, and shall say : ' I renounce thee, O Satan, with all thy pomp.' When he has said this, the presbyter shall anoint him with the oil of exorcism, over which he has prayed that every evil spirit may depart from him. Then he hands him to the presbyter, who is standing above the water, and this presbyter, filling a deacon's office, takes his right hand and turns his face towards the east in the water. Before he descends into the water, he stands facing the east above the water, and speaks thus, having first received the oil of exorcism : ' I believe and I bow myself in Thy presence and in the presence of all Thy majesty, O Father, Son and Holy Spirit.' Then he shall descend into the water and the presbyter shall place his hand upon his head and question him in these words : ' Dost thou believe in God the Father Almighty ? ' He who is to be baptized shall reply : ' I

believe.' Then he is immersed in the water the first time,
while the other releases the hand that had been placed
upon his head. The second time he shall question him in
the words following : ' Dost thou believe in Jesus Christ,
the Son of God, who was born of the Virgin Mary from
the Holy Spirit, [who came to save mankind[1],] who was
crucified [for us[1]] under Pontius Pilate, who died and rose
the third day from the dead, and ascended into heaven, and
sitteth at the right hand of the Father and shall come to
judge the quick and the dead?' He shall reply : 'I believe.'
And he is immersed the second time in the water. Then
he shall be asked the third time : 'Dost thou believe in the
Holy Spirit [the Paraclete, proceeding from the Father
and the Son[2]] ? ' He shall reply : ' I believe.' And he is
immersed the third time in the water. And on each
occasion the other says : ' I baptize thee in the name of the
Father and of the Son and of the Holy Spirit [who is
equal to them[3]].' When he ascends from the water, the
presbyter takes the chrism of thanksgiving and signs his
brow and mouth and breast with the sign of the cross and
anoints his whole body and his head and face, saying : ' I
anoint thee in the name of the Father and of the Son and
of the Holy Spirit.' Then he dries him with a towel and
leads him clothed into the church " (*C. H.* XIX. 106—135).

Baptism is followed by a laying on of hands by the
bishop. He gives thanks for the gifts that they have
received in Baptism. These gifts are specified as follows :
they are the new birth, the Holy Spirit, union with the
church, and remission of sins. " The bishop then lays his

---

[1] Probably representing later interpolations from the Constantinopolitan Creed.

[2] Clearly an interpolation dating after the addition of the Filioque
clause to the Constantinopolitan Creed.

[3] An interpolation subsequent to A.D. 381.

hand upon all who have been baptized, and prays in these words : 'We bless Thee, Almighty Lord God, because Thou hast made these worthy to be born again, and dost pour out upon them Thy Holy Spirit, so that now they have been united to the body of the church, never to be separated from it by unseemly actions. Give rather to them, to whom Thou hast granted remission of sins, the earnest also of Thy kingdom through our Lord Jesus Christ, through whom to Thee with the same Lord and with the Holy Spirit be glory for ever and ever. Amen.' Then he signs their brows with the sign of love and kisses them, saying : 'The Lord be with you.' And the baptized reply : 'And with thy spirit.' Thus he does severally to each of those who have been baptized. Then they pray, with all the people, who kiss them and rejoice in their happiness " (*C. H.* XIX. 136—141). It will be noted that each one separately receives the laying on of hands, together with the benedictory prayers. The ordinance is administered by the bishop, but the people take their part in it. For they join in by their prayers, and they give the kiss of welcome to the new brethren.

This kiss of welcome is an expression of the brotherhood of the church. This spirit of brotherhood is again illustrated by the kiss of peace in the ritual of Ordination. It is given by all the people after the prayer which accompanies the laying on of hands. " After this, let all turn to him (*i.e.* the newly made bishop) and kiss him in peace, because he deserves it " (*C. H.* III. 19). The brotherhood of the church is also recognised by the provisions made for almsgiving and care for the poor. At every Eucharist alms are to be given and these are to be distributed among the poor (*C. H.* XXXII. 160).

This brotherhood is the outcome of the unity which

marks the church. Its members are " held together in a
strict bond of union in the goodness of God" (*C. H.* I. 5).
This union then has a divine sanction.

The unity of the church naturally finds expression in
public worship, to which a special blessing is attached.
" For the Lord is present in the place where memorial is
made of His majesty, and the Spirit descends upon those
who are gathered together, and He pours out His grace
upon all " (*C. H.* XXV. 228).

It is felt not only within each local church, but as a
force binding the churches together. The local churches
have a common understanding with one another. Thus
in the case of a presbyter travelling from the church in
which he holds his commission, the " clerus " of the church
in which he wishes to settle is to obtain information
regarding him from the bishop of the church in which he
has worked (*C. H.* IX. 56).

Our Canons show that the χάρισμα of healing still
manifested itself in the church. One of the prayers for
the newly ordained bishop or presbyter was that he might
be endued with power " to heal all diseases " (*C. H.* III. 18).
And, further, the possession of this power of healing was
registered by the church by some sort of ordination.
" If anyone advances a request for ordination, saying, ' I
am endowed with a gift of healing,' let him not be
ordained before the claim is clearly established. First of
all enquiry must be made, whether the acts of healing,
performed by him, are really derived from God " (*C. H.*
VIII. 53, 54). It is not clear what exactly is meant by the
ordination here referred to. Does it simply mean admission
to an order of healers ? Or does it imply an ordination as
presbyter ? If the latter, it implies that the possession of
the gift of healing established a claim to ordination to the

presbyterate. There is however nothing in the context which makes it necessary to adopt this view.

The church possesses an authority, which is exercised both in the matter of teaching and of discipline. The entire society of the church is the authoritative body. This is illustrated by the mode of episcopal election. The power of electing their bishop rests with the whole local church, not with any official body. " Let the bishop be elected by the whole people " (*C. H.* ii. 7). And at the time of the ordination "let the people say, ' We elect him ' " (*C. H.* ii. 8). And then all the people are to join in the prayer for the bishop-elect (*C. H.* ii. 9).

The church claims obedience to its teaching. The heretics are cut off, because they do not accept the teaching of the church, which is invested with divine authority. The church however is not free to teach as it pleases: its teaching is based upon the Scriptures. It is said in reference to the heretics : " We cut them off from us, since they do not agree to the church, which is in God; nor are they with us, who are disciples of the Scriptures " (*C. H.* i. 5). The authority of the bishops is conditioned by the apostolic tradition. Their commands must be in accordance with the commands of the Apostles. This apostolic tradition must be handed on in the church unchanged. " Our brother bishops have in their own cities made each his own arrangements in accordance with the commands of the Apostles......Let our posterity beware lest they change these things " (*C. H.* xxix. 252, 253).

The disciplinary authority of the church is exercised in various ways.

It is illustrated by the treatment of catechumens. Before being admitted to Baptism, they must be present in church, in order that they may be carefully examined as to their motives and that their genuineness may be tested. If this proves satisfactory, they are handed over to a deacon for instruction. After submitting to this course of discipline they may be admitted to Baptism. " Let those who frequent the church with the intention of being received among the Christians be examined with all diligence and the reason asked why they repudiate their religion, lest perchance they are coming for the sake of mockery. But if indeed anyone comes in good faith, let him be received with joy and let him be asked concerning his trade, and let him be instructed at the hands of a deacon and let him learn in the church to renounce Satan and all his pomp. Let him keep to this during the whole time of his instruction, before he is numbered with the rest of the people " (*C. H.* x. 60—62). So then the catechumens were subjected to a strict discipline before being admitted to Baptism.

And in some cases admission to the catechumenate itself had to be preceded by a course of discipline. Those who were engaged in unlawful or worldly occupations must first of all give them up. Then, after a period of forty days, they might be admitted to " sacred discourses," by which is meant the deacon's instructions. Each of the two steps, admission to the catechumenate and admission to Baptism, could only be taken under the sanction of a " doctor of the church." " Whoever becomes an actor or a gladiator or a racer or teaches pleasures or is a hunter or fights with beasts or is a priest of idols— none of these are admitted to sacred instructions unless they are first purified from their unclean works. After forty days they become partakers of the instruction. If they are worthy, they are also admitted to Baptism. But let a doctor of the church decide on these points " (*C. H.*

XII. 67, 68). The catechumenate shall not last any fixed time, but when the doctor of the church pronounces the candidates ready, then let them be admitted to Baptism. " Let not a catechumen, who is worthy of the light, be held back by reason of the time ; but let a doctor of the church decide on this point. But when the doctor has finished his daily task of teaching, then let those who have been kept separate from the Christians join in the prayers " (*C. H.* XVII. 91, 92).

The catechumens are to be separated from the baptized at the Agapé. " Let no catechumen sit with them at the Lord's Agapé " (*C. H.* XXXIII. 172). And yet the fact that the catechumens are in a degree linked on to the church is to receive recognition. For after the celebration of the Eucharist the " bread of exorcism " is to be sent to 'them after being distributed among the communicants. " The bishop shall see that the bread purified by prayer is sent to the catechumens, so that they may be associated with the church " (*C. H.* XX. 171).

Discipline again is exercised in the case of presbyters arriving from another church. The " clerus " of the church to which he has come has to make due enquiries concerning him, before receiving him into its body and allowing him to exercise his ministry (*C. H.* IX. 56). We may assume that the " clerus," the body exercising this precautionary discipline, is the college of presbyters, with the bishop at their head.

The church has power to cut off heretics from its body. " We separate them, because they do not agree to the church, which is in God, neither are they with us, who are disciples of the Scriptures. And therefore have we separated them from the church " (*C. H.* I. 5). Thus the disciplinary authority of the church is exercised in

D. 18

cutting off heretics from its society. The church claims a judicial authority. "We, who shall judge the world in righteousness" (*ibid.*), may exercise this power.

The discipline of the church may take the form of excommunication in the case of other offences. Certain offences committed after baptism are to be visited in this way. Let one who is guilty of such offences "be excommunicated until he shows penitence" (*C. H.* XI. 66). "One who occupies a high place in civil authority, but who does not show justice, is to be removed from the flock" (*C. H.* XIII. 73). A long catalogue of sins is then given, and it is said of those who commit these sins after baptism: "Let them be expelled from the church" (*C. H.* XV. 76—79).

The discipline of the Canons of Hippolytus in regard to the separation and purification of women is curiously Levitical and may be said to indicate a Syrian or Palestinian origin for the older book of Church Order, upon which the Canons are based. "Let women after childbirth not participate in the Mysteries before they are purified. Let the time of their purification be as follows: if the child is of the male sex, twenty days; if of the female sex, forty days. Let them [*i.e.* the church authorities] not invite a woman after childbirth, but let them pray to God for the child which she has brought forth. But if, before her purification, she desires to frequent the house of God, let her pray with the catechumens, who have not yet been received or have not been counted worthy and who are mingled together with the throng" (*C. H.* XVII. 93—96). It may be noted that the periods of uncleanness mentioned here are half the corresponding periods enjoined by the Mosaic Law (Lev. xii).

The church lays down rules in regard to fasting. We

read of " the days of fasting, which have been appointed by the Canons, namely the fourth day and the sixth " (*C. H.* xx. 154). Here then we have the Wednesday and Friday fasts set down as of canonical authority. " He who adds other fasts to these acquires merit. He who resists this, without the excuse of sickness or accident or necessity, is living outside the rule and resists God " (*C. H.* xx. 155, 156). Regulations are laid down respecting the fasting of certain classes. " Widows and virgins " are to fast often (*C. H.* xx. 157). The clergy may appoint for themselves special days for fasting. The bishop however is not to bind himself to an additional fast unless the whole church[1] is fasting at the same time (*C. H.* xx. 158).

The discipline of fasting is also exercised in respect to the Passover. The week preceding the Passover must be spent in fasting. " The week in which the Jews keep the Passover should be observed by all the people with the utmost care, and they should especially see to it that on those days of the fast they abstain from every object of desire, so that in all their conversation they may speak not with cheerfulness, but with sorrow " (*C. H.* xxii. 195). Here again we have a clear indication of Jewish influence upon the original book of Church Order, upon which the Canons are based.

Fasting is also spoken of in connection with the Eucharist. " Let not any of the faithful partake of any food, unless he shall first have partaken of the Mysteries, especially on the days of the sacred fast " (*C. H.* xxii. 205). The Christian's day must normally begin with the

[1] The existing text of the Canons reads here the equivalent of " clerus." But Achelis, following the parallel passage in the Egyptian Church Order, corrects this into " populus" (λαικός), which will mean the whole local church. We have adopted the correction.

Eucharist. After that he is free to partake of his food. This injunction to begin the day with the Eucharist is of special force on "the days of the sacred fast." This may mean either the preparation for the Passover or the weekly fasts on Wednesdays and Fridays.

The public worship of the church is subject to disciplinary regulation. There is to be daily service in church in the early morning, and the clergy who fail to attend, unless reasonably hindered, are to be excommunicated. "Let the presbyters, deacons and readers and all the people be gathered together daily in church at cockcrow, and let them find leisure for prayer, for psalms and for reading of the Scriptures with prayers according to the command of the Apostle : 'Till I come give heed to reading.' But as regards the clergy who neglect to come, being hindered neither by sickness nor travel, let them be excommunicated" (*C. H.* XXI. 217, 218). Further directions are given for public worship at daybreak. " At the time of cockcrow prayers are to be held in the churches, because the Lord saith : ' Watch, for ye know not in what hour the Son of Man will come, whether at cockcrow or in the morning'". (*C. H.* XXVII. 245).

But the church also lays down stated hours of prayer for private devotions. The early morning, the third, sixth and ninth hours and the hour of sunset should all be marked by prayer (*C. H.* XXVII. 232, XXV. 233—236).

It will thus be noted that under the Canons of Hippolytus the church exercises a wide and varied disciplinary authority.

SECTION V.

THE CANONS OF HIPPOLYTUS (*continued*).

The Christian ministry : (1) Its authoritative character. (2) Ordination.
(3) Spiritual ordination. (4) Apostolic succession. (5) Sacerdotal
character of the ministry. (6) Ministry of the Laity.—Orders in the
ministry.—The bishop : (1) His election. (2) His sacred authority.
(3) His powers. (4) His position. (5) The sphere of his authority.
(6) His work.—The presbyters: (1) Their ordination. (2) Their
status. (3) Their work.—The deacons : (1) Their ordination.
(2) Their work.—The readers.—The widows and virgins.

The authoritative character of the Christian ministry
is shown by the appropriation to it of the term " clerus "
(κλῆρος). The Canons of Hippolytus seem to provide the
earliest instance of the use of the term in this sense (*C. H.*
IX. 56 ; XXVIII. 206 ; XXI. 218, 219). Of the examples
given by Lightfoot of this use of the word as meaning
the " clergy," none are earlier than Tertullian[1]. The
term implies that a privileged office was held by the
Christian minister.

Admission to the office of bishop, priest or deacon is
granted by means of a ceremony of ordination. The
outward sign of this admission is the laying on of hands
(*C. H.* II. 10) by a bishop (*C. H.* IV. 32). The ritual of
the ordination is described. In the case of the bishop
it is given in full. There is first the election by the
people ; then public proclamation is made of the bishop-
elect, followed by a space for silent prayer. Then comes
the laying on of hands, with a prayer that the new bishop
may be endued with the powers necessary for the fulfilment of his office. The kiss of peace is given and then

[1] *Philippians*, exc. on Christian Ministry, p. 247.

follows the Eucharist (*C. H.* II. 7; III. 29). The ordination of a presbyter is similar to that of a bishop, with alterations rendered necessary by the difference of office (*C. H.* IV. 30, 31).

There is a special case in which this outward ceremony of ordination may be dispensed with. If a man is brought before a heathen tribunal on account of the faith and suffers torture for it, this wins him a place in the presbyterate. He does not need episcopal laying on of hands. His confession constitutes ordination. If however he is to become a bishop, he must then be ordained. If, again, he makes confession of his faith before the tribunal and yet does not suffer punishment, he has earned the presbyterate, but in this case he requires the outward ceremony of ordination. The same holds good of the sufferings of a slave for the faith at the hands of a heathen master. Though the form of ordination has been wanting, a spiritual ordination has been obtained. When therefore the bishop completes the rite, he must omit from his prayer that part which refers to the Holy Spirit. "When one has been found worthy to stand at the tribunal for the faith and to receive punishment for Christ, but afterwards is pardoned and set free, such a one deserves the rank of presbyter in the sight of God, not in the way of episcopal ordination. On the contrary, confession stands for ordination. But if, indeed, he becomes a bishop, then let him be ordained. If a man has made confession, but has not suffered torture, he is worthy of the presbyterate; but yet let him receive ordination at the hands of the bishop. If such a one, being a slave, has endured suffering for Christ, he is like a presbyter to the flock. For although he has not received the form of the presbyterate, he has nevertheless become possessed of the spirit of the presbyterate; let the bishop therefore omit that part of the prayer which has reference to the Holy Spirit" (*C. H.* VI. 43—47).

The passages on spiritual ordination have their counterpart in the parallel passages both of the Egyptian Church Order and of the Apostolic Constitutions, and must therefore belong to the earlier lost Church Order, which underlies these writings. We have then to consider what light they throw upon the way in which ordination was regarded at the close of the second century.

They seem to exclude the idea that, in the view of the compiler of the Canons, the validity of orders depends essentially upon a mechanical succession in the laying on of hands. The fact that ordination to the presbyterate may be in certain circumstances independent of such a succession shows that the essential ground of the validity of orders, though normally it may be closely connected with this succession, is yet not to be identified with it.

The fact of such a succession of bishops remains unaffected by what is said in the Canons as to spiritual ordination. For it is expressly stated that this privilege does not extend to the bishop's office. He who receives the office of a bishop must in any case be ordained by the laying on of hands by a bishop. There will therefore, so far as the Canons are concerned, be an unbroken line of bishops, each ordained by laying on of hands by a predecessor in the bishop's office. But the Canons nowhere suggest the idea that a bishop's authority to commit to another an office in the ministry is derived from the mechanical succession which thus connects him with the Apostles.

Rather it would seem that the fundamental fact is the continuity of the church. The church possesses continuous life from the days of the Apostles. The successions of bishops, as Irenæus saw, are witnesses to this continuity. Its ministers are on the one hand the chosen representatives of this continuously living church, but on the other hand they hold their office from God. "Grant to him, Lord, the office of a bishop" (*C. H.* iii. 17) are the words of the prayer at the bishop's ordination. So then, as representing the church, the bishop ordains the candidates for the ministry. In other words, the bishop has power to ordain, not because he was himself ordained by another bishop, but because he represents the church. No one else can ordain, because no one else can be the church's representative.

The bishop can act as the church's representative because he holds the position of presidency. Thus will be seen the reasonableness of the provisions as to spiritual ordination and the reason for its being inadmissible in the case of a bishop. At a time when confession of faith before a heathen tribunal occupied an important place in the eyes of the church and martyrdom was regarded as the highest honour, it was natural that those who had shown themselves steadfast in the fiery trial should by that very fact establish for themselves a right to exercise the honourable position of presbyter in the church. But it would not be reasonable that this should also admit them to a position of presidency; nor would it be possible, for there could only be one bishop's seat (*C. H.* iv. 30) in one community. Such a one might however be afterwards chosen as president, or bishop, and he would then receive a laying on of hands in the ordinary course.

We conclude then that the Canons of Hippolytus do not warrant us in asserting that, in the view of their compiler, the Apostolic Succession of the line of bishops, continued throughout by episcopal ordination, is a primary necessity. It is rather to be described as a secondary or contingent necessity. The primary necessity is the continuous organic life of the church. But since, or so far as, the government of the church is by monarchical episcopacy, the bishop, as representing the church, performs the ceremony whereby men are admitted to bear office in it.

The sacerdotal side of the Christian ministry finds recognition. In describing the ministry of the church, the Latin version has "prælaturas et principatus" (*C. H.* III. 12). The parallel passages of the Egyptian Church Order and of the Apostolic Constitutions, in both forms of the text, show that the Greek text underlying this phrase was ἄρχοντας καὶ ἱερεῖς. The term ἱερεύς is therefore applied to ministers of the church, thus recognising the sacrificial aspect of their work. We also find the title "sacerdos" used twice of the Christian minister in the Latin version of the Canons (*C. H.* XXXVI. 188), and here again the word ἱερεύς occurs in the parallel passage in the Apostolic Constitutions. The bishop is called "princeps sacerdotum" (*C. H.* XXIV. 200). The corresponding term in the Egyptian Church Order represents, according to Achelis, ἀρχιερεύς. So the work of the bishop has a sacrificial character. The prayer at his ordination as bishop includes the petition that God will "accept his prayers and offerings" (*C. H.* III. 16).

The lay-folk may exercise a limited ministry in the church. If none of the clergy are present at the Agapé, a layman may take the lead. He may not however "sign" (*i.e.* bless) the bread. He may only break it for distribution. Then each person may offer thanks privately on his own account for his portion. "It is not proper for a layman to sign the bread, but only to break it. Let him do nothing besides. If no clergy at all are present, each may eat his own portion with thanksgiving" (*C. H.* xxxv. 181, 182).

We have now to consider the position and functions assigned to the several orders of the ministry.

The bishop is to be elected by all the people, that is by the whole local church. Regard is to be had to his character. He must be grave. The election is to take place on a Sunday, the voice of the church affirming it in the words "We elect him." Having thus voted by acclamation, they offer prayers for the bishop-elect and he is then ordained by the laying on of hands with prayer. "Let the bishop be chosen by the whole people[1]. Let him be grave, as is written in the Apostle concerning him. Then on the Sunday[2] on which he is ordained let the people say, 'We elect him.' Then, when silence has been made in the whole flock, after the acclamation, let them all pray for him, saying: 'O God, strengthen him, whom Thou hast provided for us.' Then from the bishops and presbyters let one be chosen to lay his hand upon his head and pray" (*C. H.* ii. 7—10).

It is to be noted that though the church elects and a bishop ordains, yet the authority of the newly made bishop is from God. It is God as the people acknowledge in the prayer quoted above, who has provided them with their bishop. It is God who bestows upon the man of their choice the office of bishop, as is recognised by the prayer that accompanies the laying on of hands: "Grant unto him, O Lord, the office of bishop" (*C. H.* iii. 17).

[1] The Latin version has *ex omni populo*. We have followed Achelis' emendation *ab omni populo*.

[2] The Latin version has *hebdomade*. Following the parallel passages in the Egyptian Church Order and the Apostolic Constitutions we have with Achelis adopted the emendation κυριακῇ.

The ordination prayer asks that the new bishop may be endowed with certain gifts for the fulfilment of his office. They include "the power to remit sins" (*C. H.* III. 17), but nothing is said as to the exact meaning attaching to the phrase. Then too, if we may follow the Latin version, there is the power of exorcism: "the authority to loose every bond of the wickedness of devils" (*C. H.* III. 18). There is a doubt however whether this accurately represents the Greek original of the Canons. For the *Constitutiones per Hippolytum* read in the parallel passage "authority to loose every bond according to the power which Thou gavest unto Thine Apostles," a reference to the "binding and loosing" of St Matt. xviii. 18. The word "dæmonum" in the Latin may therefore represent a gloss.

Among the other gifts, with which it is prayed that the bishop may be endowed, is the power of healing the sick (*C. H.* III. 18).

There can be no doubt that the episcopacy contemplated by the Canons is monarchical. There is only one bishop in each community. The duty laid upon a deacon is that he is to "serve the bishop and the presbyters in all things" (*C. H.* v. 34). This clearly indicates a single bishop and a plurality of presbyters as belonging to the local church. We must however take note of a phrase which occurs in the account of the ordination service. "One of the bishops and presbyters" is to be chosen to lay his hand on the head of the bishop-elect (*C. H.* II. 10). This does not however make it necessary for us to suppose a plurality of bishops in one community. It no doubt implies that the neighbouring bishops had come together for the ordination. But, once again, we read in the Latin version, in reference

to the duties of the deacons: "Let them serve those
upon whom the bishops take compassion, that they may
be able to give to the widows, the orphans and the poor"
(*C. H.* v. 36). But the plural found here in the Latin
version must be regarded as an error, for the singular,
"the bishop," occurs three times in the context. Episcopacy then is monarchical. The bishop is the president
of the local church.

The local church is the sphere of the bishop's
authority. He exercises his jurisdiction within his own
city. It is implied that his authority does not extend
beyond his own local church. "Our brother bishops
have in their own cities made each their own arrangements according to the commands of the Apostles, our
fathers" (*C. H.* xxiii. 252).

What then is the bishop's work? He has the general
duty of oversight (*C. H.* iv. 17), and this general duty is
further defined.

In the administration of baptism the leading place is
taken by the bishop. Previous to baptism, the catechumens make their confession to the bishop, who alone is
charged with this work (*C. H.* xix. 103). It is the bishop
who calls them together on the day before their baptism,
that they may make their final preparation (*C. H.* xix.
106). And then after baptism, the bishop administers
the laying on of hands to the newly baptized (*C. H.* xix.
136).

The normal custom is for the Eucharist to be celebrated by the bishop. He is to be accompanied by the
deacons and presbyters all arrayed in clean white robes.
"Whenever the bishop wishes to celebrate the Mysteries,
let the deacons and presbyters come together to him,
clothed in white robes, fairer than those of all the people

and spotlessly clean" (*C. H.* XXXVII. 201). The interval, during which the people are assembling, is filled in by the Reader and "then let the bishop pray and begin the oblation" (*C. H.* XXXVII. 204). It is, further, his duty after the celebration of the Eucharist to send to the catechumens "bread purified by prayer" (*C. H.* XX. 171).

At the Agapé and at a supper given to the poor the bishop is to offer prayer both for the guests and for the host (*C. H.* XXXII. 165).

It is the duty of the bishop to receive the firstfruits, which are to be brought to him in the church (*C. H.* XXXVI. 186).

It is part of his work to preach. He preaches sitting. This act of preaching, it is said, will be a gain both to himself and to his hearers (*C. H.* XXXIV. 177).

Ordination is the function of bishops only. On this point the Canons are quite explicit. A presbyter has no power to ordain. "A bishop is in all things on a level with a presbyter, except as regards his episcopal seat and as regards ordination, because the power of ordination is not committed to the latter" (*C. H.* IV. 32). This explicit statement must determine our interpretation of an obscure sentence that occurs in the account of a bishop's ordination. "Let one of the bishops and presbyters be chosen, to lay his hand upon the head" of the bishop-elect (*C. H.* II. 10). Taken by itself, the sentence would seem to imply that the minister of ordination might be either a bishop or a presbyter indifferently. But the statement we have quoted above excludes this interpretation. It may be that we should adopt the reading which Dr Steinschneider finds in a Bodleian codex[1]: "They shall choose one of the

---

[1] See H. Achelis, *Die Canones Hippolyti*, p. 40 n.

bishops and one of the presbyters and these shall lay their hands upon his head and pray." In this case, the meaning would be that the presbyter was to join in the laying on of hands, as ratifying the bishop's act. But even if the reading be a gloss, it probably gives the correct sense.

It is the bishop's work to visit the sick and to pray over the sick person. For this purpose a deacon is deputed to accompany the bishop and tell him of any sick people. " Let there be a deacon to accompany the bishop at all times, and let him point out to him sick persons severally. For it is a great thing for a sick person to be visited by the chief priest ; he recovers from disease when the bishop comes to him, especially if he prays over him ; because the shadow of Peter healed the sick " (*C. H.* XXIV. 199). It will be noted that the visitation of the sick by the bishop is expressly connected with that gift of healing which at his ordination it was prayed that he might receive.

We pass now to the presbyters. We find that the same ceremony of ordination is to be used for a presbyter as for a bishop, omitting only the ceremony of placing him in the seat of authority. This is for the bishop alone, being the symbol of presidency over the local church. The same prayer also is to be used, except that the reference to episcopal supervision is necessarily omitted. " If a presbyter is ordained, everything shall be done in his case in the same way as with a bishop, except that he shall not sit in the president's seat. Also the same prayer shall be prayed over him as over the bishop, omitting only the reference to the episcopate " (*C. H.* IV. 30). From this similarity in the two services it will follow that the presbyter, like the bishop, is elected by the whole church, and is ordained by the bishop by laying on of hands with

prayer.   He then receives the kiss of peace from all and
then celebrates the Eucharist.

There are only two respects in which the presbyters
differ from the bishop.   They do not occupy the presidential
seat, for the bishop takes the lead in all public functions
of the church.   And also they have not the power of
ordination.   This appertains to the bishop alone, as the
representative of the church.   "A bishop is in every
respect on the same level as a presbyter, excepting only
as regards the presidential seat and as regards ordination.
For the power of ordination does not belong to a presbyter"
(*C. H.* IV. 32).

One who has been appointed presbyter in a local
church has in every church the rank of presbyter.   He
does not require re-ordination if he leaves the church
where he holds his commission.   But before he can
exercise his ministry in any other church he must receive
admission from the clergy there.   These must first make
enquiries from his former bishop, or, if the distance be too
great, must themselves examine his character and attain-
ments and satisfy themselves as to his fitness to exercise
his office.   "If a presbyter goes away and wishes to live
in places that have not been committed to his charge, the
clergy of this place, if they are disposed to welcome him,
shall make enquiries from the bishop under whose
authority he was, lest perchance he had taken to flight for
some reason.   But if his city is too distant, let him be
examined as to whether, though he be a disciple, he yet
lacks aught that becomes presbyters.   Afterwards let him
be received into fellowship and treated with double honour,
but let him not be ordained a second time" (*C. H.* IX.
56—58).   These provisions in regard to travelling presbyters are important as showing the twofold character of

the presbyterate. On the one hand it has a local character. For licence to exercise the office in a local church is required from the local authority. Such licence is granted by the clergy, as representing the church. But on the other hand the presbyterate has a universal character. The presbyter is not merely an officer of a local church. He is a presbyter absolutely, a presbyter in the universal church. So he does not require to be re-ordained when taking up a new commission. Ordination then does not confer merely local authority: it gives a position in the church universal. Once a presbyter, always a presbyter.

The central work of the presbyters is to assist the bishop at the celebration of the Eucharist. Thus they are to join with the newly made bishop in the celebration that follows his ordination as bishop. " Let him who has been made bishop place his hands upon the oblations together with the presbyters " (*C. H.* iii. 20). So too at the regular Eucharist their place is by the side of the bishop. " Whenever the bishop wishes to celebrate, let the deacons and presbyters be gathered together to him " (*C. H.* xxxvii. 201).

The celebration of the Eucharist is followed by the distribution of cups of milk and honey. These cups are to be taken round by the presbyters after the people have been communicated by the bishop. " Let the presbyters carry other cups of milk and honey, to teach those who partake of them that they have been born as little children, because little children partake of milk and honey " (*C. H.* xix. 144).

In normal circumstances it was the duty of the bishop to celebrate. This seems to have been the original meaning of a chaotic sentence in the Latin version, of which probably the original form was this : " Let the deacon bring the elements of the Mysteries and then let the bishop begin the oblation " (*C. H.* XIX. 142)[1]. So too it is the bishop who administers the Eucharist to the people. " Let the bishop deliver to them of the body of Christ, saying, 'This is the body of Christ'; and let them say 'Amen': and let those to whom he gives the cup, saying, 'This is the blood of Christ,' say 'Amen'" (*C. H.* XIX. 146, 147).

We have however been told (*C. H.* IV. 32) that the presbyter is in all things equal to the bishop, except as regards the presidency and the power of ordination. There cannot therefore be any inherent disability in the presbyters to prevent them from celebrating the Eucharist themselves. We accordingly find that certain duties, which normally fall to the bishop, may in his absence be performed by a presbyter. " If in the absence of the bishop a presbyter is present, let all turn to him, because he is superior in God to the rest, and let them honour him as the bishop is honoured and not behave in a refractory manner towards him " (*C. H.* XXXIV. 178). In the absence of the bishop therefore the duty of celebrating the Eucharist would fall on the presbyters.

So too in the absence of the bishop a presbyter will preside at the Agapé. " Let him distribute the bread of exorcism before they sit down, so that God may preserve their Agapé from the fear of the enemy and that they may rise from meat in health and peace " (*C. H.* XXXIV. 179).

The duty of visitation of the sick falls upon the clergy in general. In this then the presbyters will take their part. One who is dangerously ill should be " visited by the clergy every day " (*C. H.* XXI. 219).

[1] Achelis, *Die Canones Hippolyti, ad loc.* p. 100.

If perhaps the tendency of the Canons of Hippolytus is to minimise the difference between the episcopate and the presbyterate, it may be said that there is also a tendency to emphasise the distinction between the presbyterate and the diaconate.

Whereas in the ordination of a presbyter the same prayer is to be used as for the ordination of a bishop, save only for slight omissions; for the ordination of a deacon, on the other hand, an entirely different prayer is prescribed. "If a deacon is ordained, let each several regulation be observed, and let this prayer be said over him ; a prayer that is applicable not to the presbyterate but to the diaconate, as becomes a servant of God " (*C. H.* v. 33). Here then is the prayer, which the bishop is to offer, as he lays his hands upon the head of him who is to be ordained deacon : " O God, Father of our Lord Jesus Christ, we pray Thee to pour out Thy Holy Spirit upon Thy servant *N.*, and to endow him together with those who like Stephen serve Thee according to Thy good pleasure ; and that Thou mayest grant to him to be able to conquer every power of wickedness with the sign of Thy cross, with which he himself is signed; and that Thou mayest grant to him a character void of offence in the sight of all men and a doctrine for the benefit of many, whereby he may guide an abundant people in the holy church to salvation without any cause of offence.   Accept his every act of service, through Jesus Christ our Lord, through whom to Thee with Himself and the Holy Spirit be glory for ever and ever.   Amen " (*C. H.* v. 39—42).

The characteristic feature of the deacon's work is service. He is " the household slave of God " (*C. H.* v. 33). He has to serve the bishop and the presbyters, not only at the time of the Eucharist, but also in their ministrations

to the sick. " Let him serve the bishop and the presbyters
in all things and not only at the time of the oblations; but
also let him serve those of the sick among the people who
have no one to attend to them. Let him inform the
bishop and pray for them, and let him secure that distribution may be made to them of things which they need,
and likewise to men weighed down with secret poverty.
Let them serve moreover those upon whom the bishops
have compassion, that they may be able to give to widows,
orphans and the poor. In this manner therefore let him
perform all his duties. Such in truth is that servant (Lat.
diaconus) of whom Christ said : 'If anyone will minister to
Me, him will My Father honour ' " (C. H. v. 34—37).

The deacon then has his duty of service at the Eucharist,
but his chief duties are in connection with the social side
of the work of the church, the exercise of hospitality and
of care for the sick and poor, which had its roots so deep
in the very nature of the church. For it is always to be
remembered that the church is a brotherhood, giving
expression to its character in acts of love and tender consideration. The deacon therefore must keep the bishop
informed as to the needs of the sick and poor. We have
already seen that a deacon is to be told off to accompany
the bishop, that he may indicate the sick to the bishop, so
that the bishop himself may visit them (C. H. XXIV. 199).

The deacon has also an office of teaching. This is
implied by the petition in his ordination prayer that he
may be endowed with " a doctrine for the benefit of many,
whereby he may guide an abundant people in the holy
church to salvation without any cause of offence " (C. H.
v. 41). The instruction of the catechumens is committed
to the deacons (C. H. x. 61).

We have seen that the deacons have the duty of

19—2

serving the bishop and presbyters at the celebration of the Eucharist. Though the distribution of the consecrated elements is normally the function of the bishop, this may if necessary be performed by the deacon. "The deacon may distribute the oblations to the people, if the bishop or presbyter give him permission" (*C. H.* XXXI. 216).

Also if no presbyters are present at the celebration of the Eucharist, the deacons are to take their place in carrying round the cups of milk and honey, which are distributed after the administration. "If there are no presbyters present to carry these cups, let them be carried by the deacons" (*C. H.* XIX. 145). This is an example of a work which properly belongs to the presbyterate, but which in case of need may be performed by a deacon.

A similar instance occurs in connection with the Agapé. In the absence of a presbyter, a deacon may take the presbyter's place at the Agapé and perform his duties up to a certain point. He may bless, break and distribute the bread. This refers to the "bread of exorcism," which was partaken of before the meal. "A deacon, in the absence of a presbyter at the Agapé, may act in place of the presbyter, so far as concerns the prayer and the breaking of the bread, which he may distribute to the guests."

The lighting of the lamps at the Agapé and at a supper given to the poor is the work of the deacon. This lighting appears to have a ceremonial character. "If an Agapé is made or if a supper is prepared by anyone for the poor on the Lord's day, then at the time of lighting the lamp, let the deacon rise, in the bishop's presence, and light it" (*C. H.* XXXII. 164).

The office of reader is definitely recognised by a formal ceremony of admission. There is to be no laying on of hands in his case. He is admitted to his office by the bishop, who delivers to him a book of the Gospels, as a symbol of the duty committed to him. The same requirements as to character must be satisfied in his case as in the case of the deacons. "Let him who is appointed reader be adorned with a deacon's virtues, and instead of imposition of hands, let there be delivered to him by the bishop a book of the Gospels" (*C. H.* VII. 48). The readers have a special place assigned to them in the church, from which to read the Scriptures. They take it in turns to read and so fill up the time as the people are assembling for the Eucharist. "Let the readers be clothed in festival robes and let them stand at the place of reading, and let one follow after the other, until the whole of the people are assembled" (*C. H.* XXXVII. 203).

There is an order of widows and virgins in the church. Admission to this order is only to be granted under due restrictions. A widow shall not be admitted to the order unless her character has been well approved by those among whom she has lived (*C. H.* VII. 50). A virgin must not be admitted until she is of full age: she must have proved herself faithful and must be of good character (*C. H.* VII. 51)[1].

[1] We have followed Achelis's emendation of the Latin text, which is here clearly corrupt. The existing text reads : 50. Neque ordinetur cœlebs. Si est sine uxore, nisi postquam testimonium pro ipso exhibitum sit ad contestandam integritatem ejus a vicinis ipsius, ita ut certum sit, eum a corruptione alienum fuisse eo tempore, quo ibi habitabat. 51. Neque alieni imponatur manus tamquam cœlibi, nisi quando ad maturam staturam perductus pro fideli habetur et testimonio commendatus est. Achelis conjectures that in the original form of these Canons §50 referred to widows and §51 to virgins. This is borne out by the parallel passages in the Egyptian Church Order and in the Apostolic

Those enrolled upon the order of widows have a special claim upon the hospitality of the church. Private individuals may show hospitality to widows by making a supper for them. But in such a case the widows must go home before nightfall. Evidently much stress was laid upon this provision, as the precaution is three times insisted upon. " If anyone wishes to prepare a supper for widows, let him see to it that they have their supper and are dismissed before sunset. If there are a large number, let him take precautions that no confusion may arise and that they be not hindered from being dismissed before evening. To each of them let sufficient food and drink be given. But let them depart before night draws on " (*C. H.* xxxv. 183—185).

Since the widows form an order and as such are the recipients of the bounty of the church, the church in its turn expects something from them. By prayer and fasting and by visiting the sick they are to discharge their duty towards the church. " A special honour is to be paid to the widows on account of their frequent prayers, their care for the sick and their frequent fasting " (*C. H.* ix. 59).

Constitutions. As the Latin text represents a translation from the Arabic version, we can see how the mistake arose. For, as Achelis remarks, *vidua* and *cœlebs* stand for kindred ideas, while in Arabic *cœlebs* and *virgo* are expressed by the same word.

It will be noted that the Latin text of the Canons supposes admission to the order to take place by a laying on of hands. But the parallel passage of the Apostolic Constitutions c. 24 has παρθένος οὐ χειροτονεῖται. Now χειροτονεῖν simply means " to appoint," but the form of the word might easily lead a translator to make the mistake of rendering it as implying a laying on of hands. On the whole, it is probable that the Apostolic Constitutions preserve the true sense of the original of the Canons and that, as is suggested by the case of the reader, the laying on of hands was reserved for the higher orders of the ministry, the bishops, presbyters and deacons.

SECTION VI.

THE EARLY MINISTRY AT ALEXANDRIA.

Constitution of the early ministry at Alexandria.—Peculiarity noted by Jerome.—Bearing of this on the doctrine of apostolic succession.

The view of the meaning of apostolic succession in the ministry, which the Canons of Hippolytus have led us to adopt, is corroborated by the practice which seems to have obtained in early days at Alexandria.

Our earliest hint as to the constitution of the ministry at Alexandria is derived from a letter written from Alexandria by the Emperor Hadrian to the consul Servianus, A.D. 134. "I have become," he writes, "perfectly familiar with Egypt, which you praised to me; it is fickle, uncertain, blown about by every gust of rumour. Those who worship Serapis are Christians; and those are devoted to Serapis who call themselves bishops of Christ. There is no ruler of a synagogue there, no Samaritan, no Christian presbyter, who is not an astrologer, a soothsayer, a quack[1]." Hadrian, as a pagan, is of course looking at the Christian religion from outside, but he is evidently a shrewd observer. He speaks separately of Christian bishops and Christian presbyters, clearly thinking of them as distinct. It is not necessary to suppose that he had any accurate idea of the meaning of the terms, but his letter may at least be taken as evidence that in the church in Alexandria in his time the episcopal and presbyteral offices were distinct. In this connection it

[1] For this letter see Lightfoot, *Ignatius*, vol. i. p. 464.

may be noted that Clement of Alexandria, who was born about the middle of the second century, knows no other mode of church government than that of bishop, presbyters and deacons. "The grades in the church here," he says, "of bishops, presbyters, deacons, I believe to be imitations of the angelic glory" (*Strom.* VI. xiii. 107). We need not then doubt that at least from the time of Hadrian's visit the body of presbyters at Alexandria had a bishop at its head.

But an allusion by Jerome to the early ministry at Alexandria raises the question as to how the bishop was admitted to his office. "At Alexandria," he says, "from the days of Mark the Evangelist down to the episcopates of Heraclas and Dionysius, the presbyters used always to appoint as bishop one who was chosen from themselves and placed on the higher grade, just as if an army were making a general, or deacons were choosing one of themselves whom they knew to be diligent and calling him archdeacon" (Jerome, Ep. 146, *Ad Evangelum*). Now Jerome had resided at Alexandria, and it is therefore not unlikely that his statement of the early practice in the church there may be well founded. Let us then see what it amounts to. The comparison of the making of a bishop by the presbyters with the making of an archdeacon by the deacons seems to imply that the bishop became such simply in virtue of the choice of the presbyters, not in virtue of an ordination to the office by the laying on of hands. The presbyters chose one of their number to be their bishop, and as a result of that choice, but without any further ordination or consecration, he took his place at their head. If Jerome supposed that the newly elected bishop received a fresh ordination at the hands of other bishops, his allusion to the practice at Alexandria would be pointless. For his object in making the allusion is to emphasise the dignity of the presbyterate, with whom alone the making of the bishop rested. He minimises the distinction between presbyters and bishop. But on the other hand any idea of presbyterian ordination is also excluded. For ordination, as Jerome goes on to say, is the distinctive function of the bishop. " What except ordination," he asks, " does a bishop do which a presbyter does not ? " (*ibid.*). We must therefore conclude that it was Jerome's belief that in the early days of the church in Alexandria, down to a period as late as the middle of the third century, the bishop became such in virtue simply of election by the presbyters without any further laying on of hands.

If then we accept the evidence of Jerome as accurate, how are we to fit in this practice with what we know of the ministry in other parts of the church ? It is surely only by means of special pleading that it can be made to fit in with a mechanical theory of transmission of orders through an unbroken line of bishops. An attempt to do this is indeed made by Dr Gore. He says of the Alexandrian presbyters, on the supposition that Jerome's evidence can be trusted, that " they were ordained, *ex hypothesi*, on the understanding that under certain circumstances they might be called, by simple election, to execute the bishop's office. They were not only presbyters with the ordinary commission of the presbyter, but also bishops *in posse*. Elsewhere there were two distinct ordinations, one making a man a bishop and another a presbyter ; at Alexandria there was only one ordination, which made a man a presbyter and a potential bishop[1]." But surely such language as this

---

[1] Gore, *Christian Ministry*, p. 143.

represents an idea of a bishop quite alien from the thought of the church of the second century. For though the function of ordination was, as the Canons of Hippolytus tell us, reserved to the bishop, yet fundamentally the bishop is thought of, not as one who ordains, but as one who presides. He is the head, the representative of the local church. It is because he stands at the head of the local church as its representative that the function of ordination rests with him and with him alone. To speak of the presbyters at Alexandria as " bishops *in posse* " is surely unmeaning. They were presbyters and nothing more. One of them might become a bishop. But this would be simply in virtue of his election to the presidency by his fellow-presbyters, not in virtue of a commission previously received from another bishop and till then lying dormant.

But while the case of the Alexandrian church cannot be fitted into the mechanical theory of transmission of orders, it is fully in accord with the doctrine of apostolic succession as explained above in connection with the Canons of Hippolytus. For the continuous life of the local church is unbroken, and although on the present supposition this continuity does not receive outward expression by the same symbolic action as was normally employed, the essential fact is unimpaired. The presbytery with its elected bishop preserves a continuity, which may equally with the normal mode of succession witness to the continuity of the church.

CHAPTER VI.

CONCLUSION.
THE LESSONS OF THE SUB-APOSTOLIC AGE.

SECTION I.

THE CONCEPTION OF THE CHURCH.

The wide range of witness.—Permanence of essential principles, but development of outward form.—The church is a divine society.—And fulfils God's purpose for the salvation of man.—The institutional and the spiritual church.—Probation in the church.—Holiness of the church.—Gifts of grace in the church.—Admission to the church.—Fundamental elements in the church : (1) Its continuity. (2) Its unity.—Unity of the church exhibited (1) In the relations between the local churches, where it is compatible with divergences of custom. (2) In each local church.—The evil of schism.—The effect of heresy.—Authority of the church: (1) In excommunication. (2) In teaching. (3) In public worship. (4) In fasting.—Discipline exercised through the ministry.—Sacerdotal character of the church.

We have now concluded our survey of all existing Christian writings outside the New Testament up to the close of the second century. We have examined their witness as to the conception of the church which underlies them. It remains for us to take a general view of the whole. The writings examined cover a period of upwards of a century. They emanate from districts widely separated from one another. But in spite of this variety of origin they have shown that, throughout the entire range of the witness examined, the conception of the church is fundamentally the same. Certain great principles are everywhere tacitly assumed or openly expressed. These great principles find outward embodiment in the organisation of the church. And it is in respect of this organisation that an element of growth and development is to be expected and is actually found. The unchanging principles find, to a certain extent, a changing expression. This change is partly the result of a gradual modification of external circumstances; and is partly tentative, as the communities feel their way towards a fuller life. In weighing the significance of this growth, it is important always to bear in mind that varying externals embody unvarying principle. This fact must also be our guide in determining how far a change of circumstances in any later period of the church's life will warrant a change in external order.

We find everywhere the underlying idea that the church is a divine society, standing in a direct relation to God. It is a sphere of grace, through which men are brought into contact with the gifts of God in Jesus Christ. In it is the way to eternal salvation. The goal, which it sets before its members, is the attainment of "the kingdom of God," in which perfect harmony with the will of God will issue in perfect happiness.

This place of the church in the scheme of salvation is in accordance with the eternal purpose of God, whose earlier dealings with men had been leading up to this consummation. So Barnabas holds that the church is the heir to the Old Testament promises and Irenæus regards the church as the goal of Judaism. This same truth, that the church fulfils under conditions of time God's eternal purpose, underlies the thought of the church as pre-existent, which we find both in Hermas and in the Pseudo-Clement.

The church, as being a spiritual sphere, fulfilling a divine purpose in regard to man's salvation, has a spiritual existence apart from its outward or institutional form. This thought gives scope for varying development according to the degree of mysticism belonging to the writer. But we may probably regard as universal the idea that the church is not merely the company of the faithful, but has also a mystical existence as the sphere of grace into which the faithful are gathered.

The definite distinction, which we find both in Hermas and the Pseudo-Clement, between the institutional church and the spiritual church, is an expression of the doctrine that the church is a sphere of probation, and that though the members of the outward church have the way of salvation open before them, it depends upon their own efforts whether they reach the goal to which the church is intended to lead them.

The relation of the church to God, and the purpose which He has connected with it, result in the fundamental fact that the church is holy. This holiness is to be realised by the growth of its members in obedience to the will of God.

Since the church is the normal way of salvation, it is richly endowed with spiritual gifts. Conspicuous among these is the gift of prophecy. The prophets are a vivid witness to the presence of the Holy Spirit in the church. It is their function, in the power of the

Holy Spirit, to interpret to men the messages of God.

The institutional church is a body with definite boundaries. It does not shade off into the world, but is sharply distinguished from it. There is therefore an external rite of admission to the church, the sacrament of Baptism. For this rite a careful preparation is needed, as the step thus taken is regarded as of decisive character. Under one aspect entrance to the church is a voluntary act; under another it is regarded as the outcome of a divine election.

Two notes of cardinal importance and of universal acknowledgment in the writers whom we have examined are the continuity and the unity of the church.

The church has a continuous life. Generations pass by, but the same church goes on. The church of the Apostles preserves an unbroken existence through the ages.

And the church is one. One church fills the whole field of God's work for man's salvation. The unity of the church is the necessary consequence of its relation to God in Christ. The church is the body of Christ, and its life is therefore one. This one universal church is represented in each place by the local church in that place. The unity of the universal church therefore determines the relations that subsist between the various local churches. The bond of a common fellowship is recognised as drawing them together. The welfare of each is the concern of all. The friendly relations between the various churches are not disturbed by differences of local custom.

Side by side with the possible variations of local custom there is an impressive unity of teaching. Everywhere the teaching of the local churches is the same. For every-where the apostolic tradition is handed down in the churches; and upon this tradition alone their teaching is based. This unity of teaching is indeed consistent with a certain latitude of opinion upon subjects which do not touch the essential doctrines of the faith. An instance of this is the millenarian belief, which in early days obtained a considerable vogue.

Further the principle of unity is to be observed, not only in the relations between the various local churches but in each local church. For each local church is to exhibit a united life. There must be no division in the Christian body in a particular place. Consequently there can only be one church in one place. The idea that various churches can be set up in the same place, forming as it were rival communions drawn from the same locality, runs counter to all the thought of the sub-apostolic age. It is a violation of fundamental principle; for it is the negation of the unity of the local church.

This unity of the local church finds varied expression. It issues in a spirit of brotherhood, which makes the weaker members a special object of care to the community as a whole. It teaches a new conception of social relation-ships. It makes public worship a necessity: for the community, whose spiritual life is one and which recognises God as the source of that life, must necessarily come before God as a community and must offer to Him united worship. Pre-eminently this note is struck in the sacred social meal of the Eucharist and the accompanying Agapé. In the Eucharist the spiritual life of the indi-vidual is deepened by living contact with the source of life; and the life of the community is also quickened by this united act, which touches the very groundwork of its existence.

Wherever monarchical episcopacy has been evolved, this unity in the local church involves obedience to the bishop, as being the representative of the church.

The spirit of schism is the negation of this unity. Schism, which is thought of as division within the church, rather than as separation from it, is sternly condemned as inconsistent with the fundamental principle of the unity of the church. It may take the form of a revolt against the authority of the ministry : or of separation from the authorised assembly for public worship, in order to form a distinct congregation. Where monarchical episcopacy has been developed, it becomes an act of schism to do anything in opposition to the authority of the bishop.

Schism cannot be justified on the ground that the church is corrupt. Those who are discontented at some fault in the local church should exercise their influence to correct the evil. They produce a far greater evil if they cause a schism. For disunion is contrary to the very essence of Christianity.

But while schismatics are thought of as still within the church and as causing disunion within the society, which should be one, the heretics on the other hand are thought of as outside the church altogether. Hegesippus is perhaps an exception to this view. He seems to speak of the heretics as exercising a corrupting influence within the church. But it is not difficult to reconcile the two views. Doubtless when heresy on a matter of fundamental importance in the Christian faith had been definitely formalised, the heretics would be excluded from the church and regarded as altogether outside it. Indeed we learn that the heretics, so far from wishing to claim church membership, despised those whom they described as mere churchpeople. But before this point was reached, there would be the corrupt influence within the church of those who were drifting from the truth, perhaps under the influence of others who were already outside the church.

The church, as must be the case with any organised body, exercises a disciplinary authority over its members. This authority resides not only in the church universal, but also in each local church. The local church may exclude an erring brother from fellowship by excommunication. It may lay down the conditions to be satisfied before such a one may be restored to fellowship. The authority of the church is exercised in its capacity as teacher, though here the authority is definitely limited; for the teaching of the church must be in accordance with the apostolic tradition. It is just because the church can prove that the apostolic tradition has, as a fact, been handed down in it, that its teaching is authoritative. In the matter also of public worship the church exercises its authority. The church appoints the time and place of worship. Only at such times and in such places as the church appoints can public worship be rightly offered. Assemblies for public worship, if unauthorised by the church, contradict the spirit of unity, which is fundamental in the church's constitution. And, further, church discipline requires that public worship should be led by the authorised ministry. Among other directions in which we find the church exercising its disciplinary authority, there is the matter of fasting. The authority so exercised is that of the whole body, the entire local church. It acts, with growing distinctness, through its own authorised ministry; and though towards the end of our period we find indications of a tendency to separate the ministry from the church as a whole and to regard the ministry as inherently possessed of a disciplinary authority

D.   20

apart from the church, yet this tendency does not belong
to the main current of thought. The church, as the spirit-
bearing community, the body of Christ, exercises a disciplinary authority over its members. The ministry has
indeed an authority committed to it, but it is a delegated
authority. The authority of the ministry is that of the
church which it represents.

The church is uniformly represented as possessed of a
sacerdotal character. It approaches God by means of
sacrifice. Its sacrifice is the Death of Jesus Christ, the
Eternal Son of God, who is Himself the great High Priest,
with whom the church stands in living union and by
means of whom it possesses the power of approach to God.
The central sacrificial act of the church is the Eucharist,
which is the characteristic service of the new dispensation.
The ministry, as being appointed to lead the worship of
a church which has this sacerdotal character, is itself
described in sacerdotal language. It is however to be
noted that the priesthood of the ministry is not that of a
separate caste. It is the authorised exercise of a power
which is inherent in the body as a whole, and which the
whole body delegates to those through whom it acts.

SECTION II.

THE MINISTRY OF THE CHURCH.

The ministry of the church.—Two types: (1) An itinerant ministry. (2) A local ministry.—Monarchical government in each local church.—Consideration of possible exceptions: (1) Rome. (2) The *Didaché*.—The three orders in the ministry.—The process of development.—Local variation in the rates of growth.—The essential principles involved: (1) The unity of the church: obedience to the bishop. (2) The continuity of the church: apostolic succession.

In the organisation of the Christian ministry the sub-apostolic age witnesses a process of development. It is easy indeed to exaggerate the significance of this development; for the changing outward forms are always the expression of a permanent underlying principle. This principle is the unity of the local church and the larger unity of the church universal. We are apt to lose sight of the permanent principle in emphasising the process of development in external form.

In the early days an itinerant ministry exhibited the harmonious relations between the local churches in the unity of the one church universal. These itinerant workers, such men as the prophets and apostles of the *Didaché*, went from church to church as need arose, or they broke new ground, by missionary effort, beyond the already organised churches; and by their roving work they proved the brotherhood of the church. For everywhere the churches bade them welcome. This itinerant ministry gradually lost its importance, as the organisation of the local churches attained a more settled shape.

In addition to these itinerants, there was from the beginning a settled ministry in each local church. This local ministry was a centre round which the life of the local church gathered. Hence the local ministry always occupied an authoritative position. It claimed the obedience of the church, for it stood for the church's unity, which it was a heinous offence to destroy. At the head of the local ministry of presbyters and deacons stood in general a single officer, whether described as president or bishop. For the most part the writers whom we have examined are explicit on this point. Monarchical episcopacy is the system of church government known to Ignatius, Papias, Polycarp, Melito, the Anti-Montanists, Dionysius of Corinth, Theophilus of Antioch, the Muratorian canonist, Hegesippus, Polycrates and his contemporaries in the Quartodeciman Synods, Irenæus and the compiler of the Canons of Hippolytus. But what of the other writers of the period whose evidence we have been considering ? We have shown that the writings of Justin imply a monarchical government in each local church. The question of church government is not raised by Barnabas, Aristides, the Pseudo-Clement, or the writer to Diognetus. They afford no evidence one way or the other. There remain two outstanding questions. What was the early organisation of the church in Rome and what are the local conditions implied by the *Didaché* as regards the ministry ?

Our earliest evidence for Rome is derived from the letter of Clement. It is hardly too much to say that this letter shows Clement as occupying a presidential position over the local Roman church. Whatever title was or was not given to him, the position, which enabled him to write to the church in Corinth as the mouthpiece of the church in Rome, must have been a unique position in that church.

The other early document proceeding from the local

Roman church is the *Shepherd* of Hermas. The evidence of Hermas must be judged in relation to the date of his writing. If we accept the late date, we know that Pius was then occupying the monarchical seat in that church. But if we disregard, as possibly prejudiced, the statement of the Muratorian canonist and, on the ground of internal evidence, regard Hermas as a younger contemporary of Clement, then the *Shepherd* gives us a second picture of the Roman church not much later than when Clement wrote to the Corinthians. If we adopt this supposition, we shall note that Hermas simply confirms what we have already learnt from Clement. But in itself the *Shepherd* supplies us with no evidence one way or the other as to whether the local church at Rome in the first quarter of the second century was or was not monarchically governed.

It remains for us to consider the *Didaché*. This archaic document mentions a local ministry of " bishops " and deacons. Did these " bishops " number a president among themselves ? If so, it must be admitted that the fact of his presidency was not thought of as having any significance in point of church order. It is probable as a matter of fact that a body of men, who united in exercising oversight over one and the same local church, must have had a leader or president. But there is no indication as to whether such a leader, if he existed, was permanently in such a position, as a monarchical chief of the " bishops." Rather the terms, in which the " bishops and deacons " are alluded to, preclude any such official authority vested in one man. The *Didaché* then seems to stand alone, among Christian writings that have come down to us from the period we are considering, in representing a condition of church government in which no single official, under whatever title, stands at the head of the local community. Some others of our documents, as we have seen, present no evidence one way or the other.   The *Didaché* alone seems to preclude a monarchical president.

Now the honour in which the *Didaché* was held by the church, as evidenced by the wide currency it obtained, shows that, with all its limitations, it was not held to violate fundamental principles.   It is indeed probable that those who afterwards used and reverenced this manual understood the title " bishop " in the monarchical sense which soon became universal.   But it is to be noticed that while the *Didaché* is not in agreement with the view that continuity is to be necessarily sought in an unbroken line of monarchical rulers, it is fully consistent with the fundamental necessity of a vital continuity in the church.

Our survey of the sub-apostolic age leads however to the conclusion that from the beginning the local churches in almost every case, though with some exceptions, were under a monarchical government more or less definite. Each body of ministers had its president.   But no doubt there was considerable difference in the degree of emphasis laid upon the monarchical character of the government in the various local churches.   The head of the local church moreover was the symbol of its unity.

Soon the ministry thus loosely organised under its local leader took a definite and permanent shape.   The three orders of bishops, presbyters and deacons emerged, the title of bishop being then appropriated to the monarchical head of the community.   This threefold order was not reached everywhere at the same time.   In some churches the development was slower than in others.   We may take it that the fully developed ministry first appears in the church in Jerusalem, where James the Lord's brother is, by universal consent in the middle of the second century, regarded as having been a bishop in the monarchical sense and where Symeon held the same office in succession to James. Early in the second century we have the evidence of Ignatius to show that the threefold order was established from Syria to Troas ; and the subsequent evidence from Asia fully confirms this fact. In Macedonia on the other hand the differentiation of the episcopal office seems to have been less rapid. Polycarp in his letter to the Philippians, though he speaks of the duties and the authority of presbyters and deacons, makes no mention of a bishop. We have seen[1] that the probable inference is that though a single officer, practically a monarchical bishop, stood at the head of the council of presbyters, yet little emphasis was laid upon the difference of position.

In regard to Corinth again the early evidence is vague. But we learn from Hegesippus that, when he visited Corinth in the middle of the second century, the full episcopal government had been established there for some time. Primus, who was then bishop, had been preceded by several occupants of the see.

The slow growth of a clearly defined monarchical episcopacy at Rome has already been noticed. Clement indeed at the close of the first century occupies a unique position in the local church. To him Hermas assigns the duty of writing to foreign churches, which as we may gather from the examples of Polycarp, Dionysius, Irenæus and Polycrates was in early days regarded as essentially the work of a bishop. But we should probably be right in saying that his official position was not yet very clearly defined. In the middle of the second century on the other

[1] See pp. 63 f.

hand we find Pius occupying a definitely monarchical position as bishop and by the close of the century we find Victor asserting a claim to excommunicate the churches of Asia.

These examples will be sufficient to illustrate the way in which by a gradual process, slow or rapid according to circumstances, the threefold order of bishops, presbyters and deacons became universally established in the ministry of the church.

There was indeed change and growth in the organisation of the ministry. But, through all the processes of change, the essential and permanent principles appear to be that the ministry is of authority, as representing the local church ; that the local church is one and that therefore the ministry representing it must be one; and that this unity finds normal expression in the one man who is appointed to preside over its deliberations.

In this we see the ground for the earnest exhortations of Ignatius that the bishop must be obeyed. He stands for the unity of the local church. He is the centre of its organised life. Hence to disobey him is to stand apart from the unity of the church.

It is in accordance with this position that the bishop as we find from the Canons of Hippolytus, was elected by the whole church. For he is not merely the president of the presbyters : he is the representative of the church.

But on the other hand he also holds a divine commission. For the church is a sacred body; and the appointment thus made by the church is held to receive the ratification of God. He receives his authority from God. If the church had been merely a human society, the election of a president of the society could only have conferred such an authority as the society might choose to grant. But the fact that the church stands in a direct relation to God is an essential element in determining the position of the ministry. The Christian minister is the officer of God as well as the delegate of the church.

We have already discussed what meaning the evidence before us leads us to give to the doctrine of apostolic succession. We have given reason for concluding that the fact of fundamental importance is that of the continuous life of the church. As fresh members are baptized into the one body, the church hands on its unbroken existence from age to age. The continuous ministry is a symbol of this continuous life. The way in which the church has as a matter of fact determined to symbolise this continuity is by requiring that those seeking orders should be ordained by bishops, who have themselves received their orders from bishops before them ; and that so a continuous chain shall be formed, going back to the earliest times. But this chain is, as we have already said, a secondary or derived necessity, not a primary or inherent necessity. So long as the church as a whole determines that its own continuity shall be symbolised in this way, it is necessary for all members of the church to acquiesce in the scheme, because otherwise they cut themselves off from the unity of the church.

It may be argued that the church might adopt some other method of symbolising its continuous life ; and indeed a variation from the normal mode seems to have been permitted for a time at Alexandria. But, however that may be, no countenance is given by any of the evidence that we have examined to the idea that it is permissible for a body of Christians to separate themselves from the episcopal order and to set up some other ministerial government of their own device. Such an act is contrary to the teaching and the principles of the sub-apostolic age, as revealed in the evidence that we have been considering ; for it cuts clean across the fundamental doctrine of the unity of the church, a doctrine which requires that there shall be only one local church in one place.

Nor is this idea an artificial one. It belongs to the innermost spirit of Christianity. Those who share that one life, which comes to them through the one Spirit from their union with the one Lord, must themselves also be one. In the fellowship of the one holy church, they are to live as brethren in the family of God.

SECTION III.

THE DEVELOPMENT OF CHRISTIAN THOUGHT.

The influence of the great movements of the second century.—Their effect in rendering explicit a position always implicitly held.—Montanism : its puritan rigorism : its prophetic claims.—Gnosticism : its syncretism : the church's appeal to tradition.—The church manifesting its life in continuous growth.

Our survey of the church from the beginning of the second century to its close has revealed a gradual development of thought and practice. This indeed was to be expected ; for the church is not a dead fossil of merely antiquarian interest, but a living organism. And moreover the early days of a movement are bound to be of critical importance in determining the relations in which it is to stand towards the forces, whether political, religious or social, outside itself. The question then arises as to the nature of the influence which external forces were able to exert upon the church during our period. How far were they responsible for a modification of the conception of the church and its ministry ? If we find that the church was led by external influences to adopt a new position, we must enquire how far the development was legitimate and whether it was a real drawing out of ideas essentially held from the first.

Now the chief religious movements of the second century, with which the church had to deal, were those of Montanism and Gnosticism. As against these dangerous separatist movements the church had to assert its own position. Under the pressure of the controversy, into which it was thus forced, a clearer consciousness arose as to what was involved in the idea of the church. Men were required to think out their position. And the stress of conflict led to a more rapid perfecting of the organisation of the church. The churches looked to their leaders to guide them in meeting the attacks of heretical or unbalanced teachers ; and this naturally led to a consolidation of the bishop's position at the head of each local church.

Let us consider first the effect of Montanism upon the church. This movement was marked by a puritan rigorism in morals : it was strenuous in fasting and forbade second marriages. Its demand was for a more visible enforcement of the holiness of the church. The Montanists stood for a ruthless strictness of principle. Any judicious relaxation of disciplinary severity was regarded by them as apostasy. They rightly contended that Christ established a society, whose note was to be holiness. Its members were to be holy not merely in adherence to sacred doctrine or to a system of ritual, but above all in life and character. The Montanist complaint against the church amounted then to this, that the note

of holiness was being transferred too exclusively to the
institutions of the church. Now no doubt a danger lay
in this direction. It constituted a temptation to which
the church was liable to succumb now that, owing to its
growth, its institutional side was necessarily attaining an
increasing importance. But the fact was that the church
was faced with a problem that required infinite tact. On
the one hand it had to guard the holiness of the body : on
the other hand it was necessary to recognise the fallible
character of human judgment. A disciplinary authority
belonged, as we have seen, to the church ; and the continual
presence of the Holy Spirit had been promised for its
guidance. But no guarantee of infallibility had been
given, and grievous wrong might be done by a too rigorous
enforcement of disciplinary measures. The problem for
the church therefore was to steer a wise course between
too great a laxity, which would result in secularising the
church, and a fanatical rigorism, which in rooting up the
tares might at the same time destroy the wheat. From
the earliest times the church on earth was regarded as a
sphere of probation, within which the divine blessings
were promised. It was not the communion of the saved ;
it was the divinely appointed sphere within which salvation might be attained[1]. The saints were such, in virtue
of their new relation to God : they were required to work
out their salvation with fear and trembling. They might
fall into grievous sin and be subjected to severe discipline[2];
but on repentance they might be forgiven and restored to
Christian privileges. But from this early position two

---

[1] Harnack on the other hand asserts that the second century
witnessed a radical alteration in the conception of the church, " the
transformation of a communion of the saved into an institution for
obtaining salvation." *Hist. of Dogma*, vol. II. p. 108, Eng. trans.

[2] Cf. 1 Cor. v. 3—6.

departures may be noted. We have already seen one instance in Hermas, who denies the possibility of the forgiveness of post-baptismal sin. He seems however to be conscious that this doctrine is a new one. For he only applies it to the future. He admits that in the past post-baptismal sin had, upon repentance, received forgiveness. His rigorism is therefore a departure from the primitive belief, possibly the result of a reaction from the worldliness of the church in Rome. The second instance of a departure from the primitive view of the church is to be found in the Montanists. The institutional church seemed to them to have departed from a true standard of holiness. Perhaps in this they were right. Quite possibly the church needed to be recalled to a higher ideal. But had they had their way the church would have been reduced to a fanatical sect, ruthlessly breaking the bruised reed and quenching the smoking flax. The Montanists lost sight of the probationary character of the church and in their pursuit of holiness would have produced a character far removed from the Christian ideal, a character in which love, patience, tenderness and gentle forbearance would have been crushed. The beautiful and tender graces of the Christian character cannot bloom in so stern an atmosphere.

Montanism in Phrygia, the country of its origin, and in the neighbouring districts of Asia was seen at once to be a force inimical to the church. It was a separatist movement, besides being of a fanatical character, and it was therefore quickly condemned. All the Anti-Montanist writers whom we have quoted belong to Asiatic churches. But from the east Montanism spread to the west, and in doing so lost the fanatical character which it had shown in the hands of its founder and first preachers. The

Montanists of the west were quite ready to remain in communion with the church. They are regarded with evident sympathy by the martyrs of Lyons and Vienne, and apparently by Irenæus himself[1]. The purpose of his mission to Rome seems to have been to enlist the sympathies of the bishop, Eleutherus, on their behalf. In the west they appeared, not as separatists, but as men who laid stress on the spiritual character of religion and on the necessity of personal holiness.

In Montanus and the Phrygian prophets the prophetical outbursts were of a wild and hysterical character and were accompanied by lives quite other than their profession of holiness would have suggested. We must suppose that the new prophecy in the case of the western Montanists was purged of its gross and unworthy elements. So the spirit of religious revival which they manifested would serve to call the attention of the church to the true gifts of the Spirit, the neglect of which had provoked a reaction. The gift of prophecy would seem to have been dormant in the church, when this movement awoke it to a fuller exercise.

We have now to consider the position taken up by the church in opposition to the Gnostics. Gnosticism represents a fusion of extraneous matter with Christian tradition. Its speculative teachers aimed at producing a philosophy of the universe. Their schemes are not Christian, nor are they properly even theistic. But upon a background of pagan thought Christian doctrines or ideas are grafted in strange syncretism. But besides being speculative, the Gnostics formed religious organisations. Practically from the first therefore they constituted rival churches in competition with the Christian churches. They claimed to be

[1] Iren. iii. xi. 9.

able to bestow spiritual privileges, which the Christian church could not give. And further they claimed to be able to satisfy the deeper intellectual needs of men. It was therefore a formidable antagonism which the church had to face. The Gnostic teaching made it necessary for the church to consider its own position. How was it to justify its teaching?

The necessity of finding a firm foothold for its opposition to Gnosticism led it to lay emphasis upon the historic fact of an apostolic tradition. That the teaching of the church had always been one and the same, that this teaching had been derived from Christ and had been handed down through the Apostles, was the fundamental fact insisted upon. The continuity of the church, as evidenced by the unbroken lines of bishops, was pointed to as guaranteeing the purity of the tradition.

Now there was nothing really new in this appeal to apostolic tradition. The teaching of the church is based on apostolic authority, at the very outset of our period, by Clement and by Ignatius. So too the writer of the *Didaché* shows his reverence for apostolic authority by the form in which he casts his teaching. He knows that the " Teaching of the Twelve Apostles " must command attention. But in early days the appeal to tradition is implicit rather than explicit. It was not at first defined as a principle. But Irenæus, to take a conspicuous example, is asserting nothing that is really new when he makes his great appeal to tradition. The force of controversy merely compels him to define the position which had in fact always been held by the church. The necessity of establishing the appeal hastened no doubt the formation of the Canon of the New Testament, so that the apostolic tradition might be more conveniently tested. It led no doubt also to a greater stress being laid upon the organisation of the Christian ministry as a witness to the church's continuity. But here again the result was really only to make explicit what had all along been implicitly held. For our investigation of the second century writings has shown consistently throughout that the thought of the continuity of the church lay ever in the background as a fundamental fact. Circumstances might require that this continuity should receive external expression in some particular form. And the church might exercise its authority to determine that such external expression should be of binding force. Under this category monarchical episcopacy, with its idea of continuity, must be placed. It is to be regarded, as we have already said, as a secondary or derived necessity ; the fundamental necessity being the unity and continuity of the church.

Thus through opposition the church was led to define ideas which at first were latent ; to render explicit what in earlier days had been implicitly held ; to embody unchanging principles in forms that were to some extent new ; to see more clearly what its permanent position in the world involved. So the church of Christ, essentially unchanged and yet ever adapting itself to meet the new needs of a new age, gives continual evidence of the presence within it of the Holy Spirit of God, guiding it " into all the truth."

INDEX.

For EU product safety concerns, contact us at Calle de José Abascal, 56–1°, 28003 Madrid, Spain or eugpsr@cambridge.org.

www.ingramcontent.com/pod-product-compliance
Ingram Content Group UK Ltd.
Pitfield, Milton Keynes, MK11 3LW, UK
UKHW012329130625
459647UK00009B/161